IMAGES
of America

CINCINNATI'S HISTORIC FINDLAY MARKET

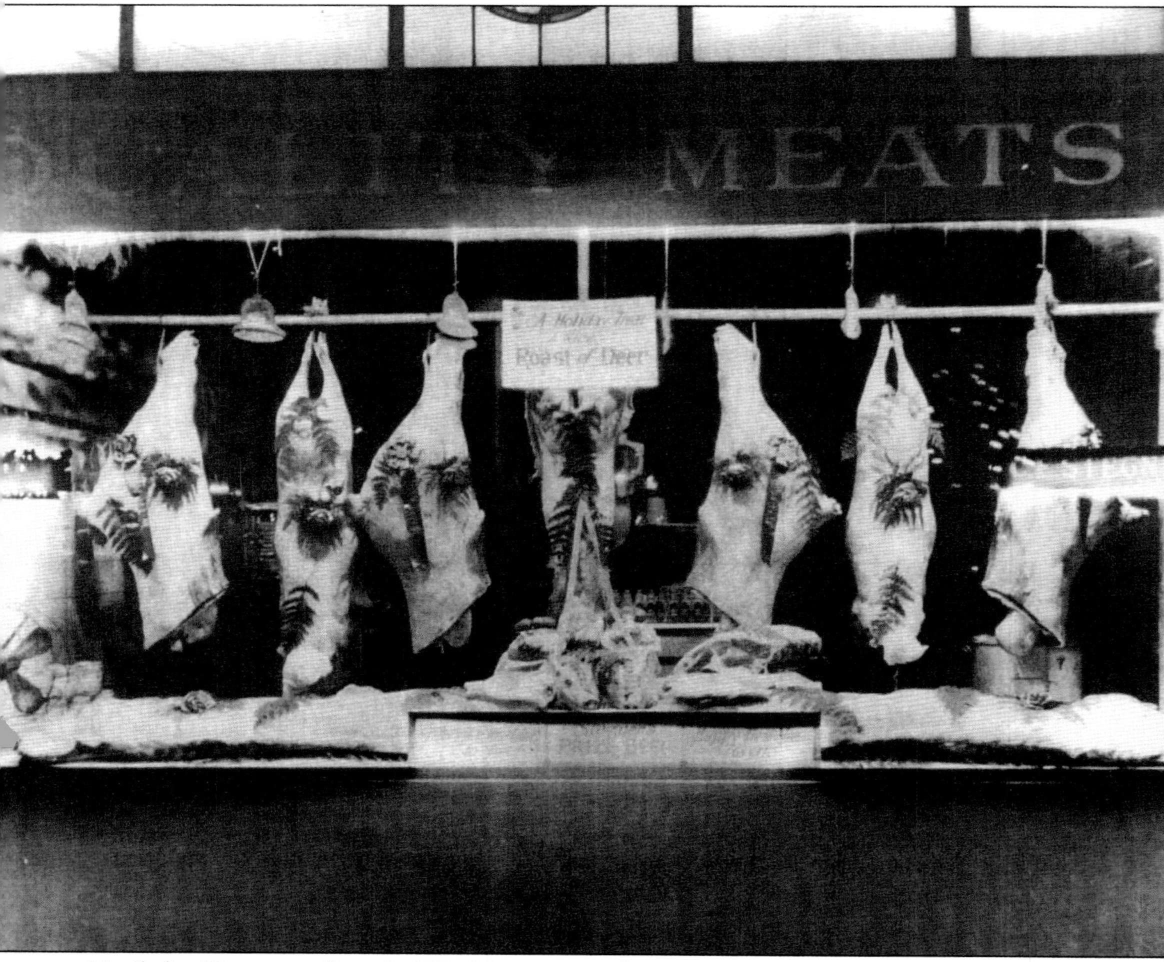

Until the Cincinnati Board of Health intervened, meat swung from hooks in the open air at Findlay Market. Exhibited in this "holiday treat" display are roasts of deer. Each carcass is decorated with blue ribbons and fern fronds to make them more attractive, and a fan blowing across the counter keeps the constant flies from lighting on the meat. (Courtesy of Peggy Schmidt.)

On the cover: Please see page 24. (Courtesy of Elaine Kunkel Bourgraf.)

IMAGES
of America

CINCINNATI'S HISTORIC FINDLAY MARKET

Liz Tilton

ARCADIA
PUBLISHING

ISBN 978-0-7385-6053-3

Published by Arcadia Publishing
Charleston, South Carolina

Printed in the United States of America

Library of Congress Control Number: 2008936157

For all general information contact Arcadia Publishing at:
Telephone 843-853-2070
Fax 843-853-0044
E-mail sales@arcadiapublishing.com
For customer service and orders:
Toll-Free 1-888-313-2665

Visit us on the Internet at www.arcadiapublishing.com

For the generations of families who have worked and shopped at Findlay Market

Contents

ACKNOWLEDGMENTS

This book would have been impossibly dull and could never have found publication without the generosity of the many families of the market. I had the pleasure of sitting at dozens of kitchen tables marveling over photographs, often with several generations of family members gathered at my shoulder, family members who could not help but tell the wonderful stories about their years on market and about the lifelong friendships formed there. They speak of one another with such fondness that it is clear to me why this market survived all others in Cincinnati. Almost all these photographs come from their collections; this is their book.

But there are many Cincinnatians who never worked at the market who love it too, and many of those contributed a great deal to this project: Lucy Schultz, whose Writing Cincinnati course at the University of Cincinnati planted the seed; Mary Stagaman, who early on showed me the market through her eyes; David and Barbara Day, designers, historians, and market lovers; the staff at the Corporation for Findlay Market, especially Bob Pickford, Cheryl Eagleson, Cynthia Brown, George Wright, and Marty Milligan; the librarians at the Cincinnati Historical Society; the shoppers who make the market such a pleasant and invigorating place to pass some time; and, finally, Deb Fritz, who always reminds me to bring home some *goetta*.

INTRODUCTION

It is not individual people or events that have made Findlay Market so special to Cincinnati; instead, in an age when technology allows for rapid flux and change, it is the stability of generations of family businesses and generations of family shoppers who continue to meet every week and exchange produce or meats or dairy products across Findlay Market counters that makes it unique. On market, it is not the more famous Cincinnati names like Pete Rose or Neil Armstrong or Marge Schott that stand out; it is the market names of Bender, Catanzaro, Gaudio, Gibbs, Heist, Kroeger, Kunkel, Luken, Roth, Silverglade, Simpson, Yunger—names of families who have owned and operated Findlay Market stands for generations—that shine.

Established in 1852, Findlay Market is Ohio's oldest public market in continuous operation. James Findlay, the man after whom the market is named, arrived in Cincinnati from neighboring Pennsylvania in 1793 and quickly opened a small store near the Ohio River. Findlay eventually opened larger stores, served in the military, helped establish a public library in Cincinnati, became governor of Ohio, and served in the U.S. Congress. After living for some time in Cincinnati, Findlay and a business partner purchased wooded property north of the city's limits in an area then known as the Northern Liberties; the property they bought became known as Findlay's Woods, and although Findlay always dreamed of opening a market on that site, he died before he realized his plan. Upon his death, however, the executors of Findlay's estate donated Findlay's Woods to the City of Cincinnati with the stipulation the city use it to establish a public market and name it in honor of James Findlay.

From its beginning, Findlay Market has been part of a complex, marginal community, which may account for one reason it has become such a beloved Cincinnati institution. The market was originally opened outside Cincinnati's city limits—in an area referred to as the Northern Liberties because of its location north of Northern Row, the street marking Cincinnati's northernmost boundary (and now renamed Liberty Avenue). And because the Northern Liberties lay just beyond city jurisdiction, the area was known for a host of social liberties, such as prostitution, bootlegging, and thievery, taken there. City officials eventually sought to annex the Findlay Market area to protect the housewives who shopped there from those questionable Northern Liberties characters, but the rebellious spirit of Findlay Market was not quelled by annexation, and this rebelliousness may account for one reason it has outlasted every other municipal market in the city.

The fact that the Findlay Market house was so solidly constructed of cast and wrought iron may be another reason the market was not razed as were Cincinnati's other public markets. The market house was originally an open shed without sides, and although it has been renovated three times, it is the openly visible cast-iron supports that remain the market house's most identifiable architectural hallmark.

Findlay Market is now located at the heart of Cincinnati's historic downtown Over-the-Rhine neighborhood, a neighborhood established by German immigrants after its annexation to the city and named because, to get to it, people had to cross one of the few footbridges over the Miami and Erie Canal, a water crossing that reminded the German settlers of crossing over the Rhine River of home. Over-the-Rhine remains an increasingly vibrant, edgy downtown neighborhood today; it is an area always in flux and often a challenge to the city government, but Findlay Market has remained the heartbeat and primary market for the people living there.

But Findlay Market is more than just a market; it represents a network of relationships that weaves through and is indispensable to Cincinnati's city fabric. All Cincinnatians know the national baseball season cannot begin without the Findlay Market opening day parade, coordinated and hosted since 1919 by members of the Findlay Market Association. On opening day, grown-ups skip work, children skip school, and a local barbershop hangs a sign in its window that reads, "Gone to the funeral: Grandma died again." And in the year when opening day was canceled due to the baseball players' strike, the Findlay Market opening day parade indomitably carried on, and Cincinnatians turned out in record numbers to cheer it. All this so that Cincinnatians can line the streets and watch what has over the years become the city's largest annual parade wind its exuberant way through Over-the-Rhine and to Fountain Square, the city's center.

Beyond its Over-the-Rhine neighborhood, however, Findlay Market is literally and civically supported by the Greater Cincinnati population. In 2001, a young African American man was shot and killed by a white police officer in Over-the-Rhine, a tragedy that set off days of riots in the neighborhood and received national media coverage; much property was damaged, including some Findlay Market businesses. The city's nerves were on edge and tension remained palpable in Over-the-Rhine, which threatened business in the beloved market. In an attempt to support the vendors who for generations have made their livings on the market, an organized group of volunteers calling themselves the Friends of Findlay Market made a citywide call for shoppers to come downtown and support the market on the Saturday after the riots were calmed. Shoppers in record numbers rallied from all over the city and its sprawling suburbs to show their tangible support.

Some of today's Findlay Market shoppers were weighed as children on the same butchers' scales that are still being used to weigh their meats; many of the vendors and stall owners and farmers doing business on market are the third or fourth generation to do so, and the same is true of the shoppers there. Because of this history, Findlay Market is more than simply a place to Cincinnatians—it is an institution where people of Cincinnati's every socioeconomic level, religion, race, age, political party, and sexual preference stand shoulder to shoulder to buy their meats, cheeses, produce, baked goods, and flowers and to exchange recipes with one another and then eat together under the bright outdoor canopies.

One

FAMILIES ON MARKET

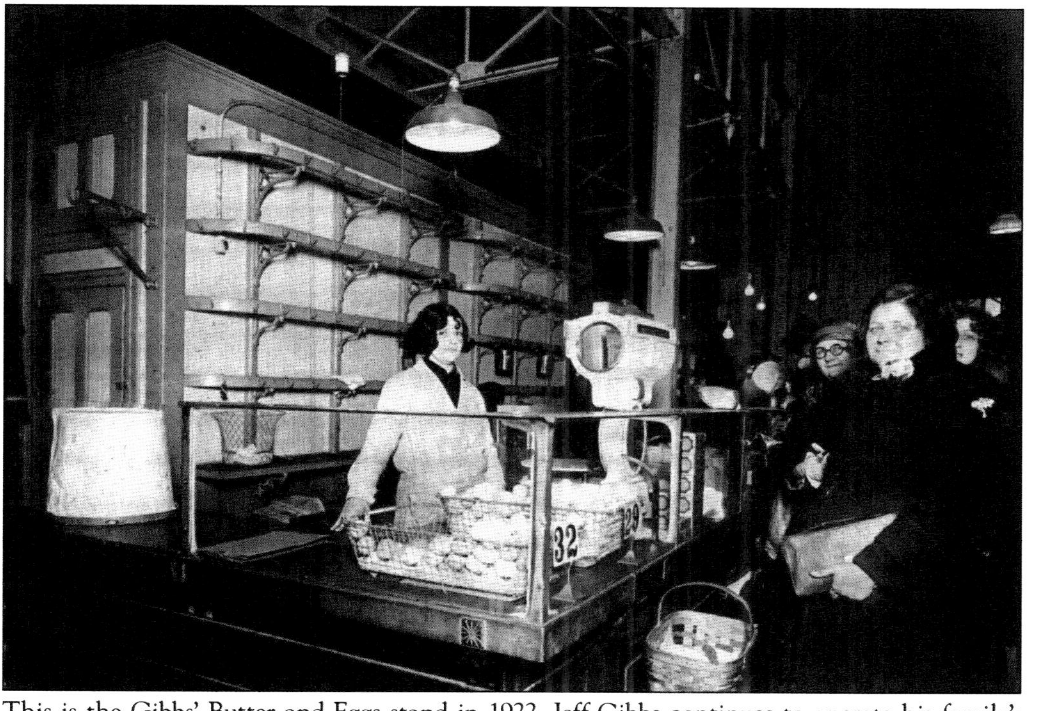

This is the Gibbs' Butter and Eggs stand in 1922. Jeff Gibbs continues to operate his family's stand in this exact spot today, and although the business has expanded to include many other food items, Gibbs still cuts his big squares of butter from blocks like the one shown on the left here. These loose eggs are separated in baskets according to size and the price is marked per dozen. (Courtesy of David Day.)

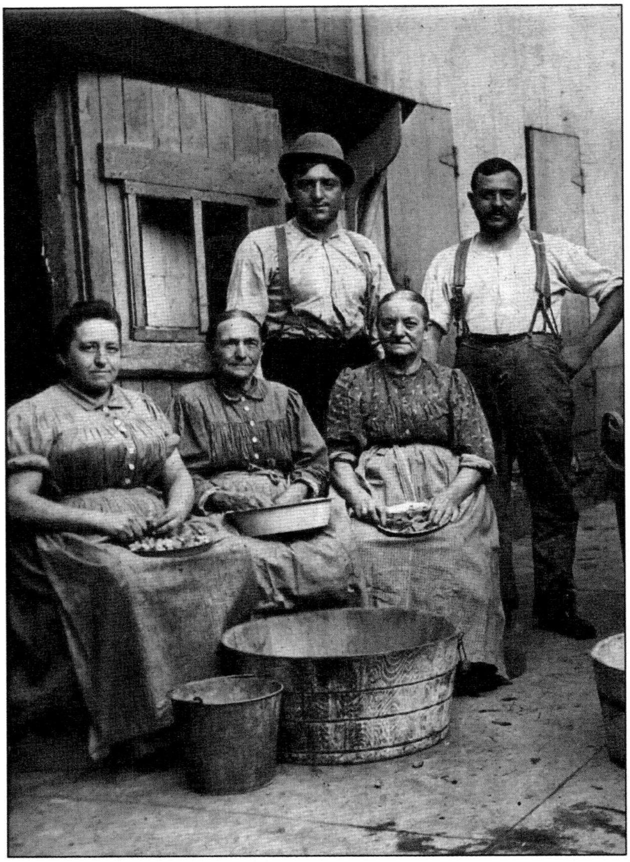

These folks gather for an 1898 pickling day. Soon after arriving in Cincinnati from Germany, Theodor Kunkel opened his Findlay Market pickle and sauerkraut stand the year the market began, and generations of Kunkel's descendants continued the business without interruption for over 150 years. Taken in the alleyway behind the Kunkel residence at 2112 Vine Street, these photographs document the family and neighbor effort of preparing bushels of pickled vegetables for market. The photograph at left includes, from left to right, family members Amelia and Agatha Kunkel, Mollie Meyer, and Frank and William Kunkel. Below, beans fill the women's aprons and hands, a man in the background is posed with a long knife to core a head of cabbage, and two dogs perch on the ever-present wooden barrels used to store the pickled food. Goods were hauled from home to market for sale. (Courtesy of Elaine Kunkel Bourgraf.)

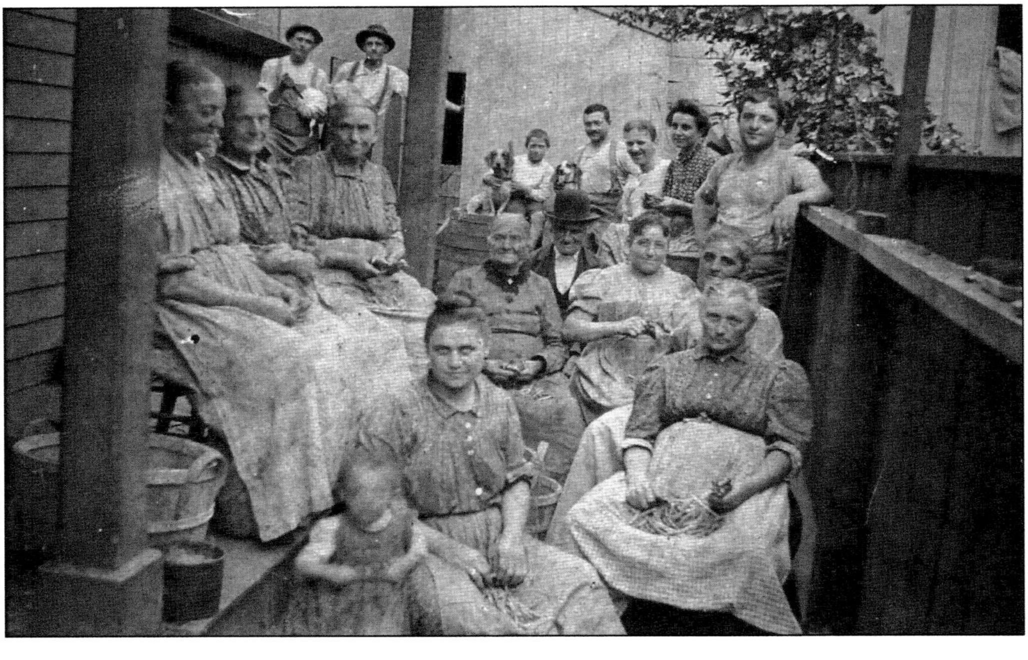

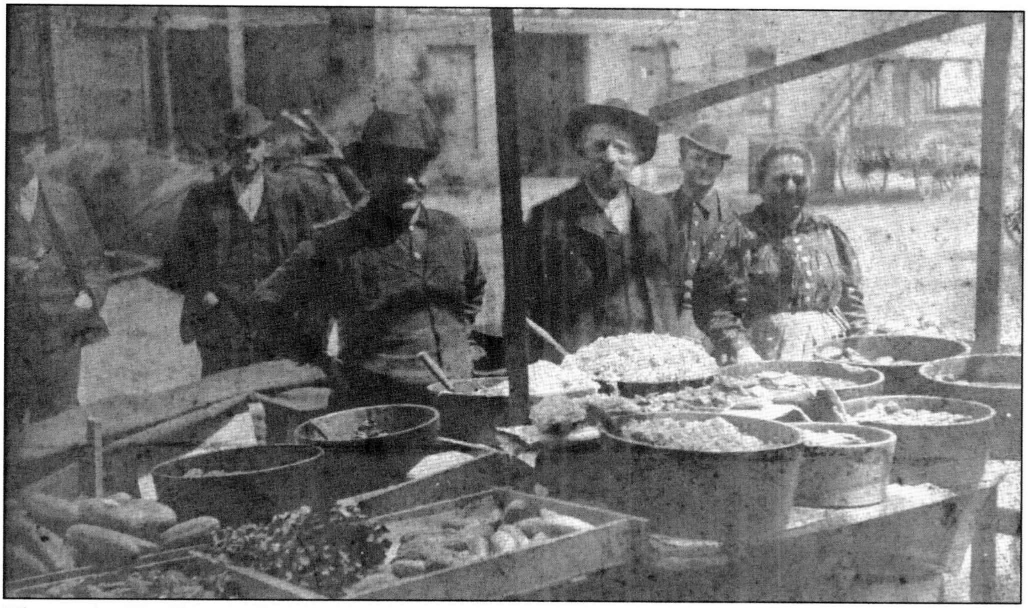

This is the Findlay Market stand to which the Kunkels hauled their pickled vegetables. In the crocks are sauerkraut; turnip kraut; sour, dill, and sweet pickles; pickled onions; pickled beets; and pickled beans. The smell of sauerkraut and pickles still carries a strong memory for many Findlay Market shoppers and vendors. From left to right are Herman Richman, William Kunkel, Frank Kunkel, and Mollie Kunkel. (Courtesy of Elaine Kunkel Bourgraf.)

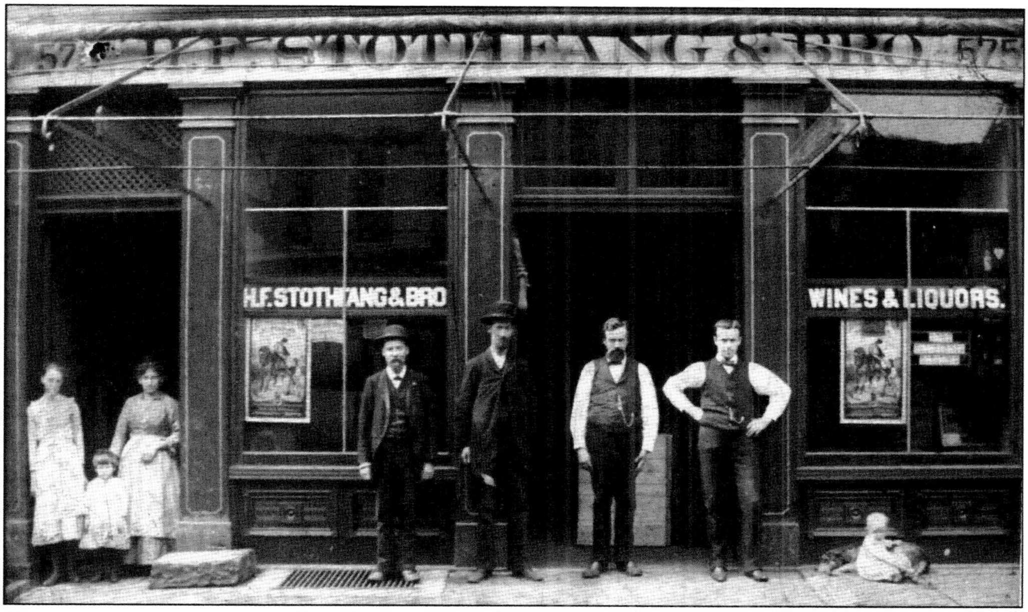

German immigrants arrived in Cincinnati and Over-the-Rhine holding their beer close, so it is entirely likely the late-19th-century market men may have shared a well-earned, after-market-hours drink with their fellow vendors, a drink that could easily have come from the neighboring H. F. Stothfang and Brothers Wines and Liquors shown here on Central Avenue in 1895. (Courtesy of the Stothfang family.)

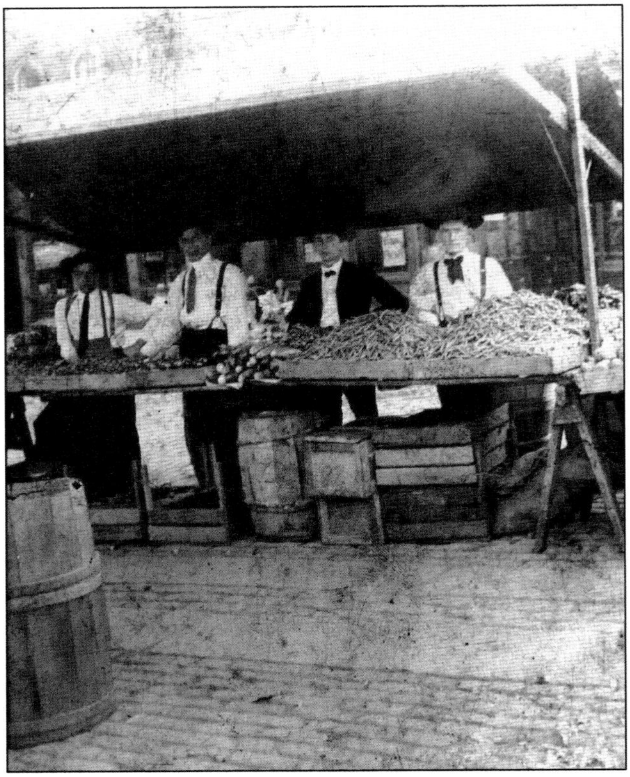

Anthony Beck, second from left, operated this 1911 Findlay Market stand for most of his life. Like most vendors, he alternated between Findlay and Court Street Markets, two markets that were never open on the same day. Beck's father and grandfather worked the market before him; Lorenz Beck Sr. began the business in the late 1850s, making him one of the original Findlay Market merchants. (Courtesy of Jane Beck Sansalone.)

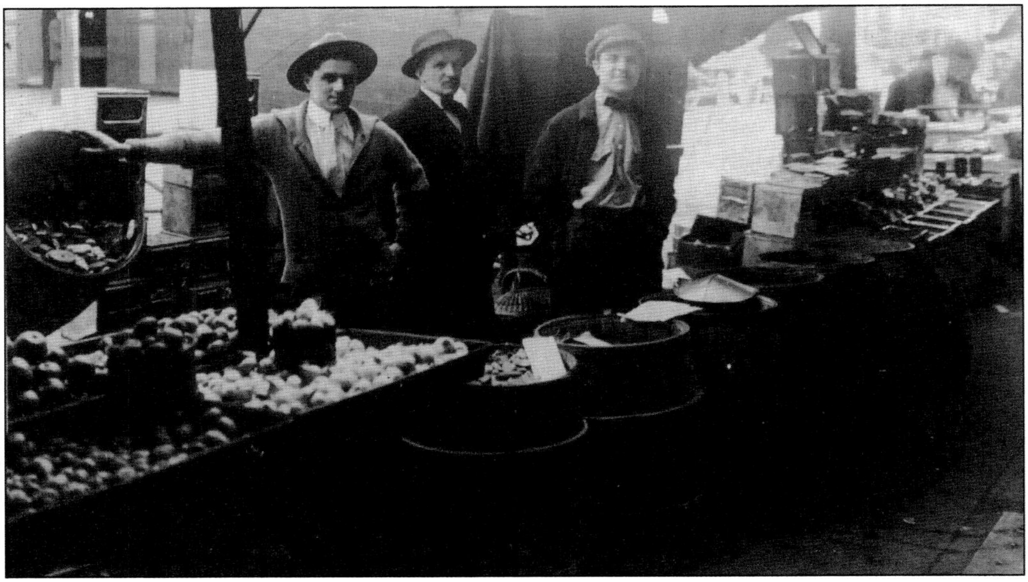

William Naish (center) established his cookie business in the early 1900s. Cookies fill each barrel, and the crates behind the men read, "National Biscuit Company." Freshly baked cookies were picked up from local bakeries and sold on market. Naish demanded high-quality cookies, which may explain why people still recall his stand as a favorite. Shown in 1912 are sons Charles (left) and Robert. (Courtesy of the Naish Gambetta family.)

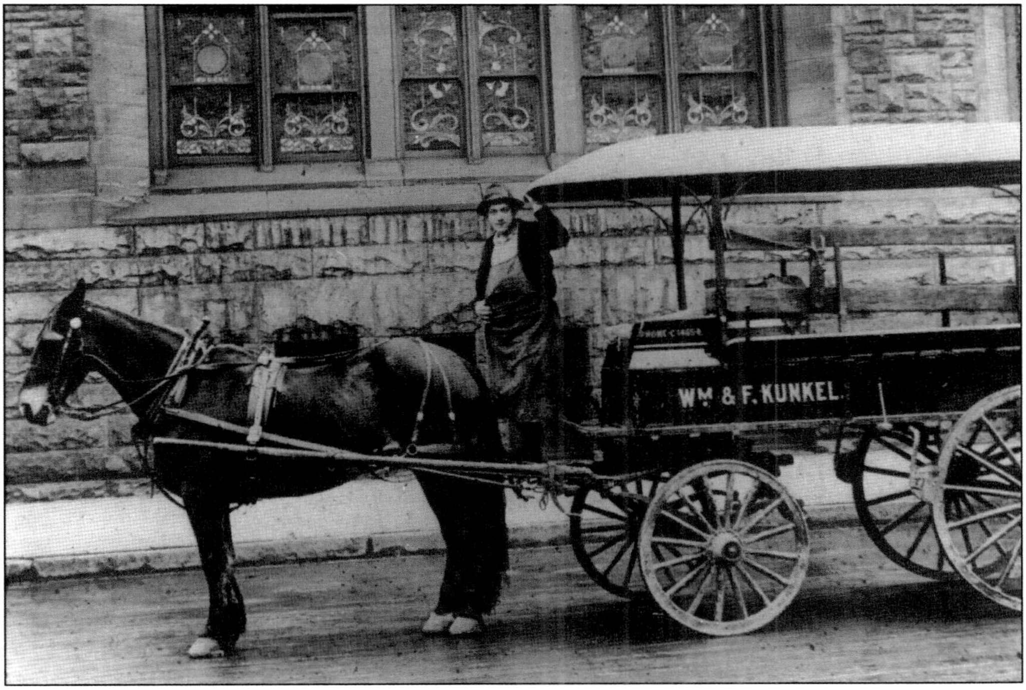

Before the automobile became common, families hauled goods from home or from warehouses to market in horse-drawn wagons. Shown here in 1915, an aproned Ted Kunkel drives the Wm. and F. Kunkel business wagon. Stenciled on boards of the driver's seat is the telephone number C-1465 R. Below, on the business card from this same period, the telephone number is Canal 1465-R, indicating that the Miami and Erie Canal was still a strong neighborhood presence and a city thoroughfare. The business card suggests the Kunkels operated, as was the practice for most market families, at both Findlay and Court Street Markets. The two markets were opened on alternating days to service different neighborhoods while allowing vendors a presence at both locations. (Courtesy of Elaine Kunkel Bourgraf.)

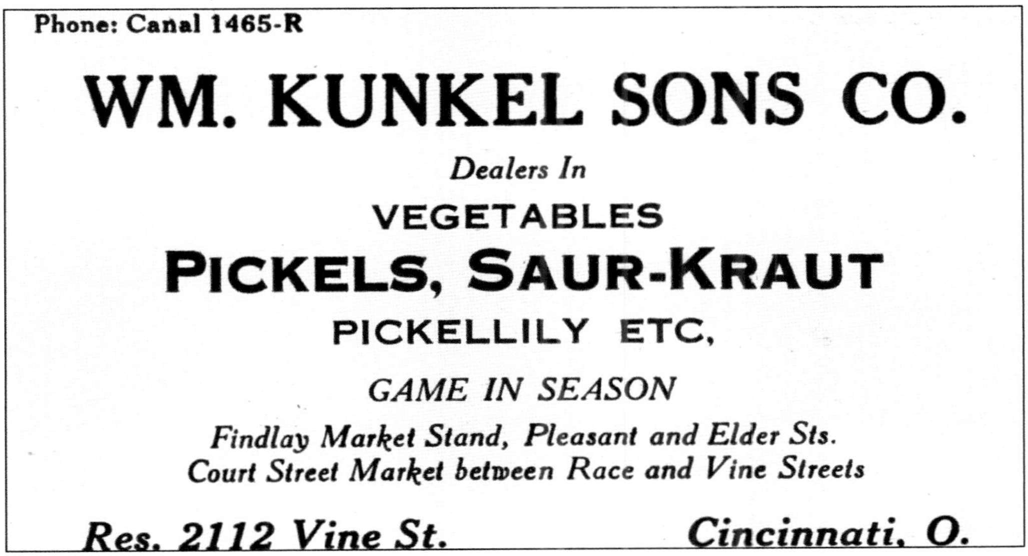

Phone: Canal 1465-R

WM. KUNKEL SONS CO.

Dealers In

VEGETABLES

PICKELS, SAUR-KRAUT

PICKELLILY ETC,

GAME IN SEASON

Findlay Market Stand, Pleasant and Elder Sts.
Court Street Market between Race and Vine Streets

Res. 2112 Vine St. *Cincinnati, O.*

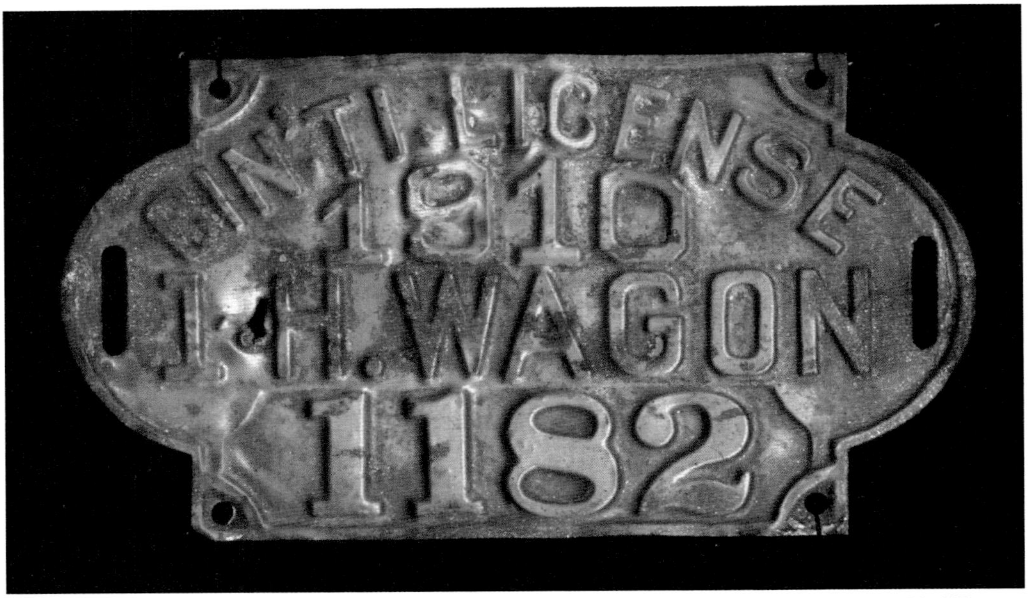

This license plate from the Kunkel business wagon reads, "Cin'ti License, 1910, 1-H. Wagon, 1182." In other words, this licensed a 1910 one-horse wagon. By 1890, the wagon-building industry had made Cincinnati the world's center for the trade. However, when the world turned in mass to the automobile, Cincinnati industry stuck with the wagon, thus missing its opportunity to become the nation's automobile center. (Courtesy of Elaine Kunkel Bourgraf.)

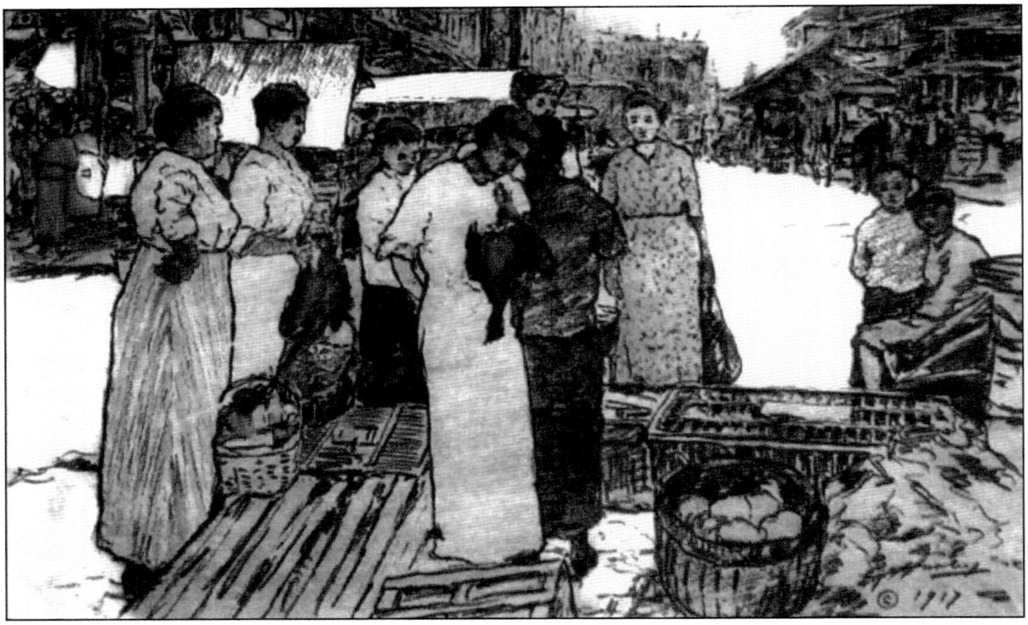

More horses and buggies line the street next to the Findlay Market house in Edward Timothy Hurley's *Women with Chickens* etching. Of note is Hurley's focus on women and their darker skin tones, neither of which are often associated with this period in Findlay Market's history. In the early 1900s, German immigrants composed most of the population living in the Over-the-Rhine Findlay Market neighborhood. (Author's collection.)

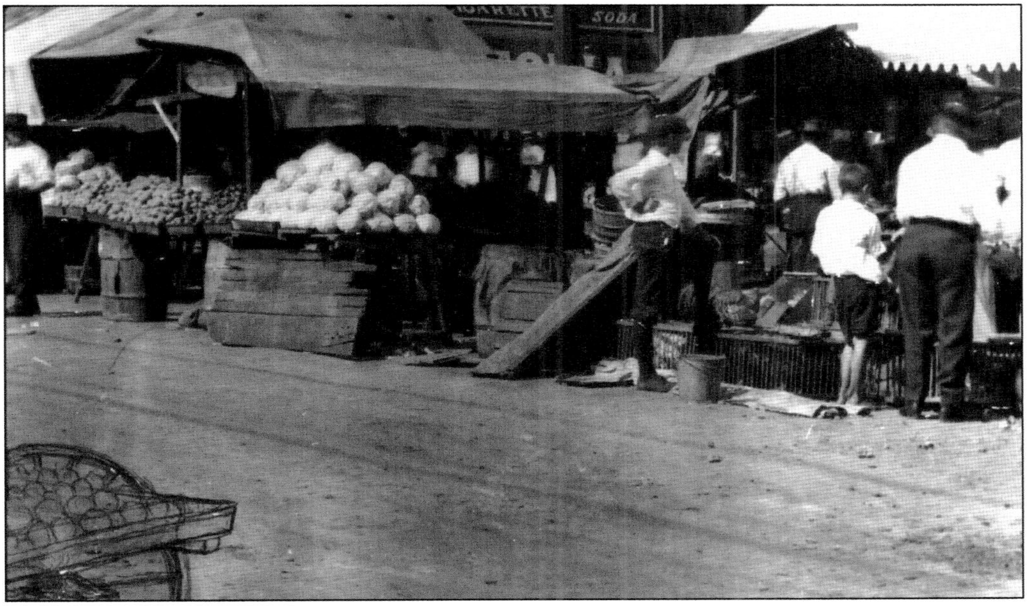

In the bottom left corner of the photograph above, notice the hand-penciled drawing of a grapefruit-loaded pushcart. One can safely assume the drawing is from the hand of Cincinnati artist Edward Timothy Hurley because he almost exactly reproduces this scene in his colored etching titled *The Lost Grapefruit* below. Under the mentorship of his Cincinnati Art Academy instructor Frank Duveneck, Hurley became a skilled artist and etcher, and for 52 years, he also designed at Cincinnati's now-famous Rookwood Pottery. Hurley photographed many Cincinnati scenes like this one and later reproduced them in art; early-20th-century Findlay Market was a particular Hurley favorite. This scene captures mounds of displayed cabbage (possibly the Kunkel family's), and the boy in the foreground rests his foot on a coop filled with chickens. (Above, courtesy of the Cincinnati Historical Society; below, author's collection.)

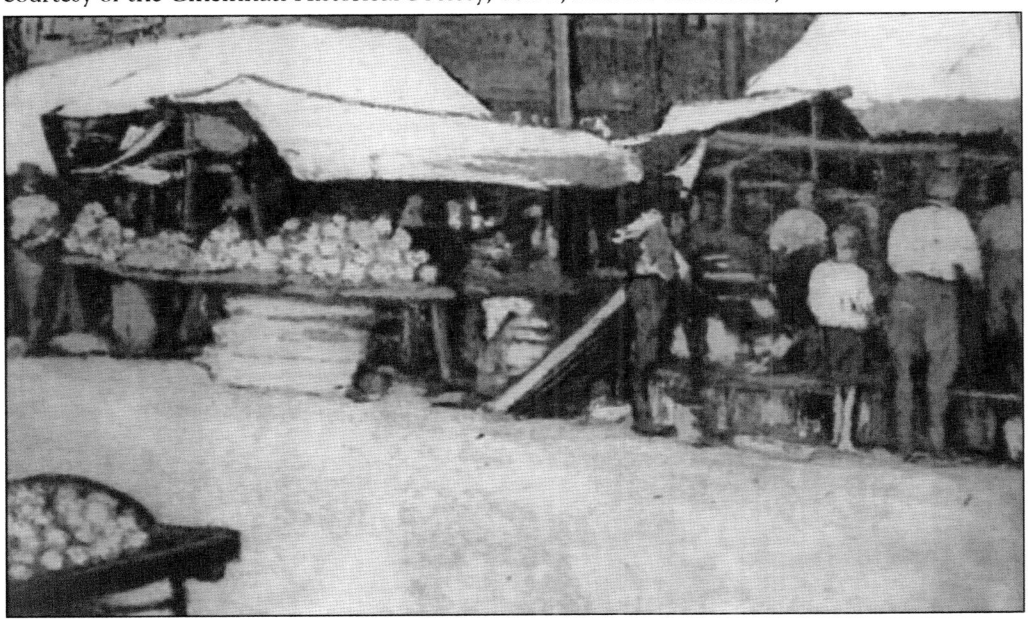

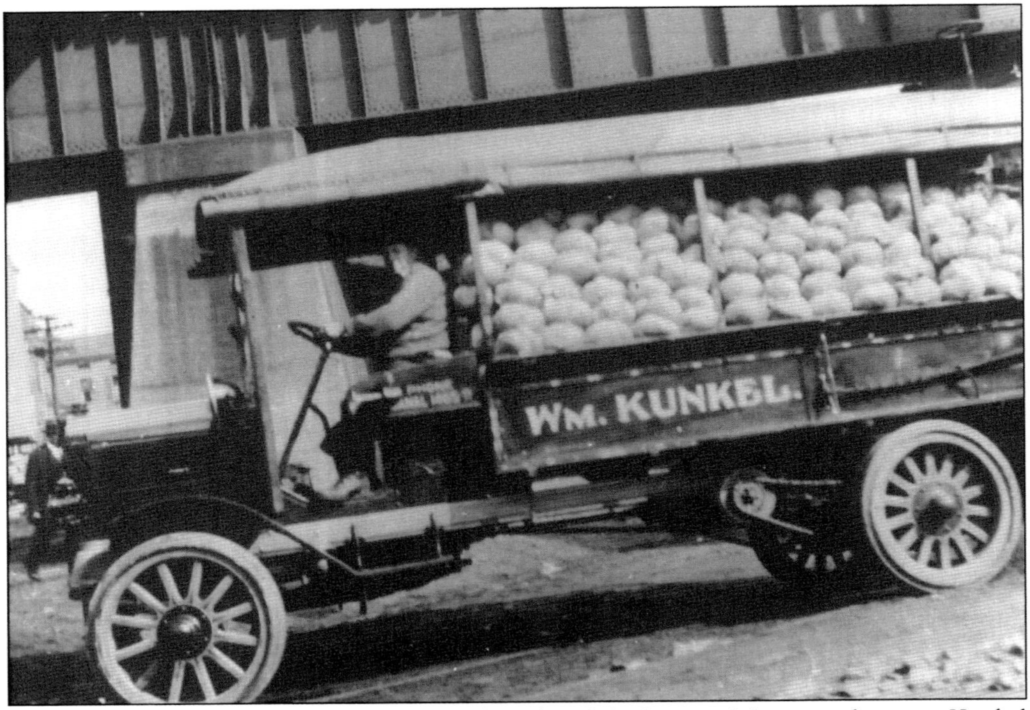

Once again driven by Ted Kunkel, this truck replaced the business's horse and wagon. Kunkel hauls cabbage from the Cincinnati, Hamilton and Dayton Railroad (CH&D) rail yards where vendors bought produce shipped into Cincinnati. This photograph was taken in 1919, only a year before construction began transforming the Miami and Erie Canal into present-day Central Parkway. The blotter below marks this transformation as its telephone prefix shifts from *canal* to *parkway*. The blotter shows other shifts as well: William Kunkel appears the sole business owner, and he has moved his business from outside to inside, now occupying a presence inside the "butcher house." For a long time, only meat could be sold inside the market house; all other vendors remained outside. (Courtesy of Elaine Kunkel Bourgraf.)

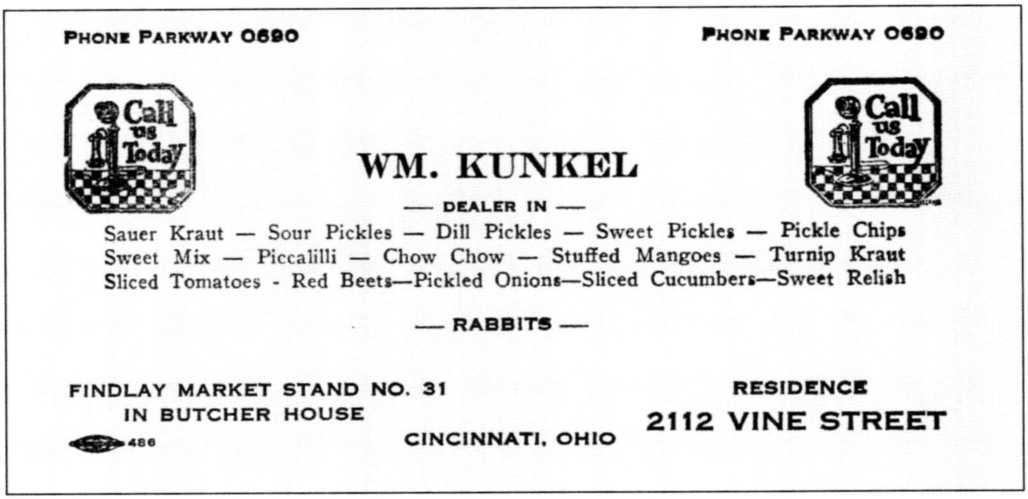
PHONE PARKWAY 0690 PHONE PARKWAY 0690

Call us Today

WM. KUNKEL

— DEALER IN —

Sauer Kraut — Sour Pickles — Dill Pickles — Sweet Pickles — Pickle Chips
Sweet Mix — Piccalilli — Chow Chow — Stuffed Mangoes — Turnip Kraut
Sliced Tomatoes - Red Beets—Pickled Onions—Sliced Cucumbers—Sweet Relish

— RABBITS —

FINDLAY MARKET STAND NO. 31
IN BUTCHER HOUSE

RESIDENCE
2112 VINE STREET

CINCINNATI, OHIO

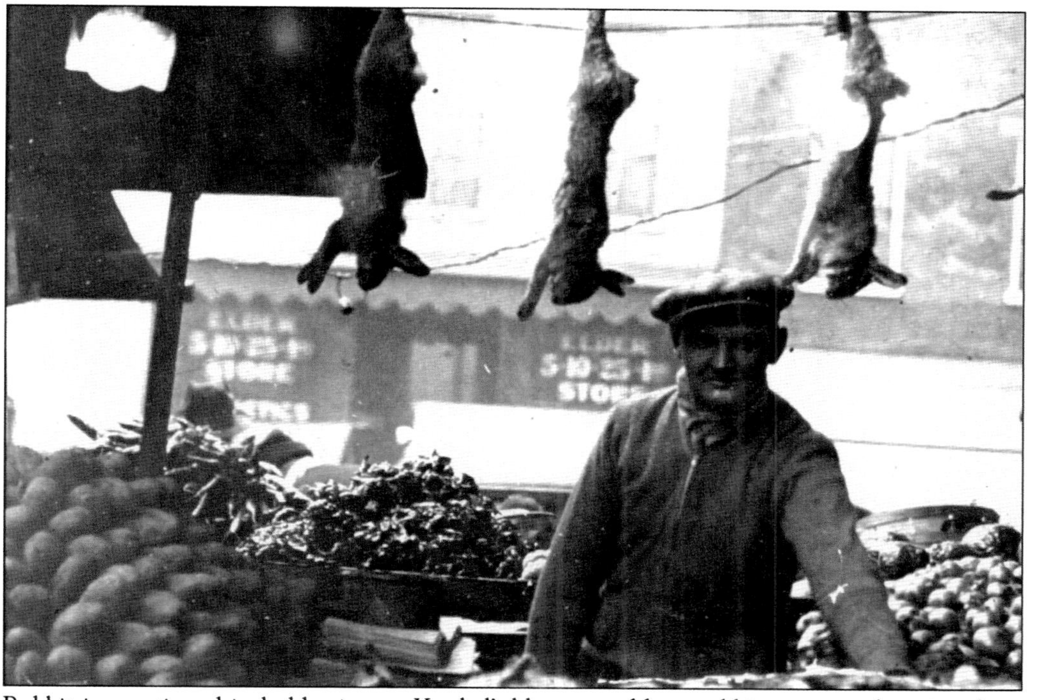

Rabbit is mentioned in bold print on Kunkel's blotter, and here rabbits are seen hanging from the electrical wire strung above Jim Kirsch, who worked for George Wunderlich at Wunderlich's vegetable stand for many years. Rumor has it that the sale of rabbit was eventually discouraged because lots of the neighborhood cats disappeared. In this photograph, a paper bag wrapped around the exposed lightbulb focuses the otherwise diffuse light more directly onto the produce. The Wunderlich family sold produce at Findlay Market until 2001. Below, George Wunderlich heads out to Findlay Market in his new truck. (Courtesy of Donald Wunderlich.)

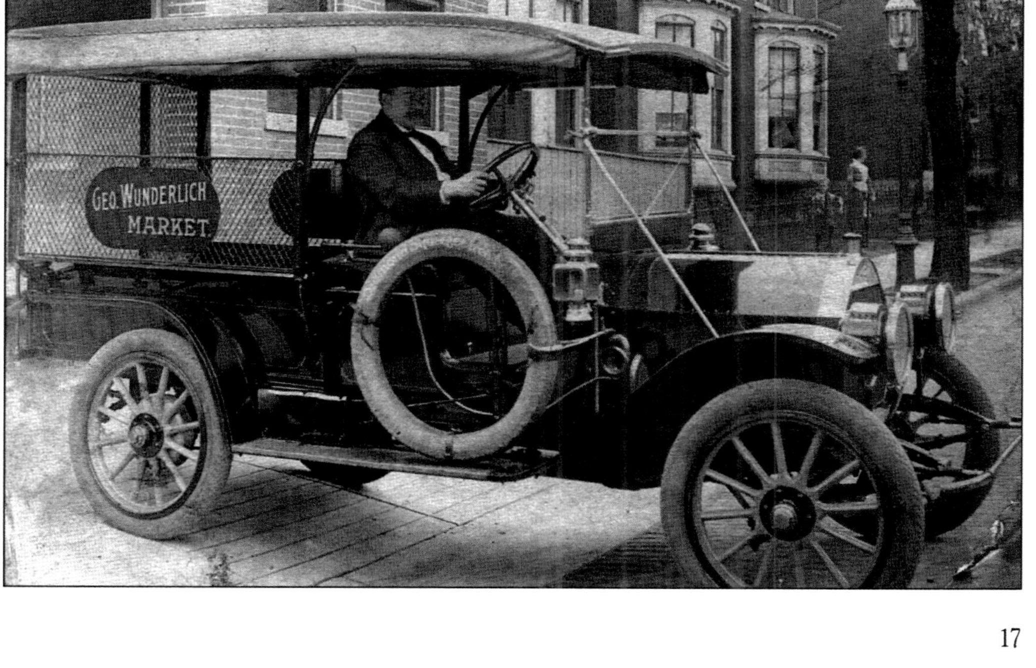

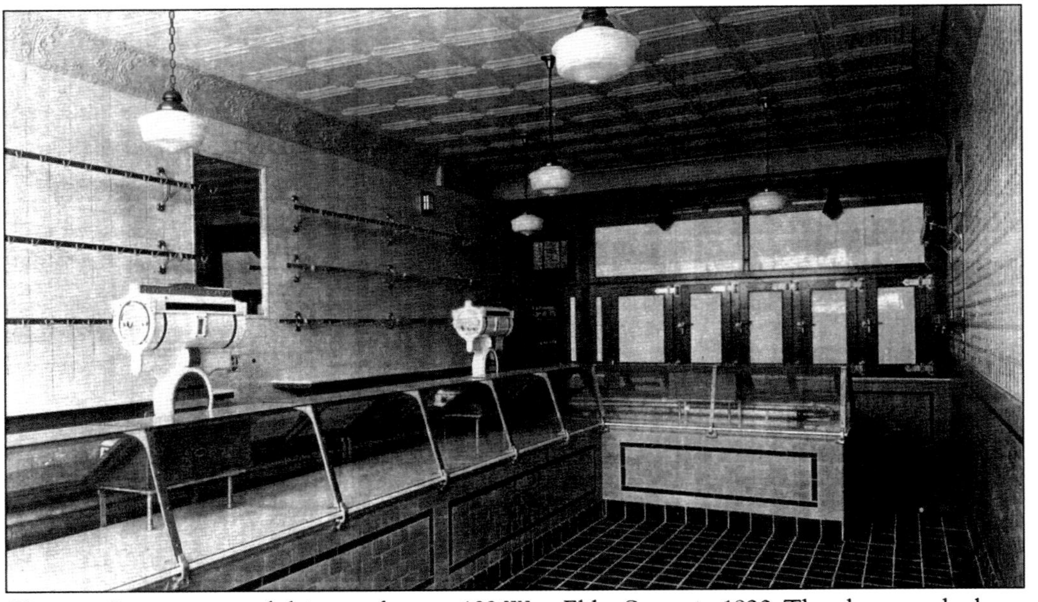

Clarence Stegner opened this storefront at 102 West Elder Street in 1920. The photograph above was taken before the space was occupied, whereas the photograph of the same space below was taken after Stegner had been in business for a few years. In the latter photograph, fresh meat hangs on every available wall hook and is piled high on the wooden barrels lining the wall opposite the counter. Deep sawdust spread on the floor absorbs blood and other juices dripped from the meat. Several of the men behind the counter wear what is known as a market or a peddler's cap. (Courtesy of Peggy Schmidt.)

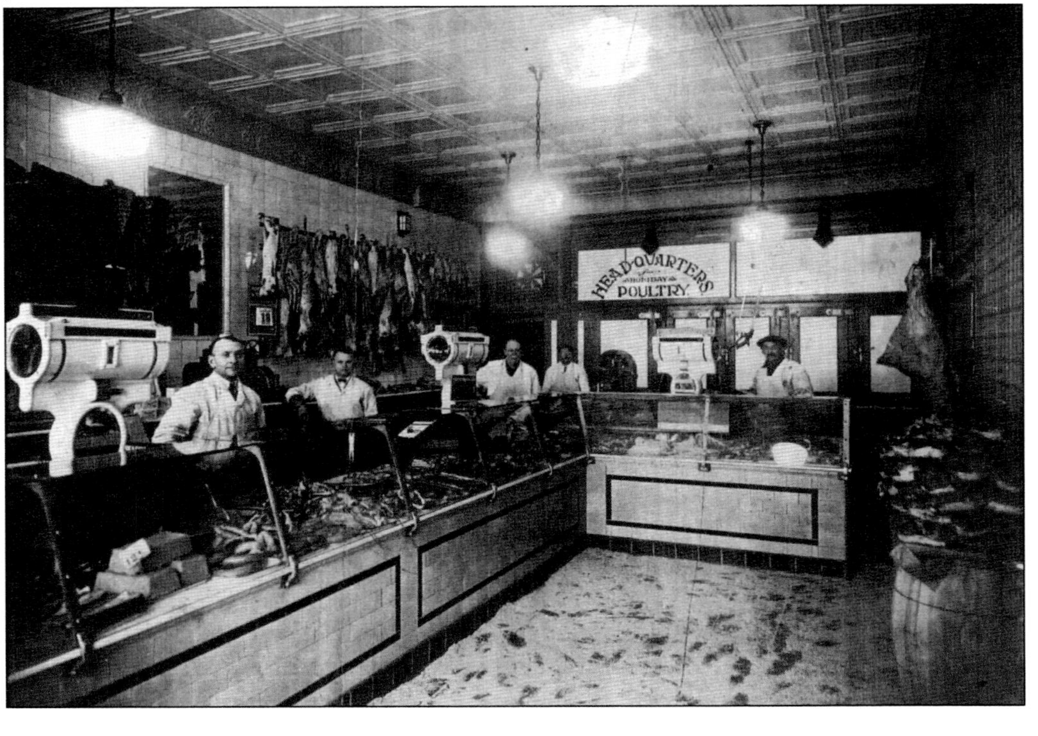

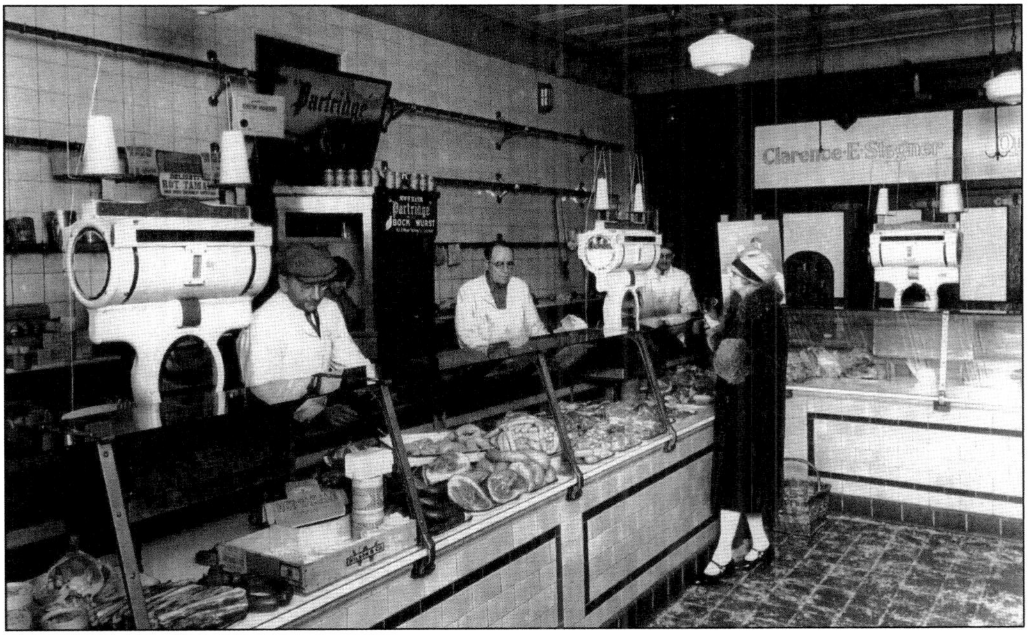

In this later image showing the interior of Clarence Stegner's meat business, sawdust remains on the floor, but the walls are empty of meat. Stegner, left, wears his peddler's hat, and butcher's string is rigged in spools above him. Although shoppers' baskets are quickly making a comeback, not many women would wear a fur coat, a hat, and heels to Findlay Market today. (Courtesy of Peggy Schmidt.)

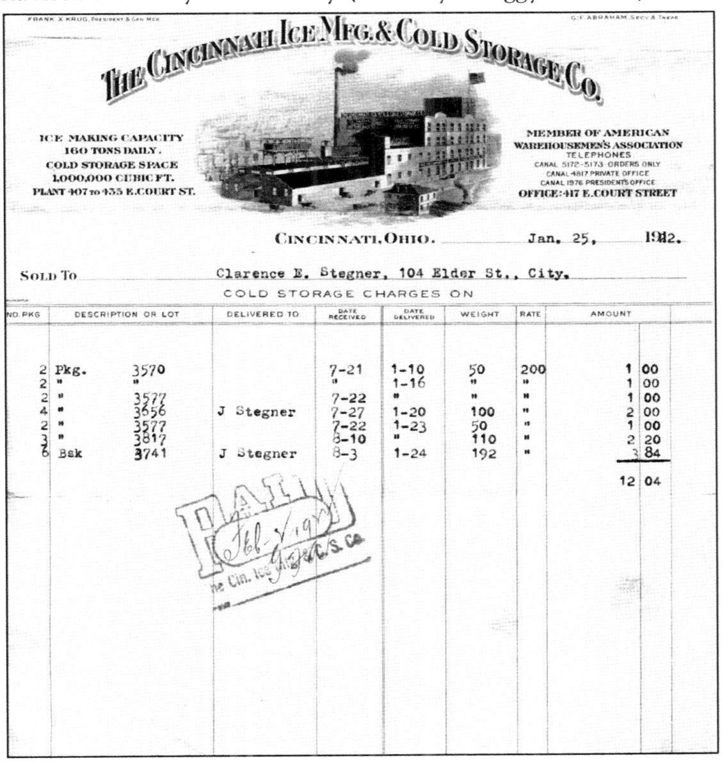

FRANK X. KRUG, PRESIDENT & GEN. MGR. — G. F. ABRAHAM, SEC'Y & TREAS.

THE CINCINNATI ICE MFG. & COLD STORAGE CO.

ICE MAKING CAPACITY 160 TONS DAILY.
COLD STORAGE SPACE 1,000,000 CUBIC FT.
PLANT 407 TO 435 E. COURT ST.

MEMBER OF AMERICAN WAREHOUSEMEN'S ASSOCIATION
TELEPHONES
CANAL 5172-5173 ORDERS ONLY
CANAL 4817 PRIVATE OFFICE
CANAL 1976 PRESIDENT'S OFFICE
OFFICE: 417 E. COURT STREET

CINCINNATI, OHIO. Jan. 25, 1932.

SOLD TO Clarence E. Stegner, 104 Elder St., City.

COLD STORAGE CHARGES ON

NO. PKG	DESCRIPTION OR LOT		DELIVERED TO	DATE RECEIVED	DATE DELIVERED	WEIGHT	RATE	AMOUNT
2	Pkg.	3570		7-21	1-10	50	200	1 00
2	"	"		"	1-16	"	"	1 00
2	"	3577		7-22	"	"	"	1 00
4	"	3656	J Stegner	7-27	1-20	100	"	2 00
2	"	3577		7-22	1-23	50	"	1 00
3	"	3817		8-10	"	110	"	2 20
6	Bsk	3741	J Stegner	8-3	1-24	192	"	3 84
								12 04

PAID

The luxury of refrigeration came slowly to the market, so most businesses relied on shipped-in ice to keep goods cold in display cases during the day. At night, most businesses hauled their spoilable goods to a cold storage facility for safekeeping until the next market day. Here is an invoice for ice and cold storage charged to Clarence Stegner. (Courtesy of Peggy Schmidt.)

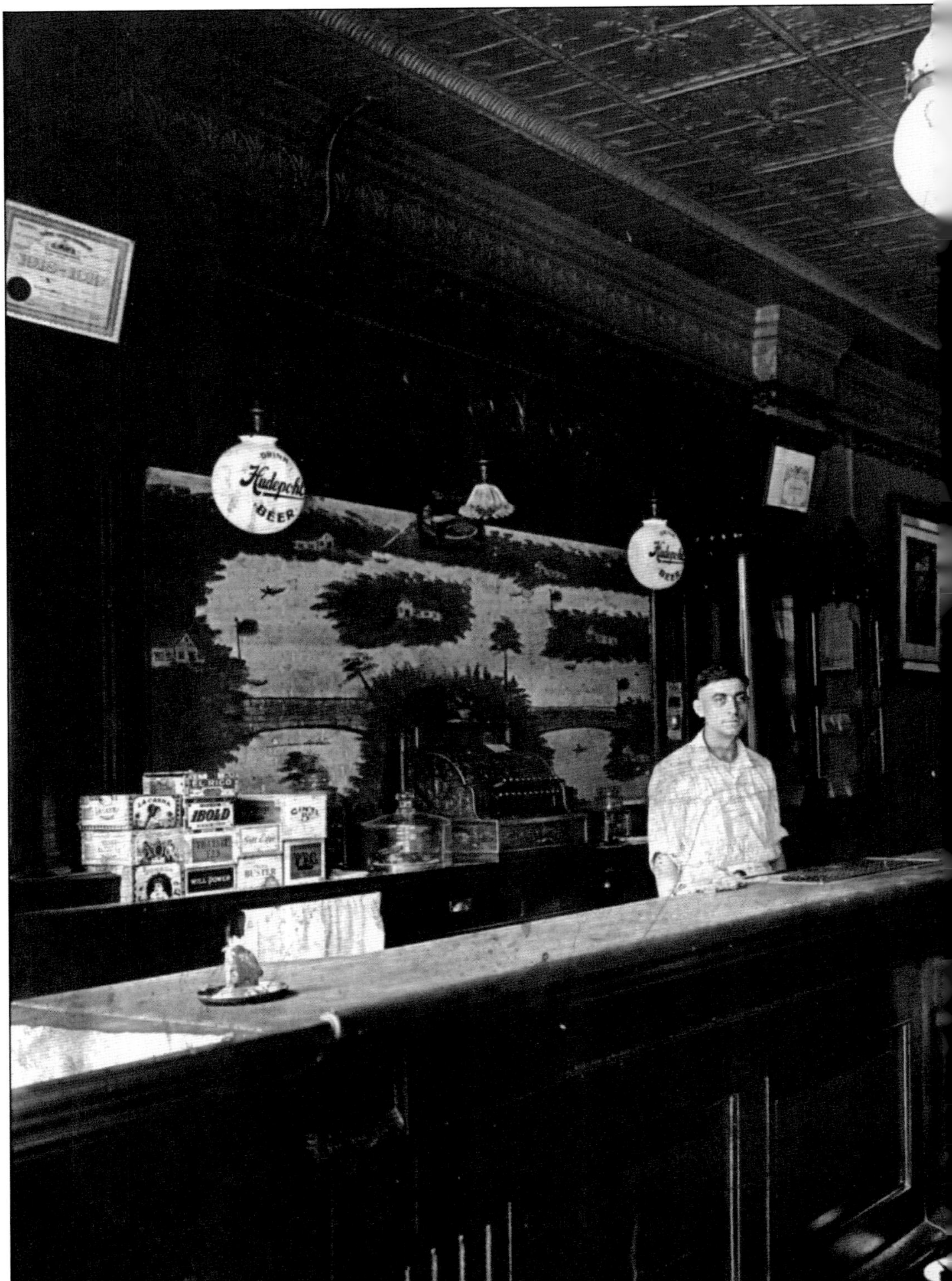
DRINK
Hudepohl
BEER
IBOLD

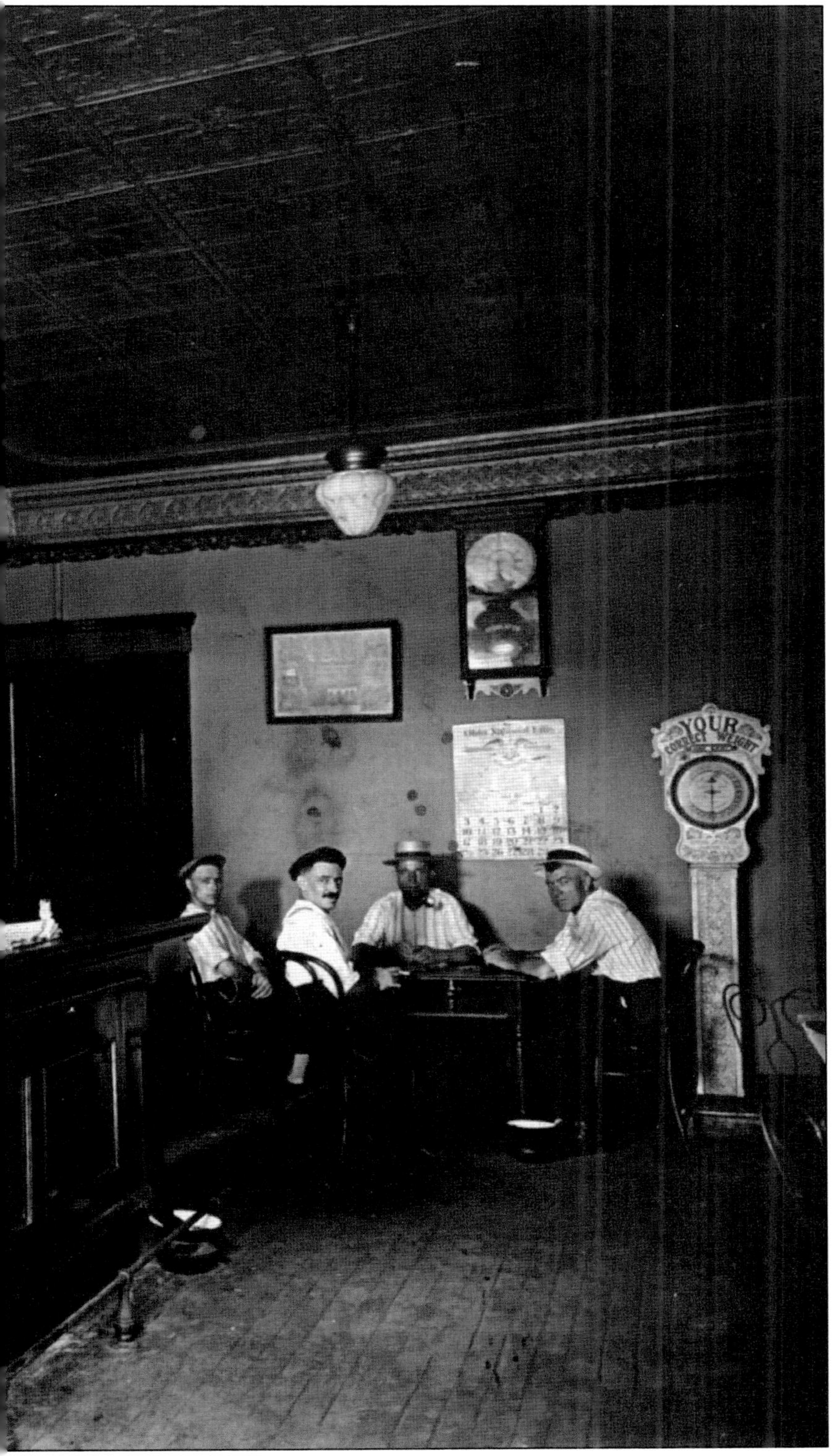

In 1921, Yunger's Cafe was born. At the age of 16, Frank Junker arrived from Romania alone at Ellis Island where his name was changed to Yunger; he eventually opened Yunger's Cafe. Taken in July 1921 according to the wall calendar, this image shows the café's interior the year it opened: spittoons line the floor at the bar's foot rails, four men play cards, and, for a penny, people can learn their correct weight on the tall scales. Because this was taken during Prohibition, no liquor is visible on the shelves (which does not mean there was none hidden on the dumbwaiter!), but someone has left some pie on a plate on the bar. "Uncle Pete" Wagner stands behind the bar; his son, Pete Wagner, eventually conducted Cincinnati's Pete Wagner Orchestra. (Courtesy of the Yunger family.)

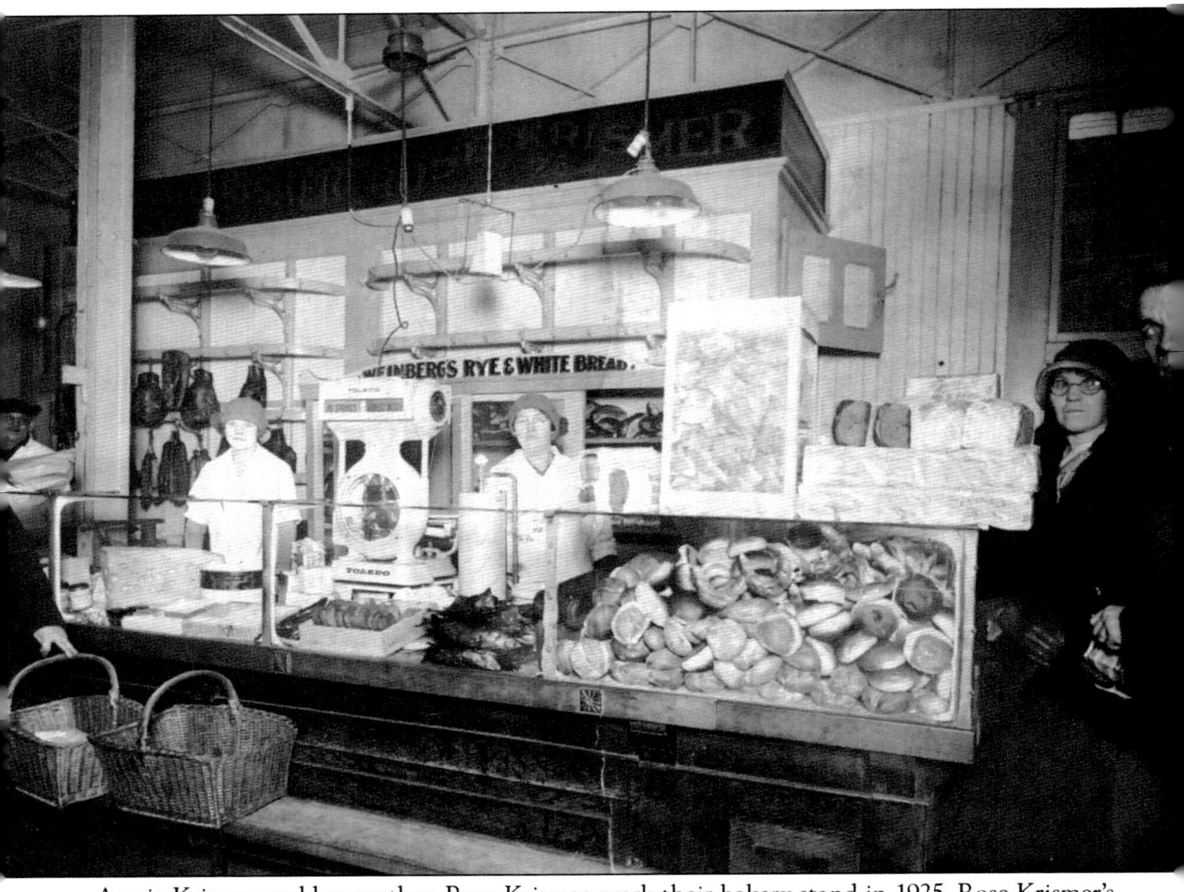

Annie Krismer and her mother, Rose Krismer, work their bakery stand in 1925. Rose Krismer's husband was killed by a train on his way home from the market. Family legend tells that he had worked late into the night, but since his horse knew the way home, William Krismer usually fell asleep in the wagon. On this night, however, the horse stopped on the railroad tracks, and Krismer was killed in his sleep by a train; the horse arrived home without him. His death left Rose to rear seven children on income earned from this stand. In the stand beside them and wearing the dark peddler's cap is George Kisker of Kisker Meats. Rose's grandsons, Cliff Kist and Jimmy Krismer, continue to work at their own stands in the Findlay Market farm shed today. (Courtesy of Jimmy Krismer.)

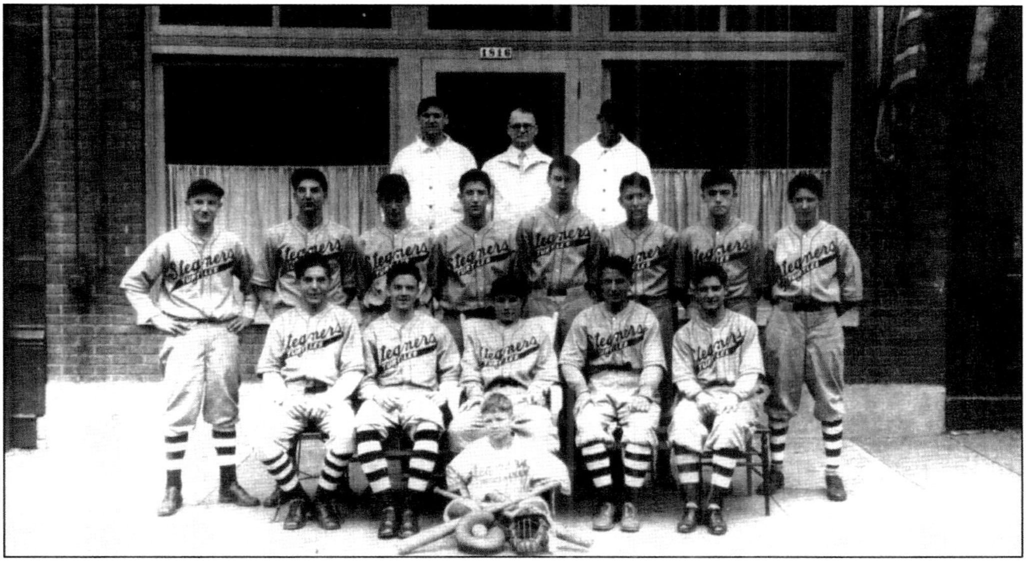

By the time this 1928 photograph of the Stegner Turtles baseball team was taken, Clarence Stegner (back row, center) had expanded Stegner Meats into Stegner Products Company, which now included both mock turtle soup and chili con carne. His business had outgrown the 102 West Elder Street storefront and had moved around the corner to a larger space at 1816 Race Street. (Courtesy of Peggy Schmidt.)

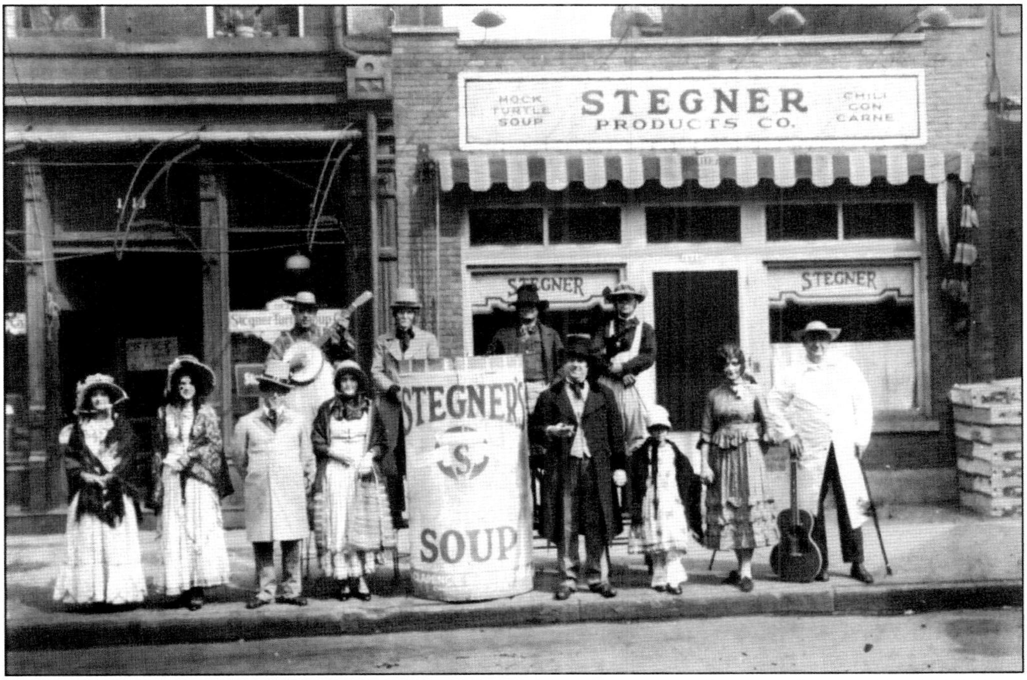

In 1928, Clarence Stegner (third from left) poses with a giant can of soup in front of his 1816 Race Street store with a group of others in period costumes. The occasion for the costumed event is unknown. Stegner's mock turtle soup eventually became so popular the company began canning it and its other soups for wider distribution. (Courtesy of Deborah Ooten.)

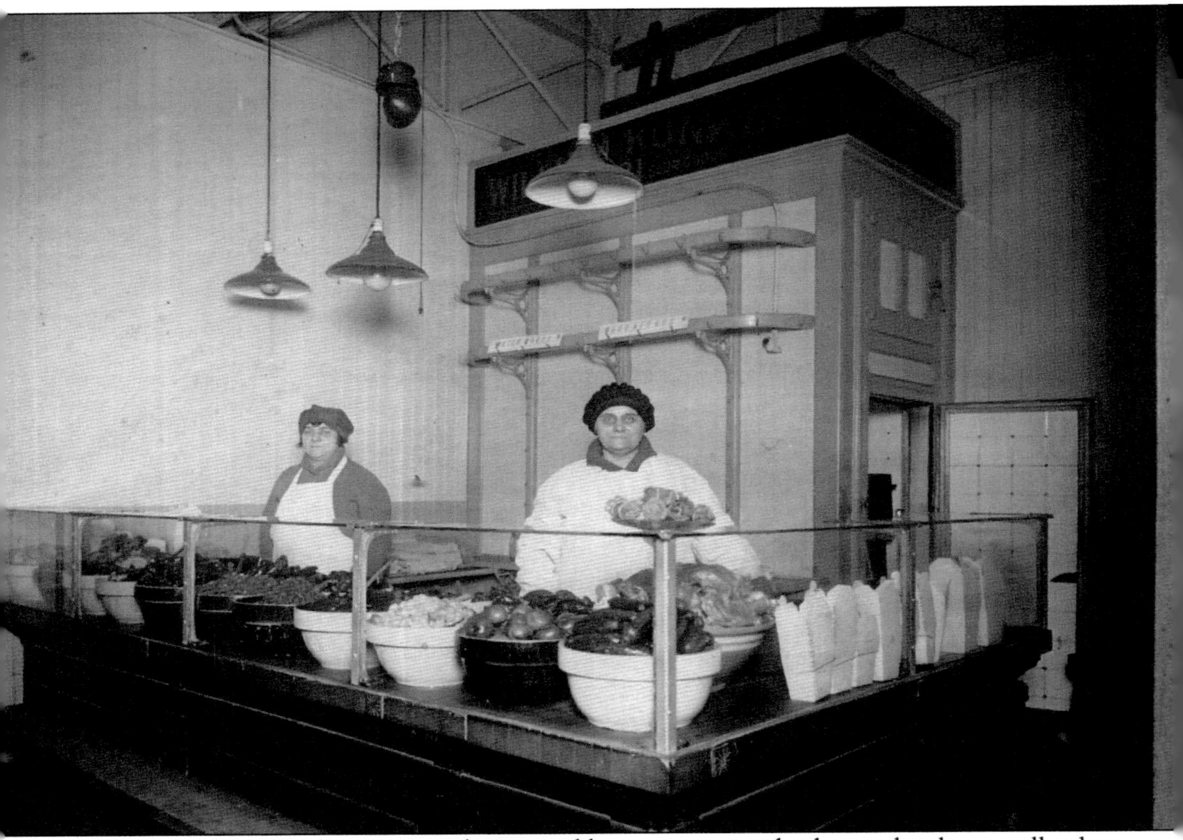

Until the 1930s, only meat merchants could rent space inside the market house; all other vendors had to sell outside. This image of Mollie Kunkel Steding (left) and her mother, Teresa Kunkel, working in their family sour goods stand was taken in the 1930s, shortly after the market house opened to nonmeat businesses. On their counter in large crocks are every kind of pickled vegetable, and the sour goods are boxed for customers in the carryout containers stacked on the right. Behind the women on the empty meat hooks are Watercress and Sassafrass signs. The door to the refrigerator is opened at the rear of the stand, and one can see the tiled insulation inside. Ice was kept in the small space above, while those items requiring refrigeration were stored and cooled in the bottom section. Also in this view, one clearly sees the convenient shelf on which shoppers could place their laden baskets. The women wear what is known among market vendors as a peddler's hat. (Courtesy of Elaine Kunkel Bourgraf.)

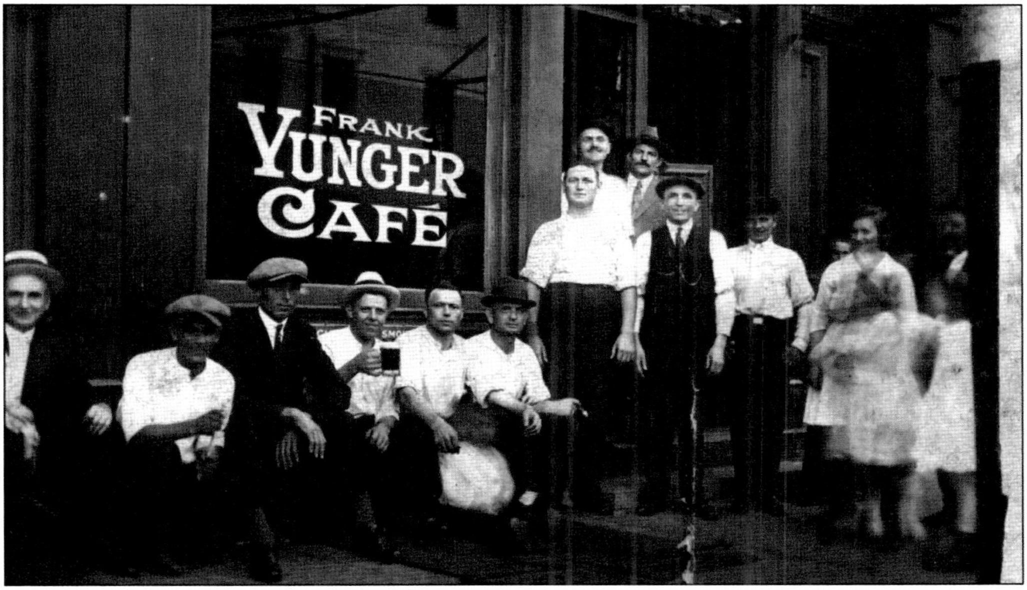

Prohibition ended in 1933, and these neighbors celebrate on the steps of Yunger's Cafe. During Prohibition, Frank Yunger closed his café; to the delight of Findlay Market vendors, shoppers, and neighbors, he reopened when he could legally sell liquor. Frank Yunger sits to the right of the man holding the beer; his son and future café owner, Frank M. Yunger, blurs between his knees. (Courtesy of the Yunger family.)

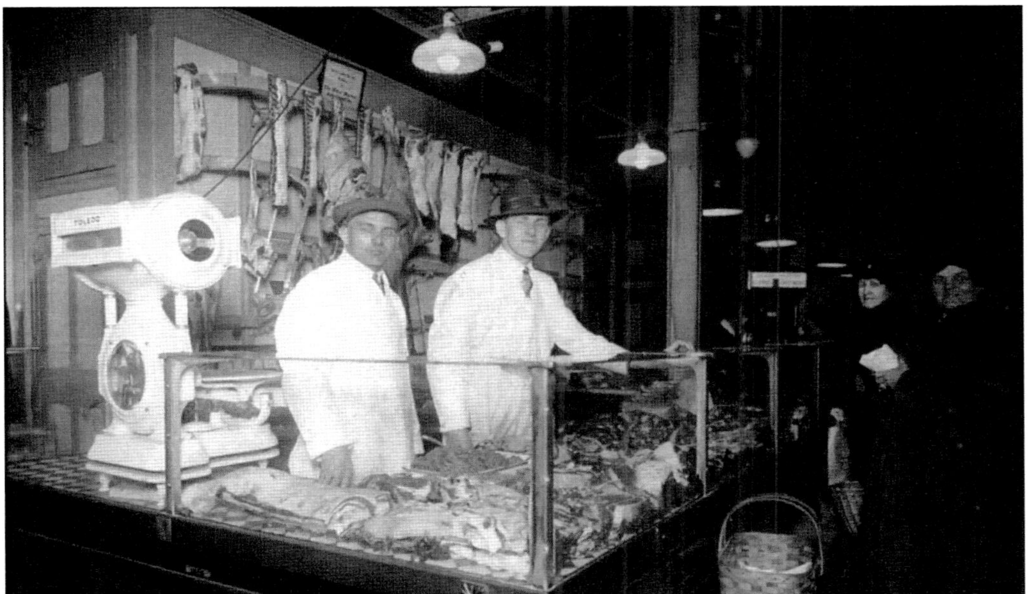

John Mueller (left) and Ernst Mueller (no relation) work John Mueller's meat business. For a long time, only meat was sold inside the market house. On hooks behind the men hang the saws used to trim meat for customers. In this image, Mueller's meat case is full; later, during World War II, however, meat supplies became severely limited, although Mueller managed to stay in business. (Courtesy of Johanna Mueller Ritzi.)

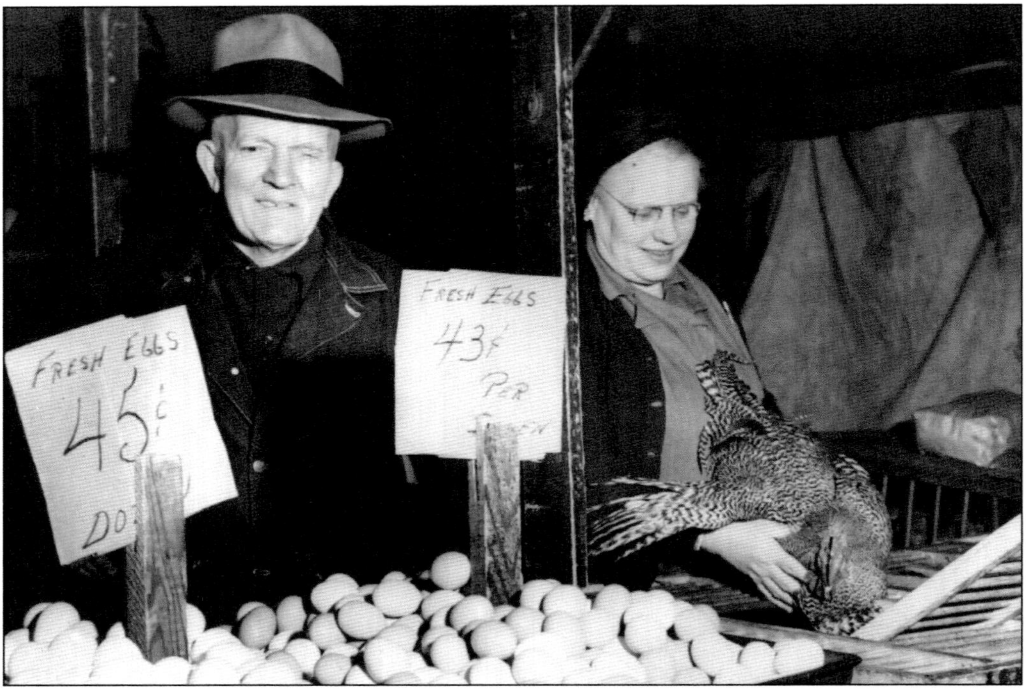

William "Blind" Beck stood alone on market for many years, but when he began to lose his eyesight, his wife, Kathryn, shown here with the chicken, took this spot beside him. It is not entirely clear what Kathryn Beck plans to do with the chicken. (Courtesy of Jane Beck Sansalone.)

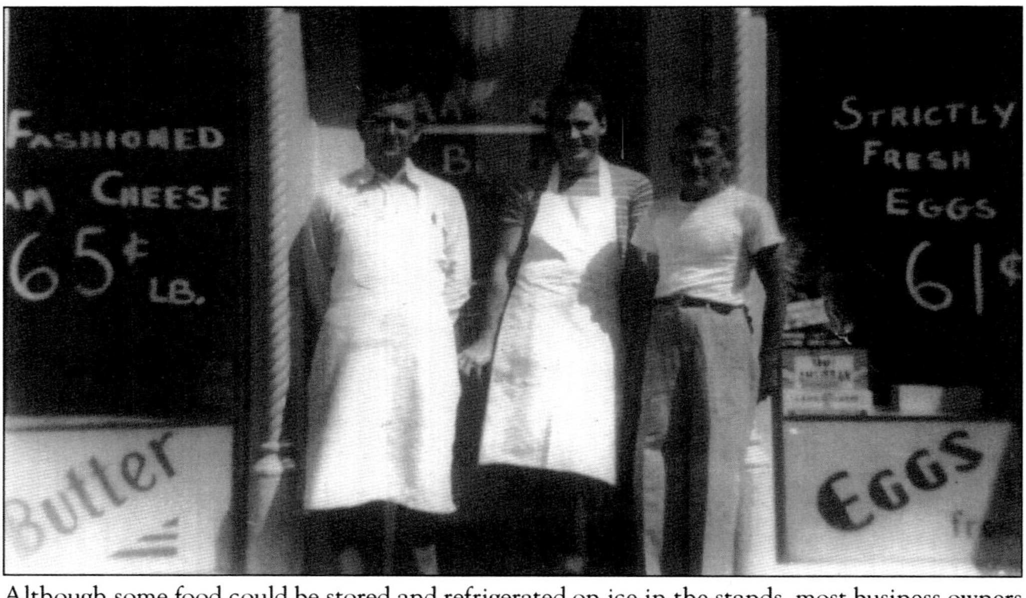

Although some food could be stored and refrigerated on ice in the stands, most business owners kept or rented warehouse spaces off market and hauled fresh goods to market each morning. This is the Gibbs warehouse at 1720 Race Street, around the corner from the market. In the center is Russ Gibbs, who operated the business and was a Findlay Market mainstay for many years. (Courtesy of David Day.)

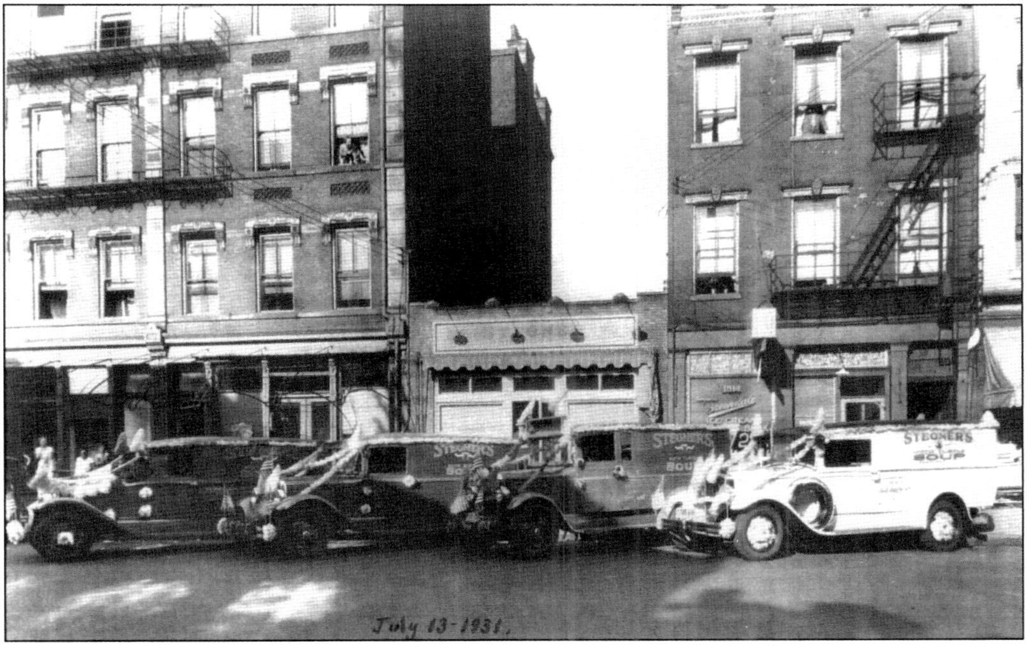

By 1931, when this photograph was taken, Clarence Stegner had already grown Stegner Meats into Stegner Products Company and had begun locally marketing Stegner's mock turtle soup; in the next several years, the business continued its expansion, and by 1936, it was called Stegner Food Distributing Company. Throughout the Stegner company's growth, Clarence Stegner never moved the business more than a block from its original Findlay Market home, and Stegner remained a strong presence on market. The trucks lined up above delivered Stegner's soup daily to local restaurants; the image below indicates the business's expanding fleet. (Courtesy of Peggy Schmidt.)

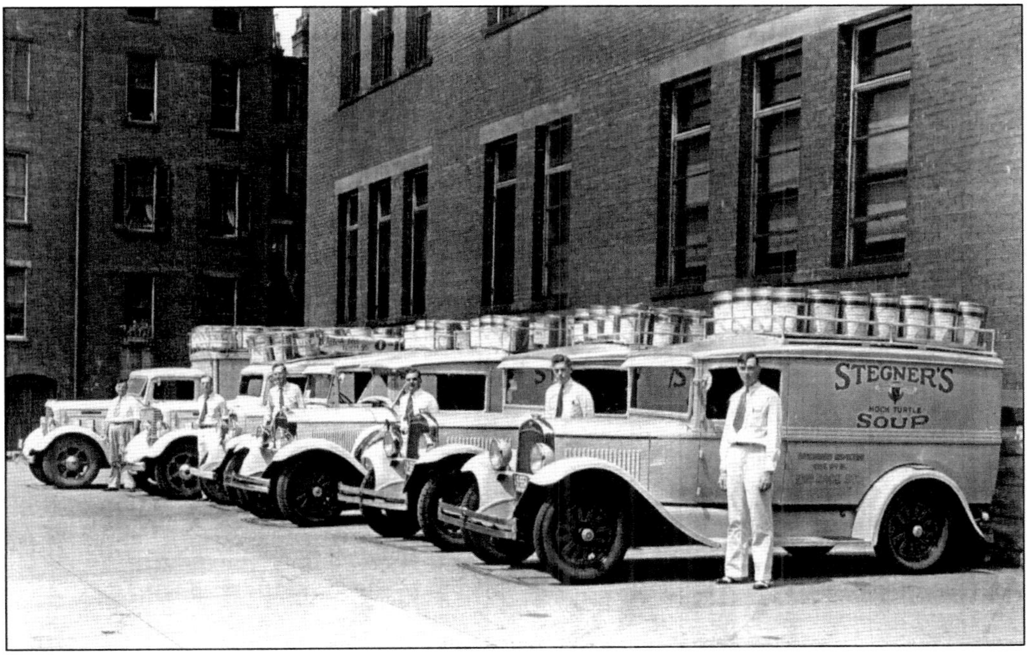

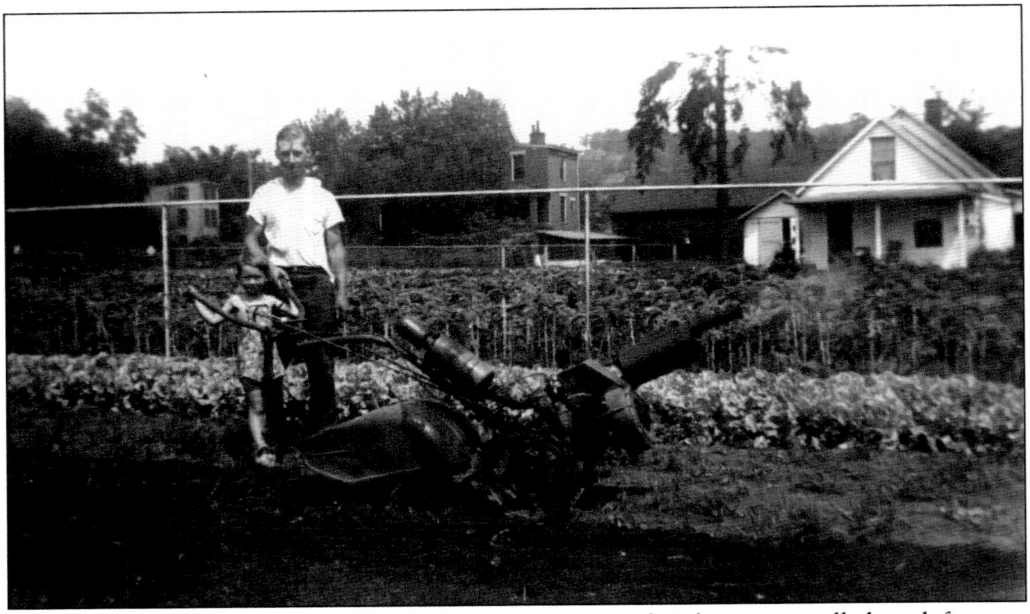

Farmers hauling to market a truckload of produce grown at their homes are called truck farmers. Shown in 1937 with the rototiller used to prepare their soil, truck farmers Doc Krismer and young Jimmy Krismer grew all the produce they sold at market on their Kirby Road three-acre family lot. In the background grows kale; in the foreground is lettuce. Below, cold frame boxes and three greenhouses fill the photograph and show how completely the property was used for farming; produce was grown on-site, prepared for market in the white shed beside the family home, and driven to market every market day in the family truck parked outside the shed. Although he sold his greenhouse business, Jimmy Krismer continues on market every Saturday the farm shed is open. (Courtesy of Jimmy Krismer.)

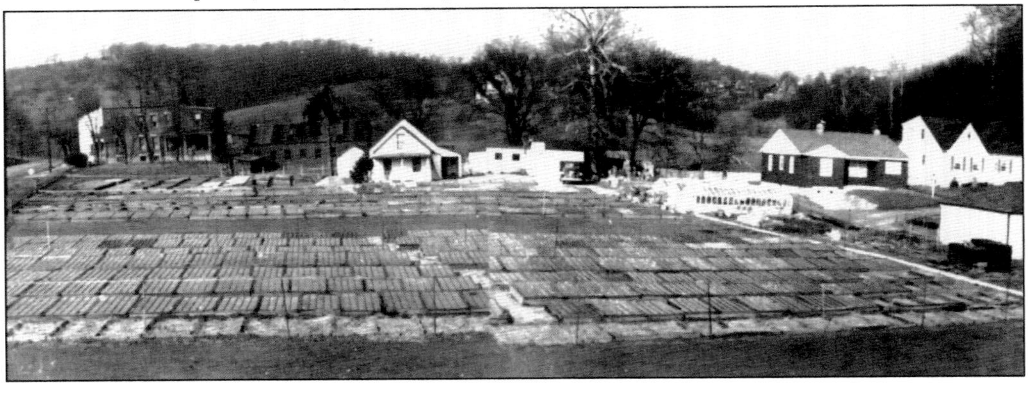

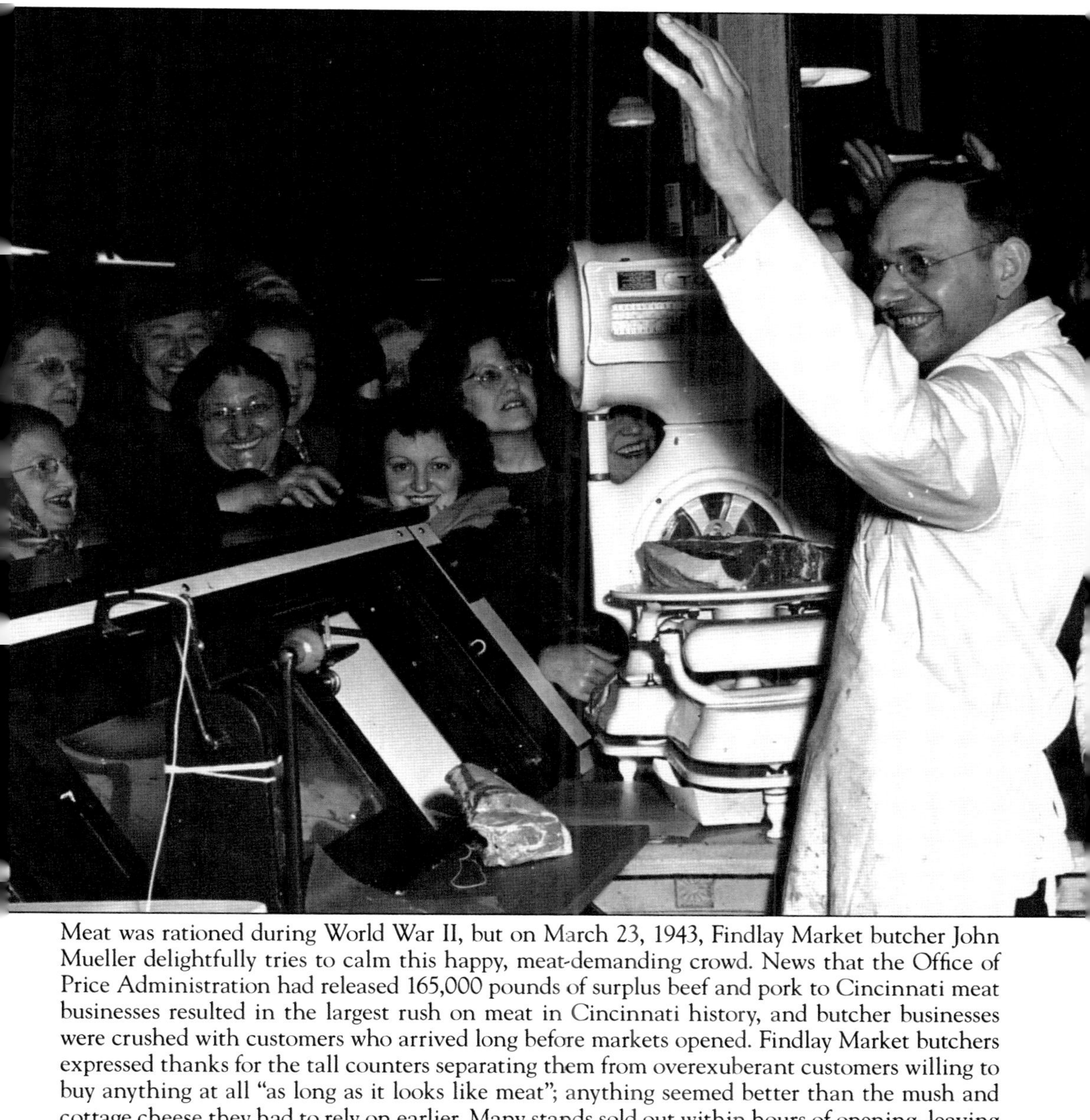

Meat was rationed during World War II, but on March 23, 1943, Findlay Market butcher John Mueller delightfully tries to calm this happy, meat-demanding crowd. News that the Office of Price Administration had released 165,000 pounds of surplus beef and pork to Cincinnati meat businesses resulted in the largest rush on meat in Cincinnati history, and butcher businesses were crushed with customers who arrived long before markets opened. Findlay Market butchers expressed thanks for the tall counters separating them from overexuberant customers willing to buy anything at all "as long as it looks like meat"; anything seemed better than the mush and cottage cheese they had to rely on earlier. Many stands sold out within hours of opening, leaving most of their would-be customers completely meatless again for the remainder of the weekend. (Courtesy of Johanna Mueller Ritzi.)

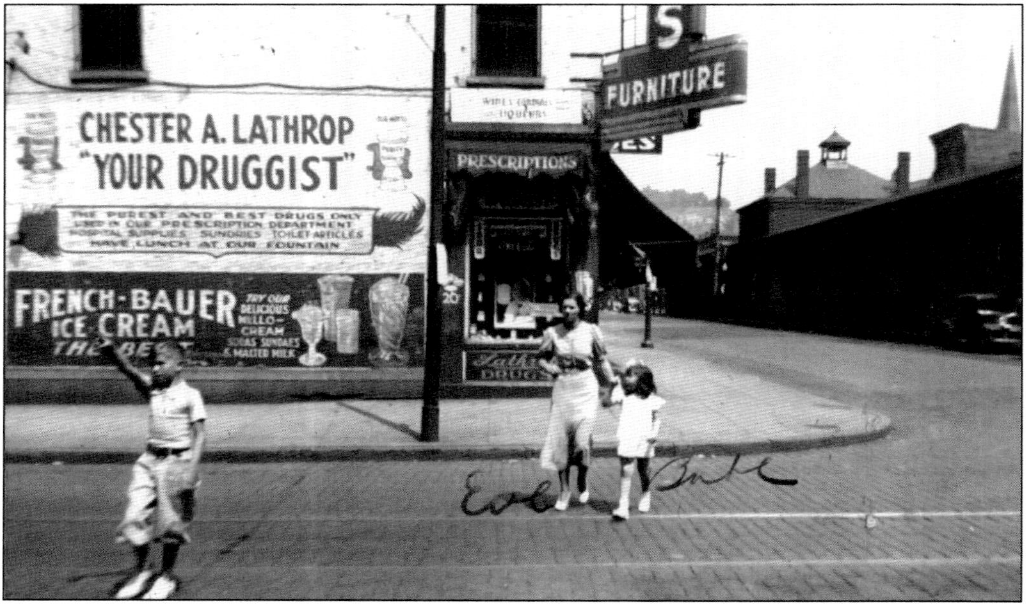

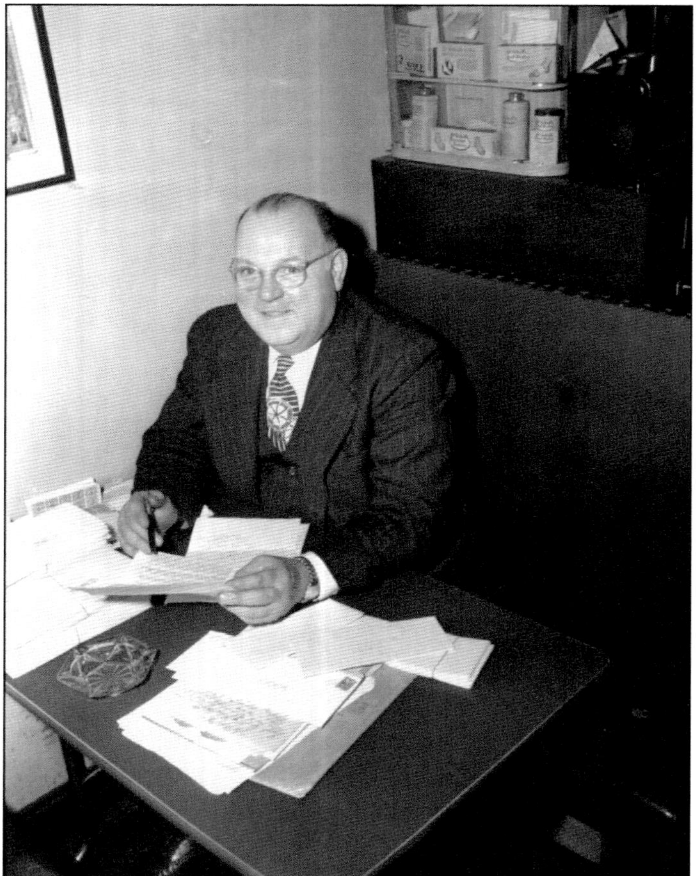

Behind these Yungers who are crossing Elm Street is the wall advertising Chester A. Lathrop, "Your Druggist," on Findlay Market; in the background is the 1937 Findlay Market house on a Sunday. Lathrop's corner store was a source of delight for his neighbors, not only because Lathrop was a fun-loving man (the Yungers called him "Uncle Chester") but also because one could buy a banana split for 20¢ and a Coca-Cola for a nickel. At left in 1963, Lathrop works at a booth in his drugstore; on the shelf behind him are Dr. Scholl's foot-care products such as the bunion reducer and the arch binder. (Above, courtesy of the Yunger family; left, courtesy of Deborah Ooten.)

Barbara Yunger takes a break from cooking hot meals served at Yunger's Cafe in 1937. Seen against the backdrop of the French-Bauer ice-cream advertisement on the Elm Street wall of Chester A. Lathrop's drugstore (now Leader Furniture), one sees evidence in her posture of how hard women on market worked. Yunger and her family lived above the café. (Courtesy of the Yunger family.)

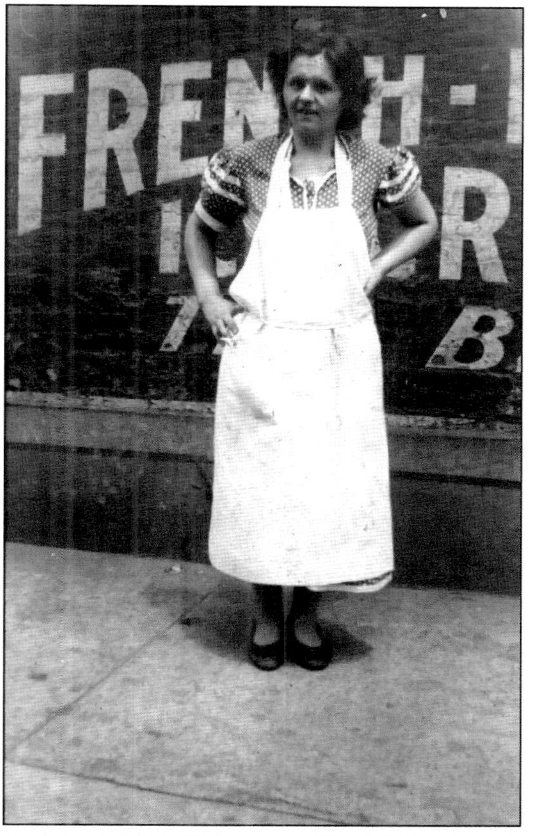

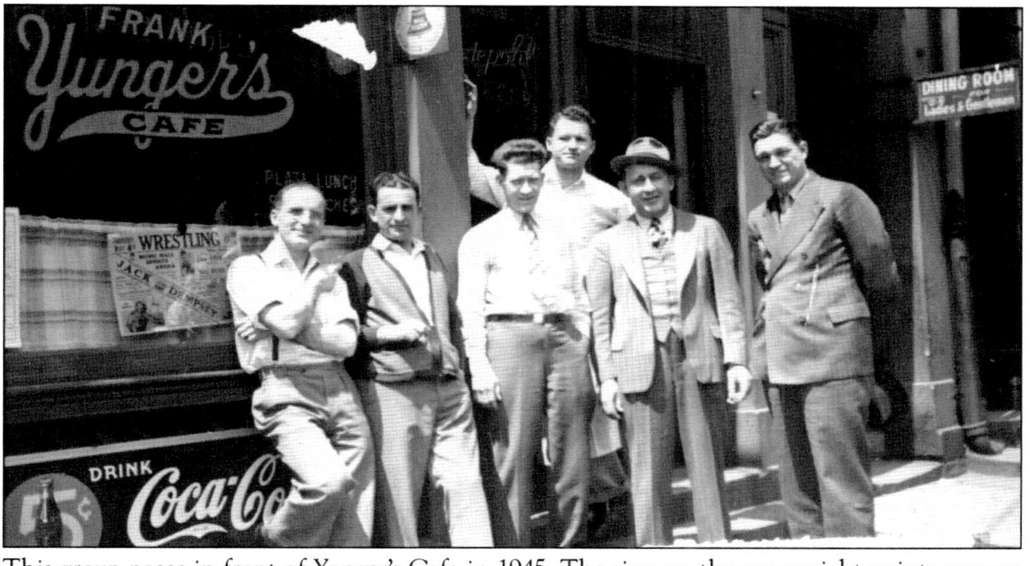

This group poses in front of Yunger's Cafe in 1945. The sign on the upper right points women into the café dining room from a side entrance; for a long time, it was considered improper for women to be in or to enter through the bar. On the window is posted a notice for a Jack Dempsey boxing match at the music hall sports arena. (Courtesy of the Yunger family.)

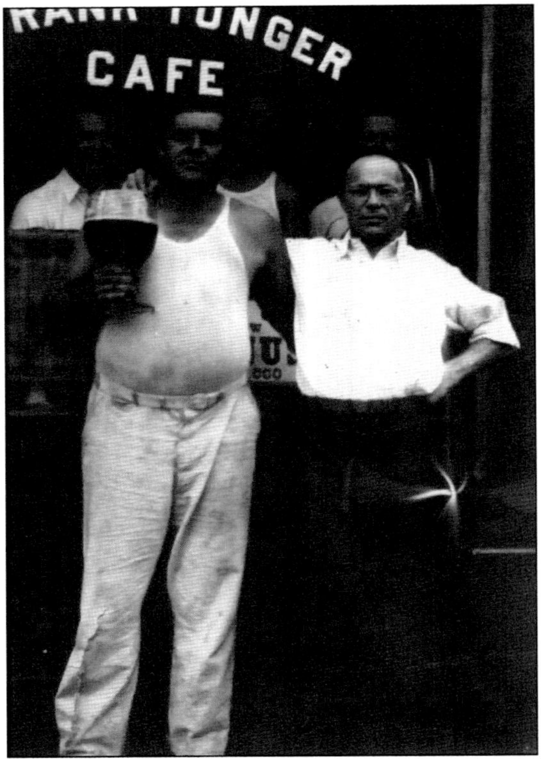

Now that is a mug of beer! Yunger's Cafe was a local café, meeting place, and watering hole for many Findlay Market vendors and their Over-the-Rhine neighbors. Most customers lived close enough to walk from home to the café, thank goodness. (Courtesy of the Yunger family.)

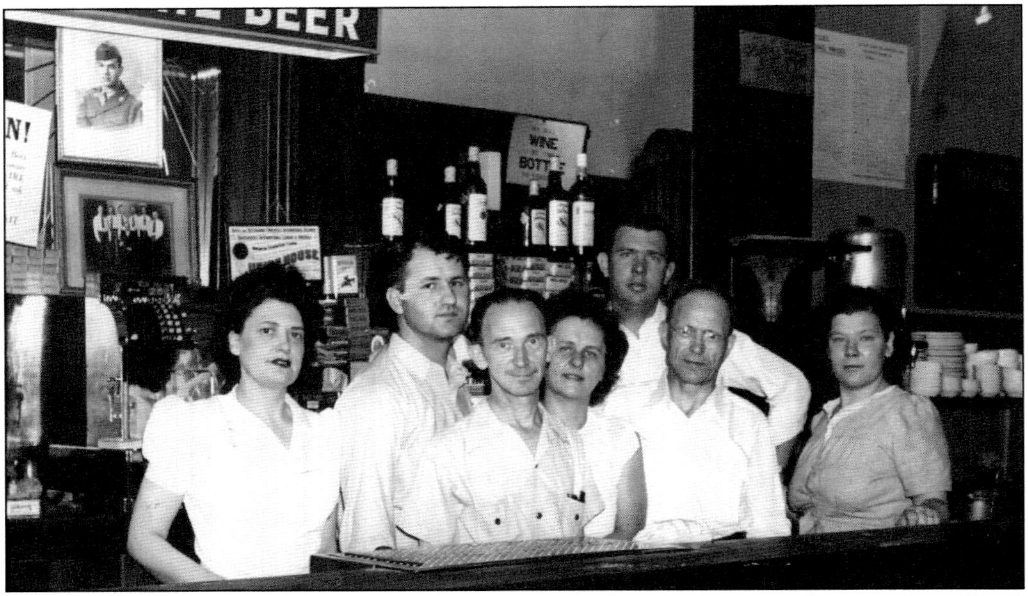

This is Yunger's Cafe's 1945 crew, including owner Frank Yunger, wife Barbara, and son Frank M. Yunger. Above the register is a picture of uniformed son Robert; also above the back bar is a photograph of the café-sponsored bowling team. Plates for the steam table stack in the background, and a sign on the wall reads, "Elderly people please cross streets at intersections *extra carefully.*" (Courtesy of the Yunger family.)

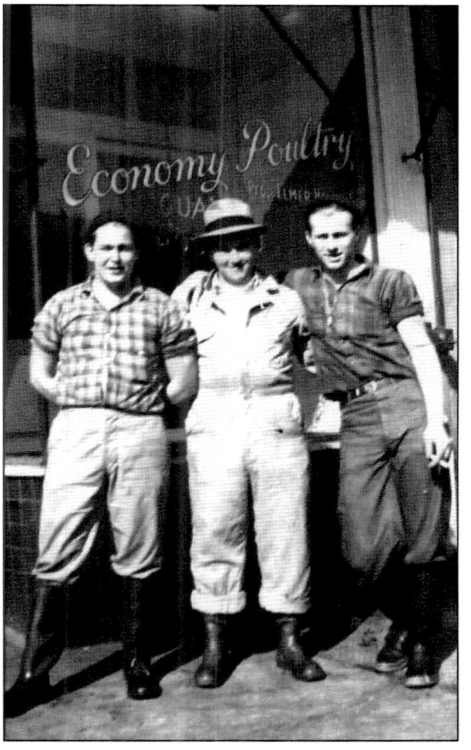

Ray Heist (at right, center) and two employees stand before Heist's Economy Poultry, a storefront business on Elder Street across from the Findlay Market house. The rubber boots worn by all the men indicates the mess in which they worked killing and dressing fresh poultry for their many customers. The Heist family opened Economy Poultry at Findlay Market in 1938, and although the name has changed to Heist Fish and Poultry, the business still operates in the same location today. In 1982, Ray Heist turned ownership of the business to his son, Tim (who, with his wife Barbara, still owns it), but Ray continued working there for another 15 years. Below is the family truck; in the truck's bed are the chicken coops used to transport live chickens to market. (Courtesy of the Heist family.)

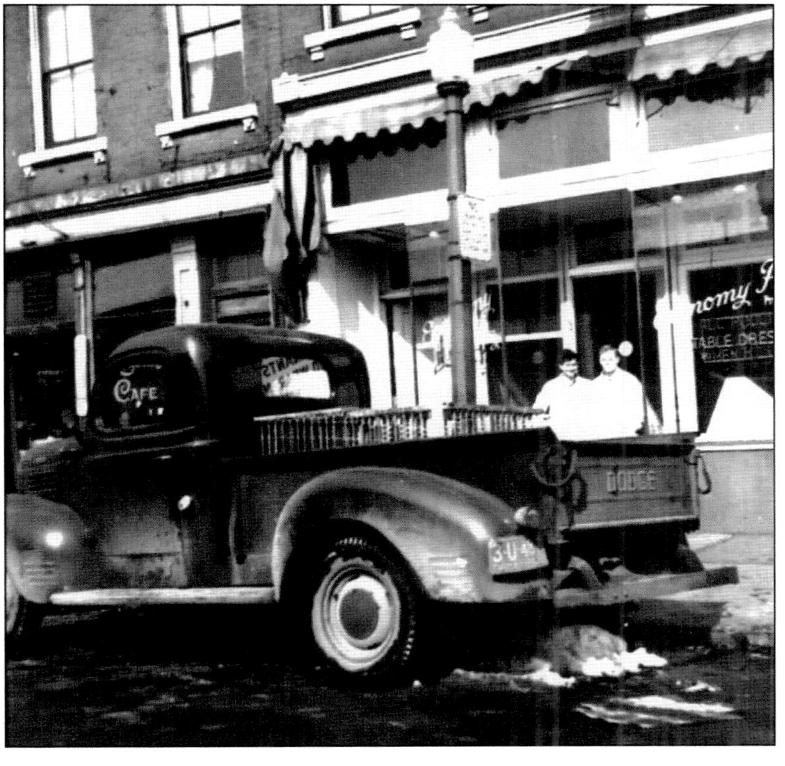

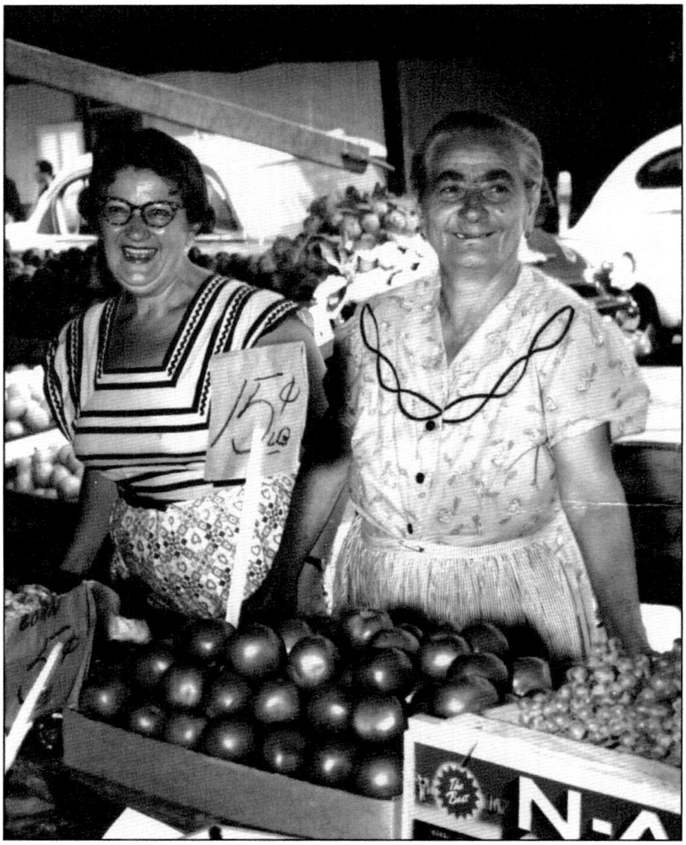

Charlotte Spagnolo (left and below, right), her daughter May (left), and her son Teddy (below, left) work busy Saturdays. Charlotte Spagnolo owned this stand. The physical labor involved in operating a stand on market is missed on most shoppers. Everything from the produce to the crates to the sawhorses to the oilcloth to the signs to the paper bags to the string of lights seen in this photograph had to be hauled in, set up every morning, removed, and hauled out every night. Vendors often begin their days by 2:00 or 3:00 a.m., gathering product in their homes or in their trucks and getting them to market by the time the market bell rings at 6:00 a.m. (Courtesy of Larry Schmolt.)

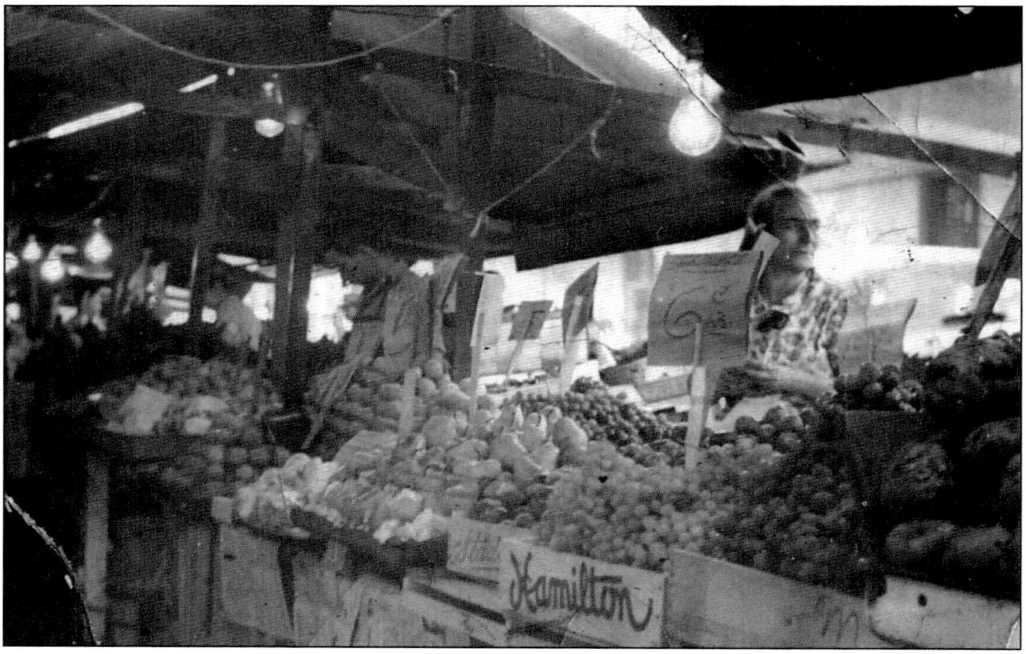

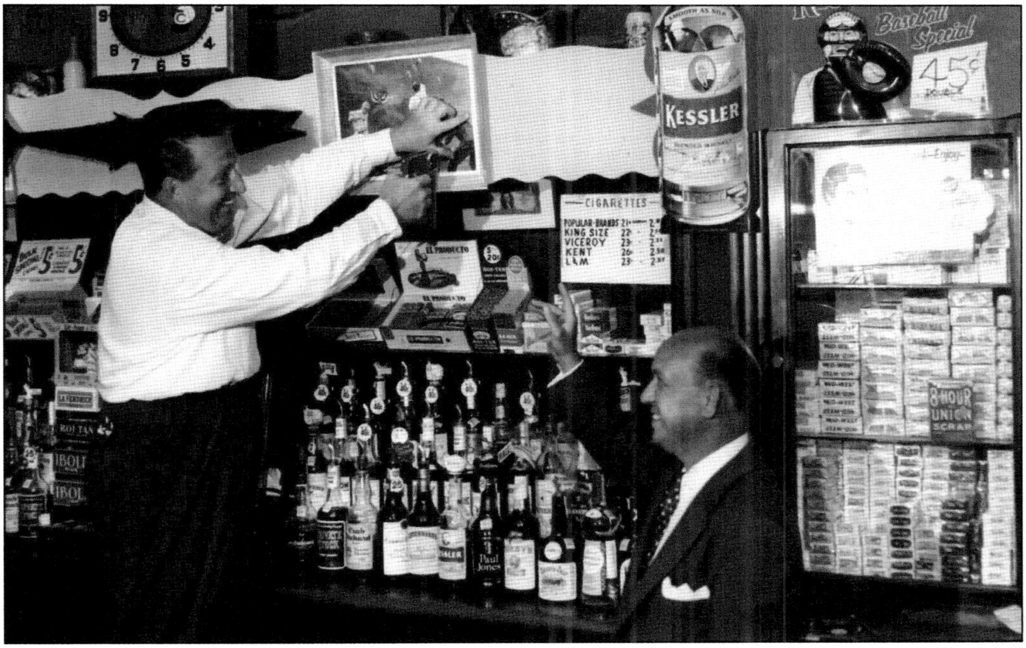

Harold Brooks (right) and Bernie Cohen hang a picture in Brooks's Elder Cafe at 128 West Elder Street across from the market house. Brooks bought the café in 1941 and ran it until 1965. He worked many jobs to buy his café; bookmaking for "gentleman betters" was the most lucrative. On Saturday nights, Brooks hired a piano player and Brooks sang; it is said he had a beautiful voice. (Courtesy of the Brooks family.)

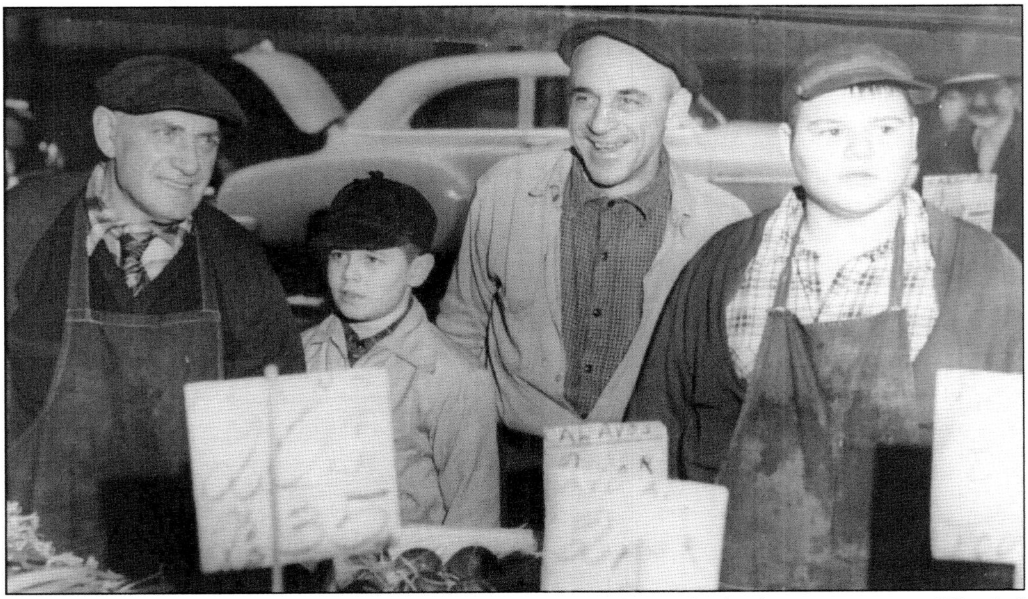

Ted, Bernie, Joe, and Nick Kunkel Jr., seen from left to right, embody the generations of Kunkel men at work together in their produce stand outside the market house around 1945; during this same time period, women in the family typically handled the family pickle business at their stand inside the market house. (Courtesy of Elaine Kunkel Bourgraf.)

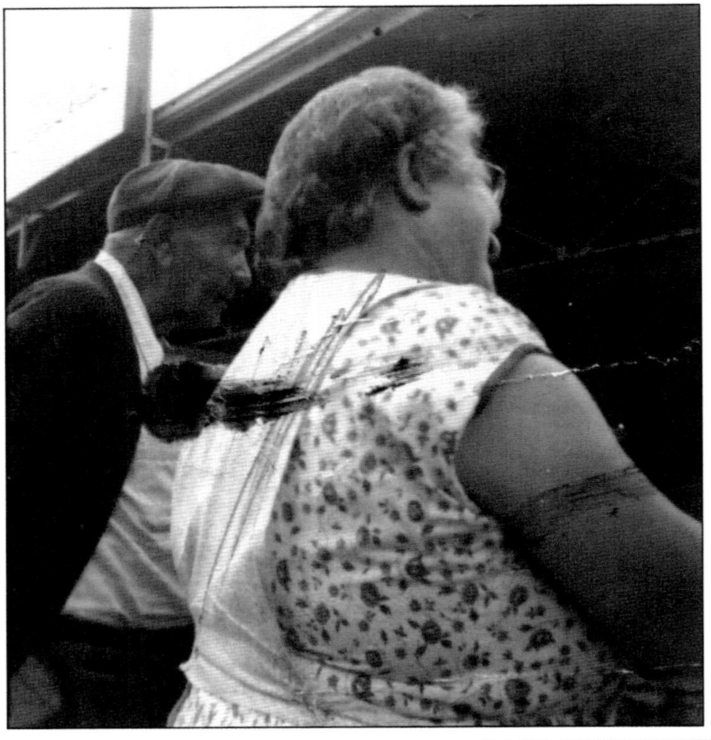

At left are husband and wife Joe and Lena Caito, who operated stands on both Findlay and Court Street Markets. Joe Caito spoke very little English; Lena communicated with him in Italian. It is said that Lena was the family workhorse responsible for the business's success. The two were joined on market by their seven children; today their grandson Frank Gaudio and his son John Gaudio operate the family business at almost this exact location. Below, and many years later, Lena Caito weighs tomatoes. (Left, courtesy of the Gaudio family; below, photograph by Jane Gahl.)

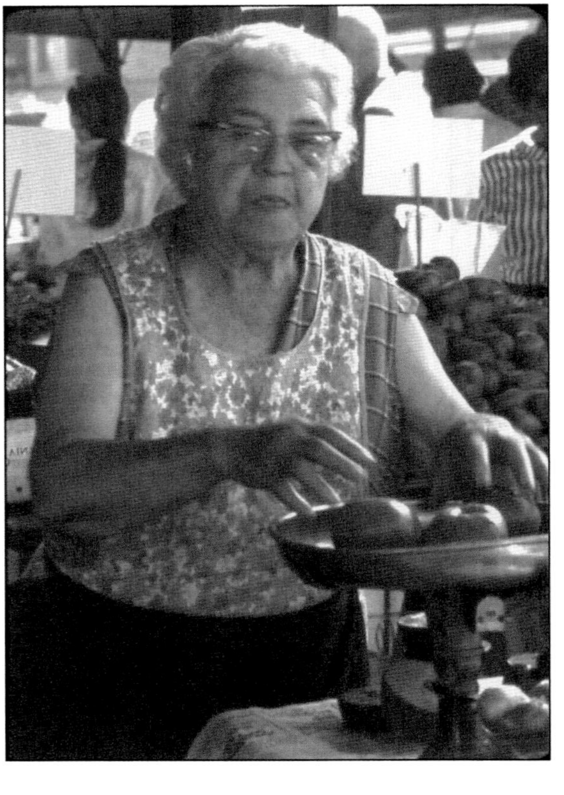

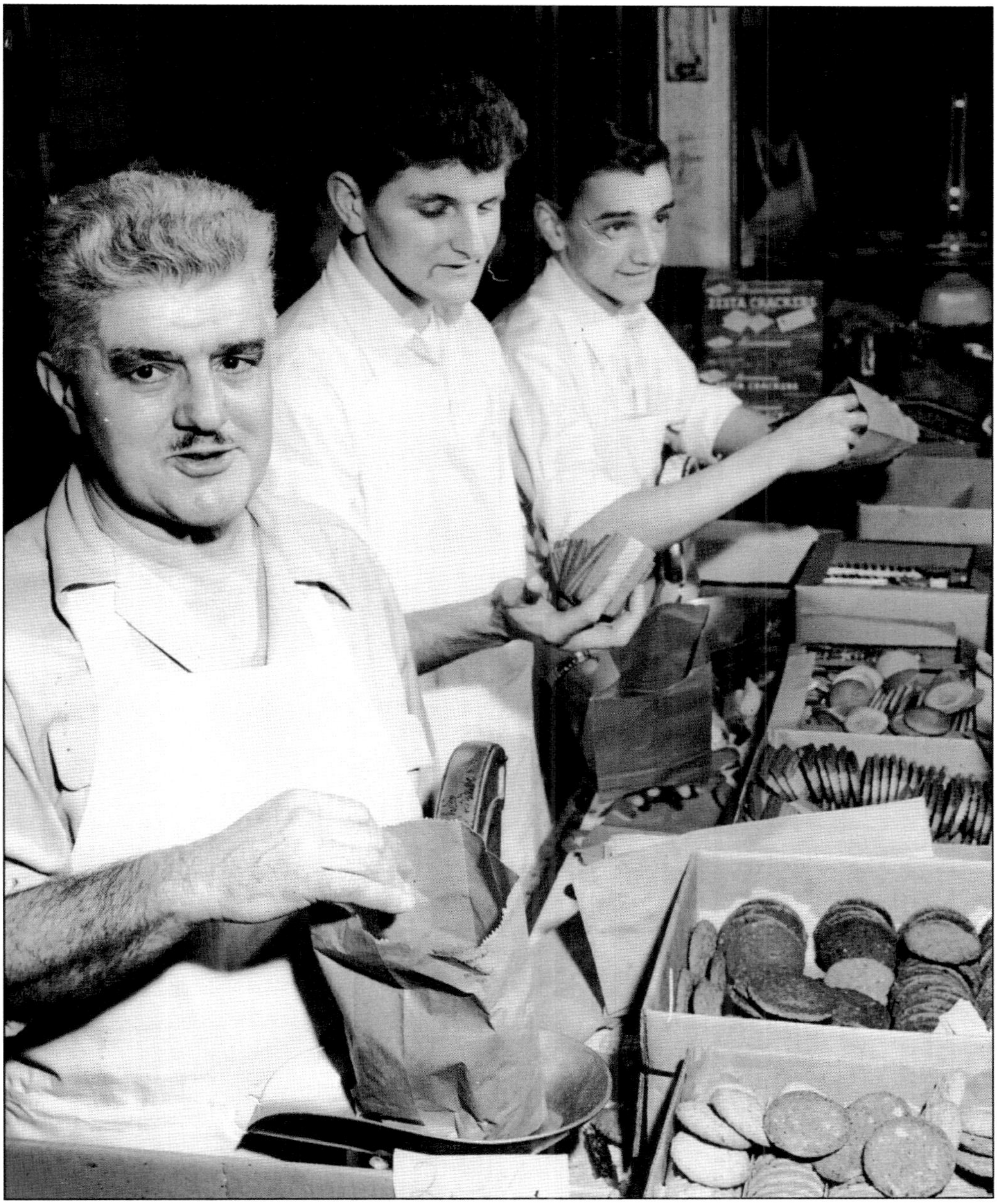

"Charlie, could you sell me a cookie that won't make me fat?" was a request repeated by many of Charles Naish's cookie customers. Naish (left) took over this cookie stand from his father, William, and later Charles's son, Bill Naish (pictured next to Charles), ran the business. Fresh, high-quality cookies were bought early each week either from local bakeries like Mrs. Allison's or Strietman Bakery or they were trucked in from Illinois and sold on market. The Naishes knew their customers' favorite cookies, and with hands busily filling different varieties in bags, the Naishes winked and smiled and chatted with their regulars. The Naishes sold cookies, potato chips, and pretzels in bulk, placed individual orders in paper bags, and weighed them; math was calculated either in their heads or scribbled on slips of paper, but it had to be done right and fast so the customer was never kept waiting. (Courtesy of the Naish Gambetta family.)

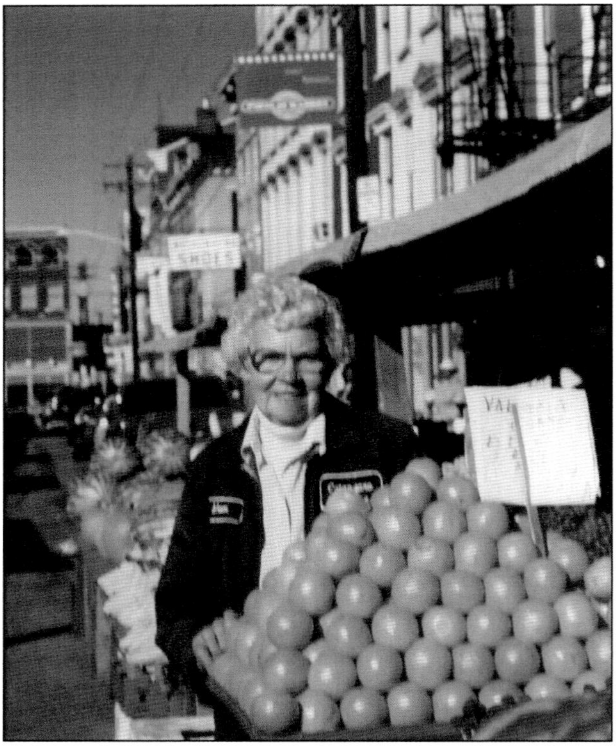

Olivia Catanzaro works at her produce stand. Over the years, Catanzaro was eventually joined at her stand by her children, her grandchildren, and her great-grandchildren; Findlay Market teemed with happy Catanzaros. The family became one of the best-loved and most influential contemporary families on market, and Saturdays would find a whole slew of them at work there. (Courtesy of the Catanzaro family.)

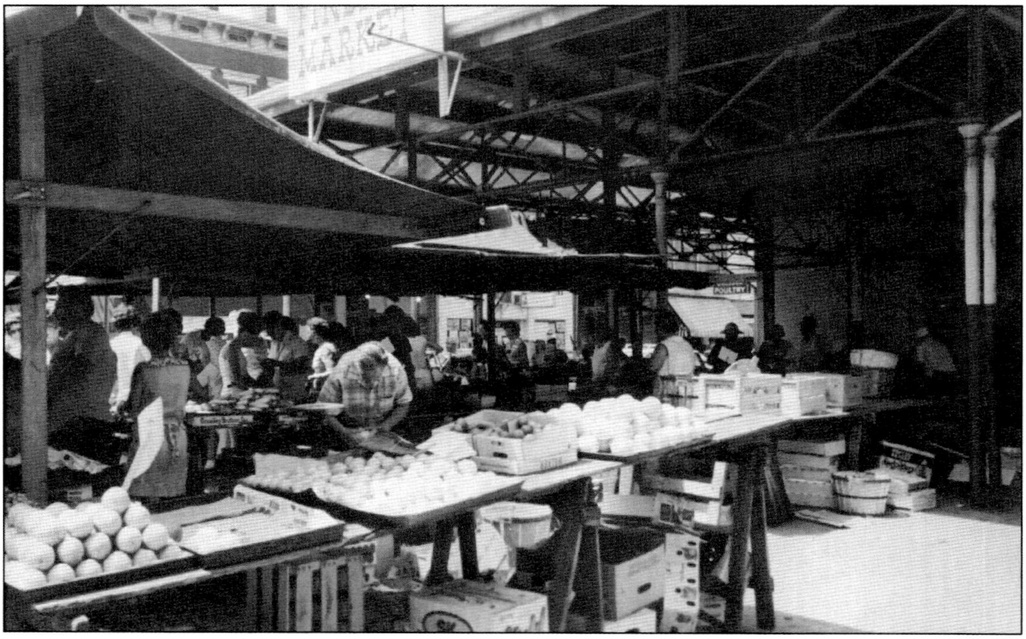

This photograph shows the Race Street entrance to the market and the Gaudio produce stand. At the entrance to the market house and standing in the shadows in his white paper hat is the "Horseradish Man," who would grate fresh horseradish so pungent that it made the eyes burn. The Horseradish Man also cracked and grated fresh coconut there. (Courtesy of George Wright.)

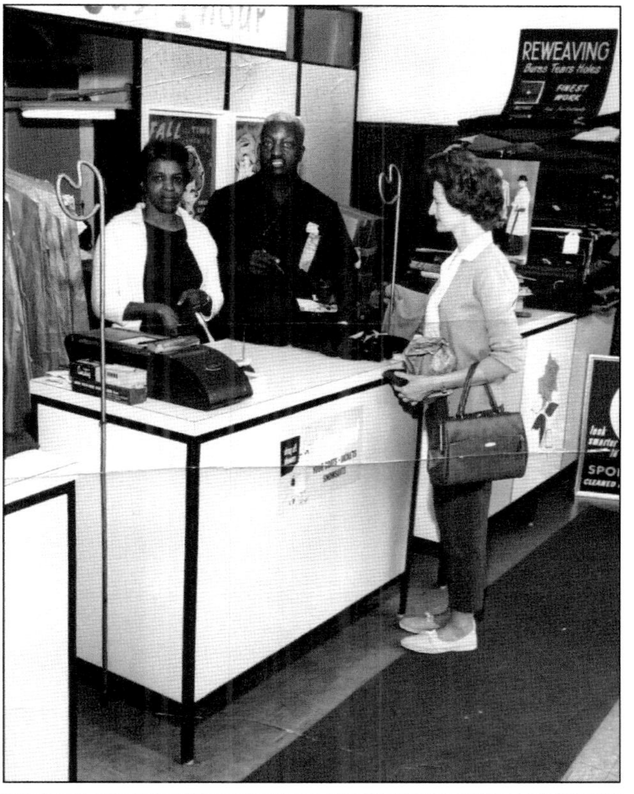

Reconstruction of Cincinnati's West End in 1962 prompted Dorothy and Curlen Hudson (left and right behind the counter at right) to move their Hudson Brothers Dry Cleaning to 1720 Elm Street. Hudson Brothers Dry Cleaning became a neighborhood meeting place where for 46 years loyal customers have been considered a part of the Hudson family. Below, Duane Hudson Morgan (right), daughter of Dorothy and Curlen Hudson, visits with police officers Ray Scarlotta and A. Brown in front of the family business. Because the Hudsons offered discount dry-cleaning rates for police officers, firefighters, and meter readers over so many years, they nurtured very special relationships with Cincinnati's uniformed employees. The sign hanging above the inside counter reads, "Fresh as a Flower . . . in Just One Hour." (Courtesy of the Hudson family.)

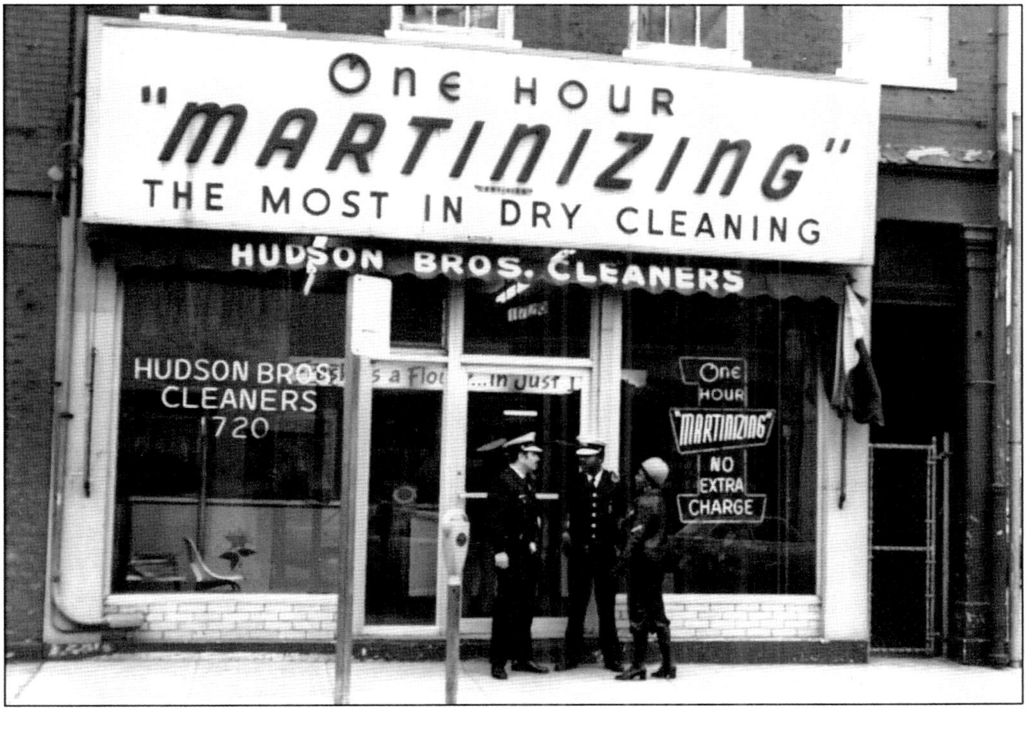

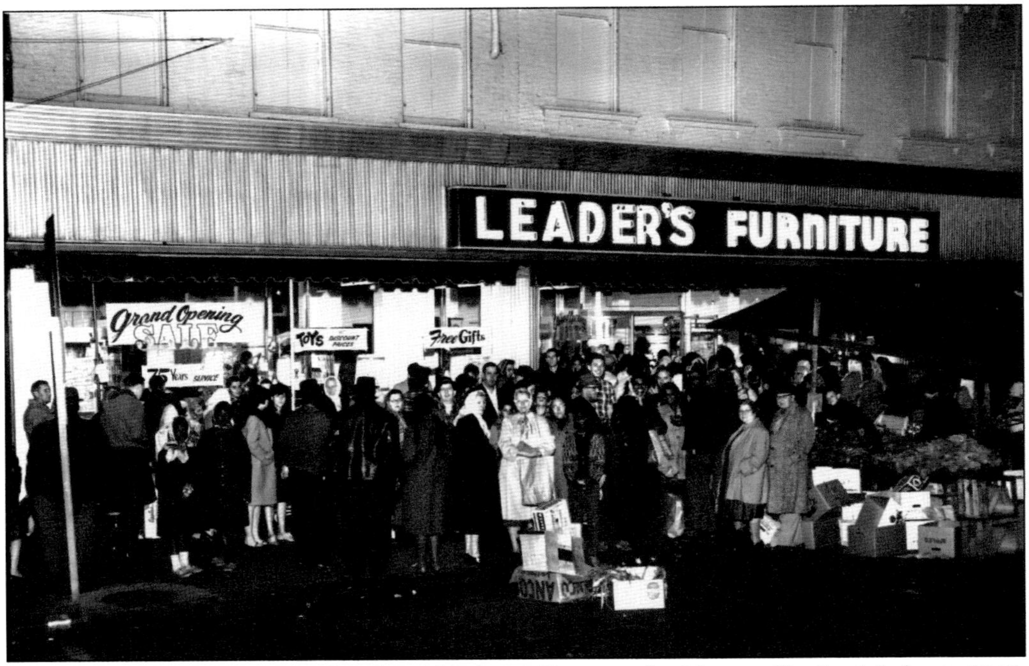

When Leader Furniture moved to the old Solway's Furniture building on Findlay Market in 1963, its grand opening event drew big crowds on a busy market night. Below, the president of nearby Provident Bank (right) draws the winning tickets for raffle prizes, and the crowd swells out the front door onto Elder Street. The market bustled until late several nights each week, and Leader Furniture matched market hours by keeping its doors open late too (notice the Catanzaro's produce stand open and busy on the right side of the photograph above). Brothers Gary and Gerald Mallin own Leader Furniture, which was started by their father and his business partner; Gary's son William has now joined them. (Courtesy of the Mallin family.)

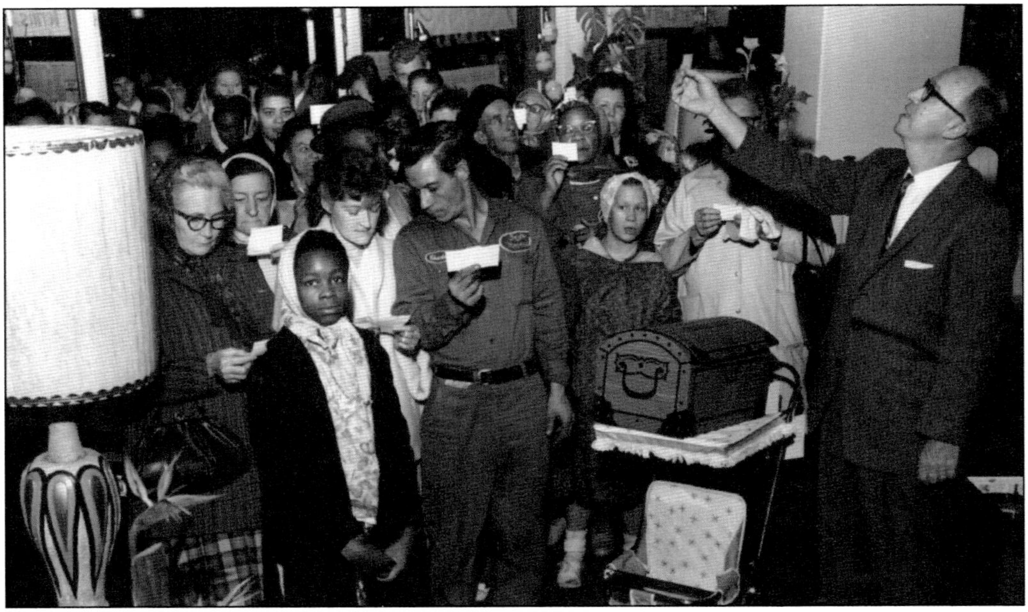

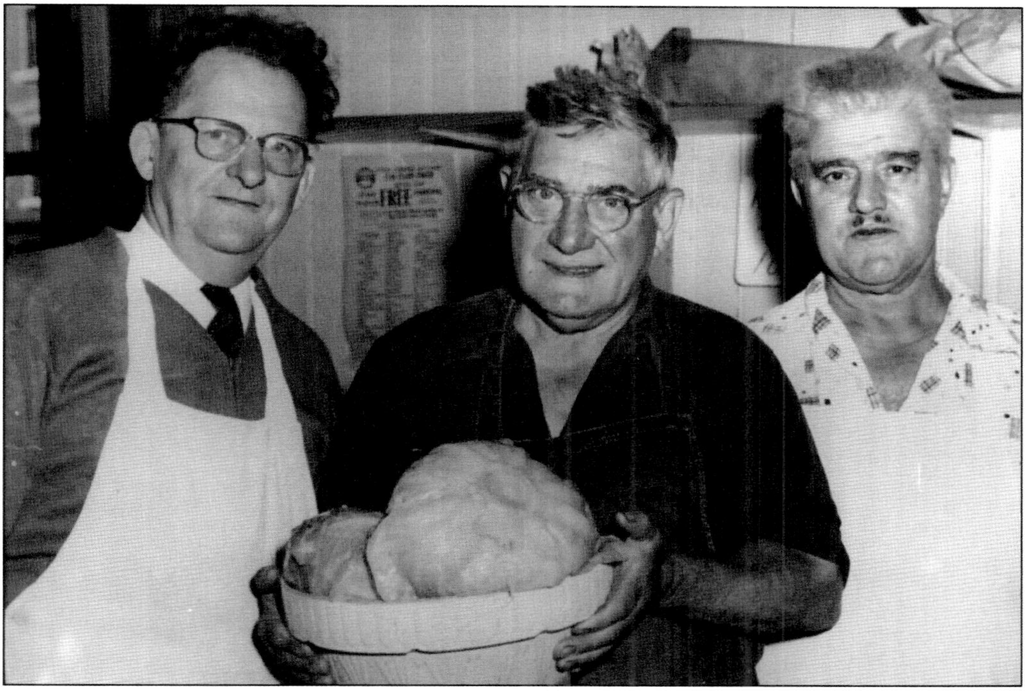

Wilson Spies, Ted Kunkel, and Charles Naish (left to right), all three longtime Findlay Market vendors, pose together inside the market in the photograph above. Spies sold meats and cheese and specialty foods; Kunkel sold sauerkraut and pickles; Naish sold cookies. Below, Joe Kunkel, Ted Kunkel's brother, visits his indoor pickle and sauerkraut stand; the Kunkel men operated a produce stand outside while the women worked the pickle stand inside. Below, notice the rows of pickle jars and the racks of paper bags on the wall. The sign in the display case points to pickled pig's feet for $1 per pound. (Courtesy of Elaine Kunkel Bourgraf.)

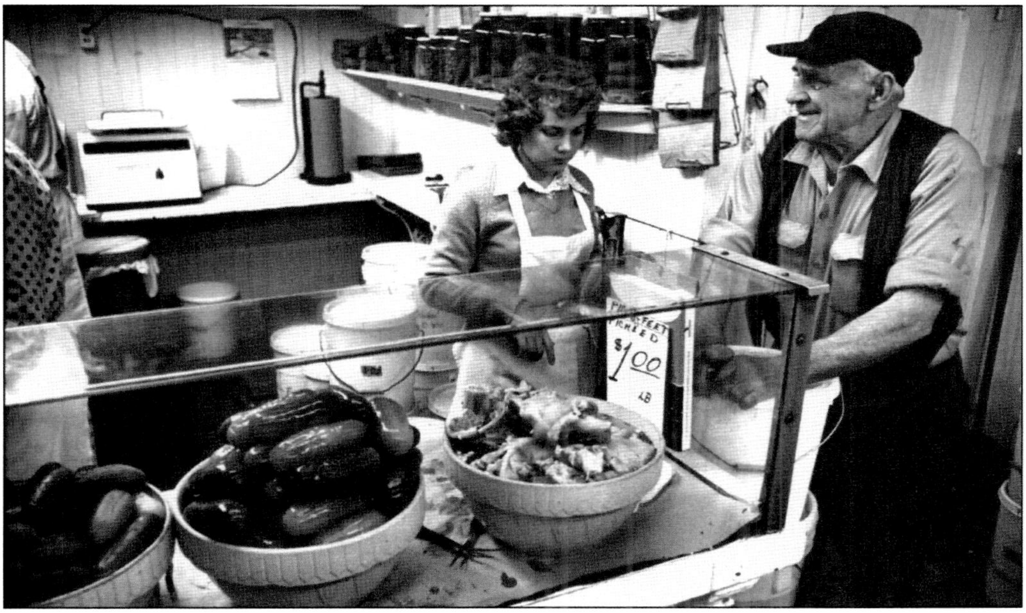

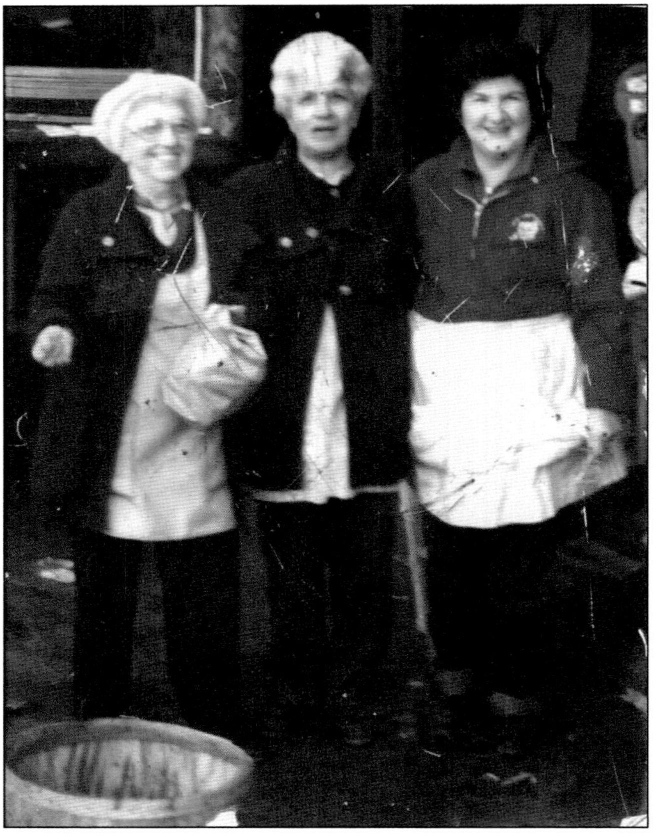

At left are Annie Schawilje, Mary Hauser, and Carol Kirn (left to right) at the stand originally established by Annie's parents, Joe and Lena Caito. After Lena Caito reduced her involvement at the stand, Annie became the "feisty" presence at market, often insisting, "Lady, don't put your nose up to the corn!" or "Lady, don't dig your fingernails into the tomatoes!" In the right side of the photograph is the parking meter on Race Street; behind the women is the family truck used to haul produce from the warehouse and cold storage to market and back. Below, Annie Schawilje (right) and her nephew Frank Gaudio work together at the family stand Frank now operates with his son John Gaudio. (Courtesy of the Gaudio family.)

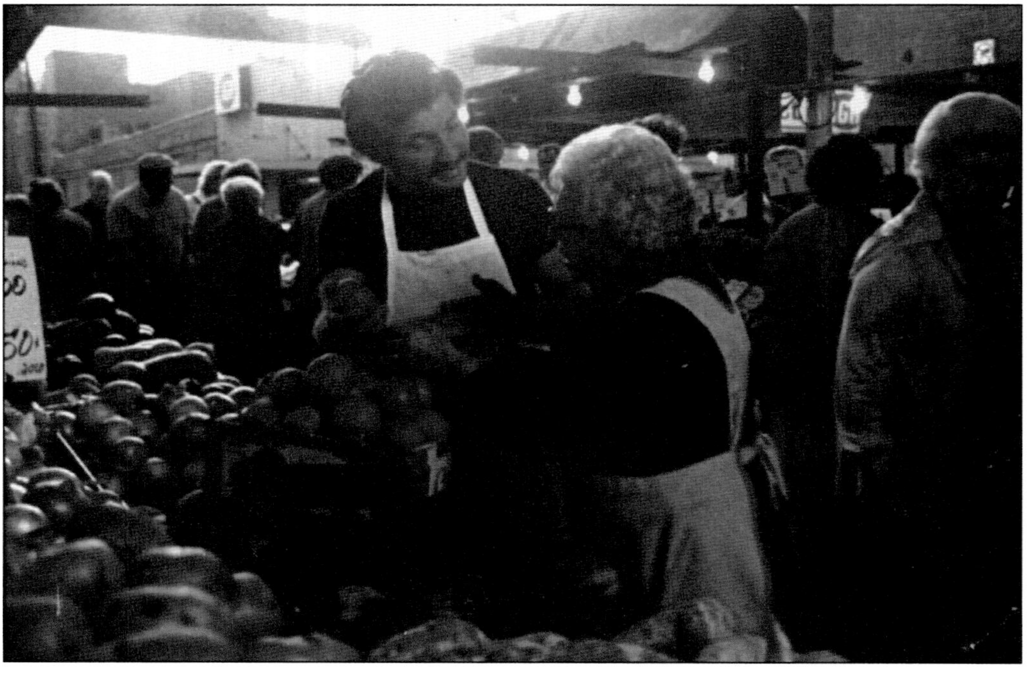

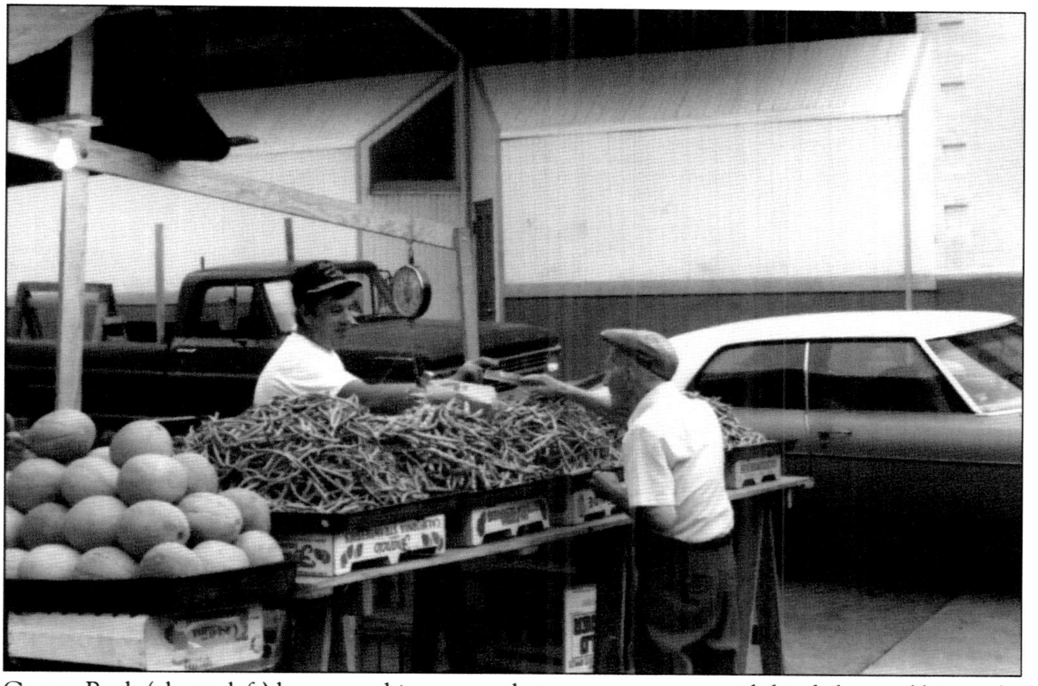

George Roth (above, left) began working on market as a young man with his father and his uncle, and he still sells his produce every market day at Findlay Market. The photograph above shows Roth working his stand sometime in the 1970s. In the photograph below, Roth (left) and his son Mark Roth work during a Taste of Findlay Market event that for many years was held every autumn. Below, George Roth wears a market hat, a black peddler's cap in the style of many market vendors. There was apparently a big football game the day this photograph was taken because the Roths have set up their television set on a crate behind them. (Courtesy of George Roth.)

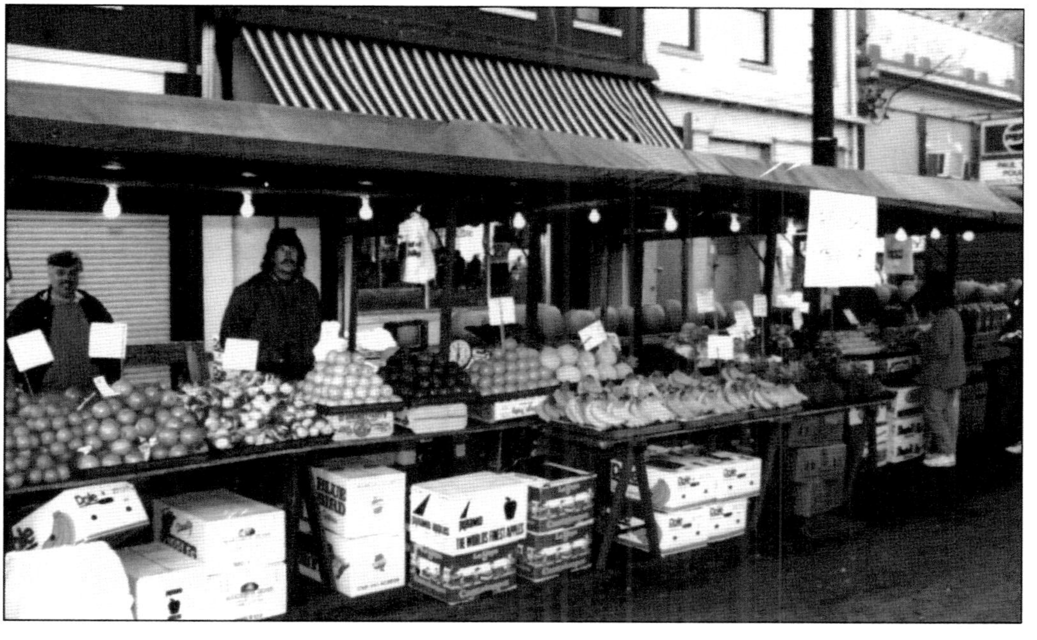

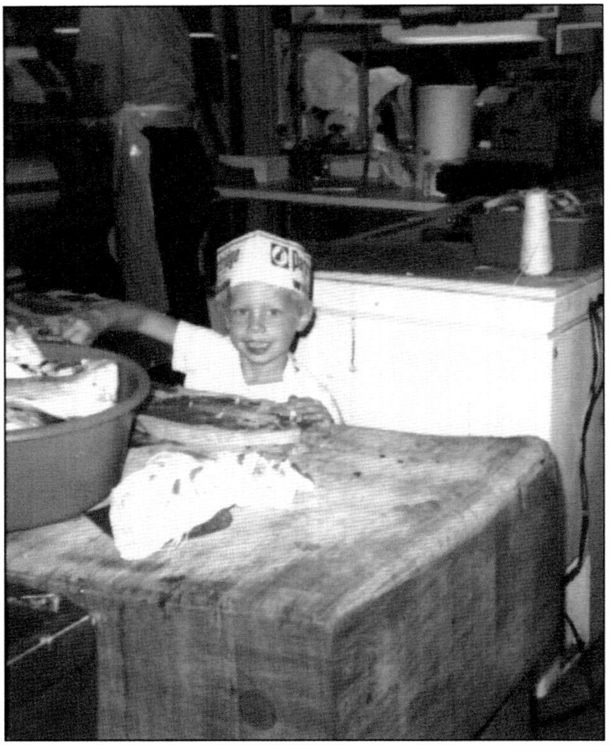

For as long as the market has existed, children have worked there alongside their parents and grandparents; those children who grow up with the market ingrained in their lives and who continue working there as adults affectionately refer to themselves and to one another as "market rats." Young market rat Mark Kroeger looks comfortable and happy behind a huge butcher's block at left. Below, the same but older Mark Kroeger prepares sausage by hand at the stand he and his family continued to operate. Until the Kroegers sold their business, they displayed in their stand the German document certifying Mark's grandfather as an official sausage maker. (Courtesy of the Kroeger family.)

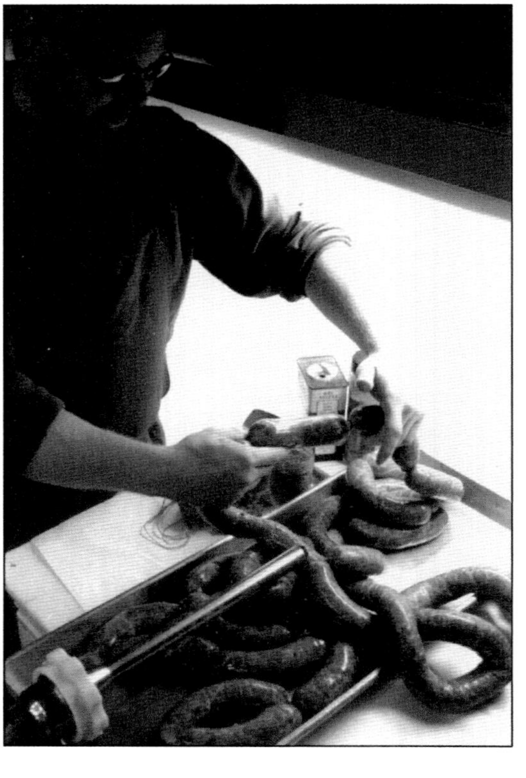

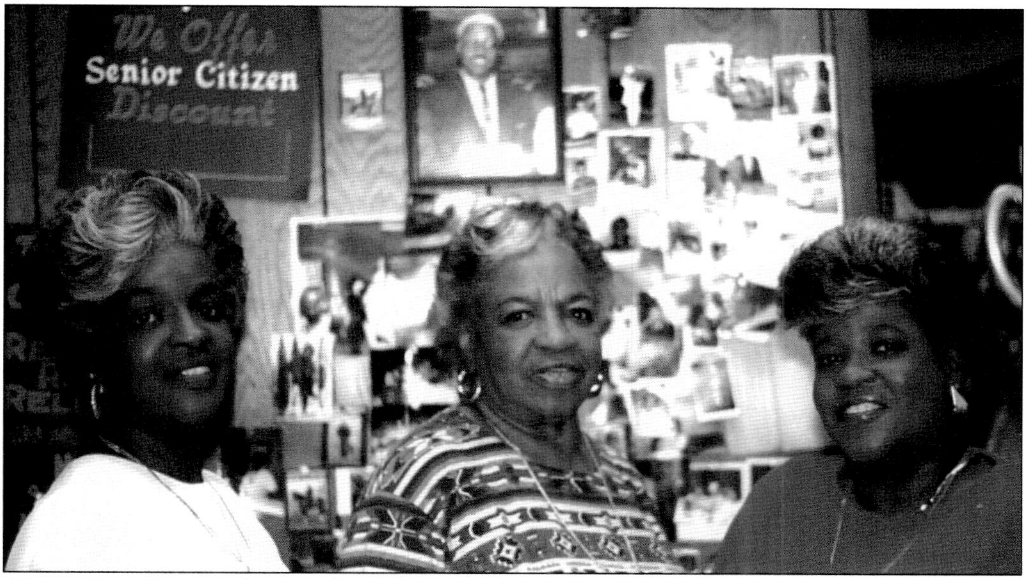

Above, Dorothy "Cookie" Hudson Phipps (left) and Duane Hudson Morgan (right) pose with their mother, Dorothy Hudson, at their Hudson Brothers Dry Cleaning business at 1702 Elm Street. After their father's death, Cookie and Duane joined their mother in running the family's business; the sisters took full responsibility for its operation in 2000. A photograph of their father, Curlen, hangs on the wall behind them. Below, Cookie (left) and Duane receive the key to the city of Cincinnati from Mayor Mark Mallory for their long and distinguished service to the city and for consistently maintaining a strong example of a minority-owned business; Cookie and Duane are quick to remind people that minority-owned businesses includes those run by women. The sisters retired and closed Hudson Brothers Dry Cleaning in November 2008. (Courtesy of the Hudson family.)

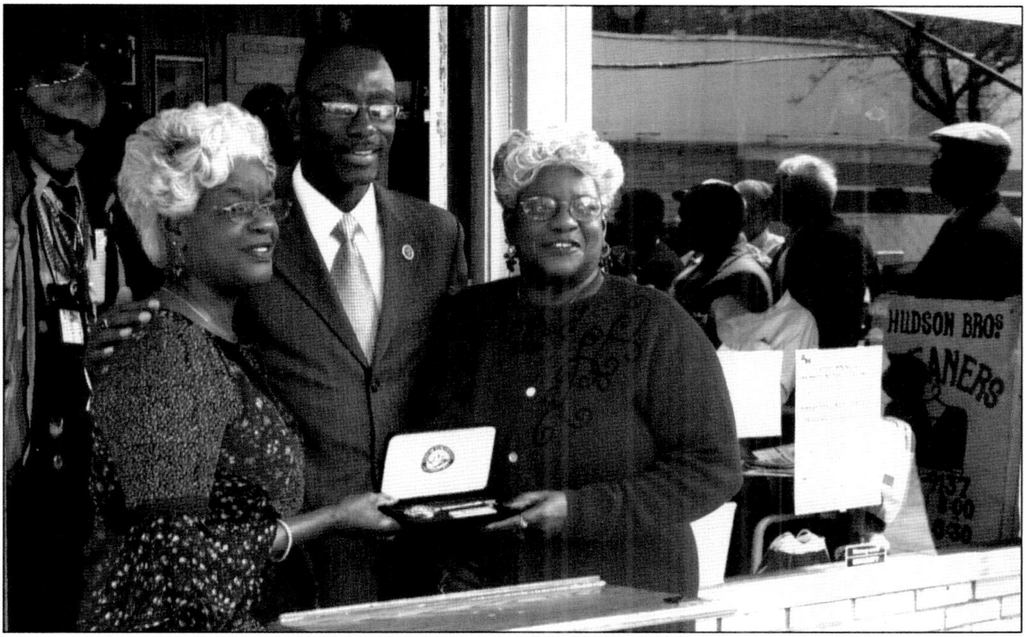

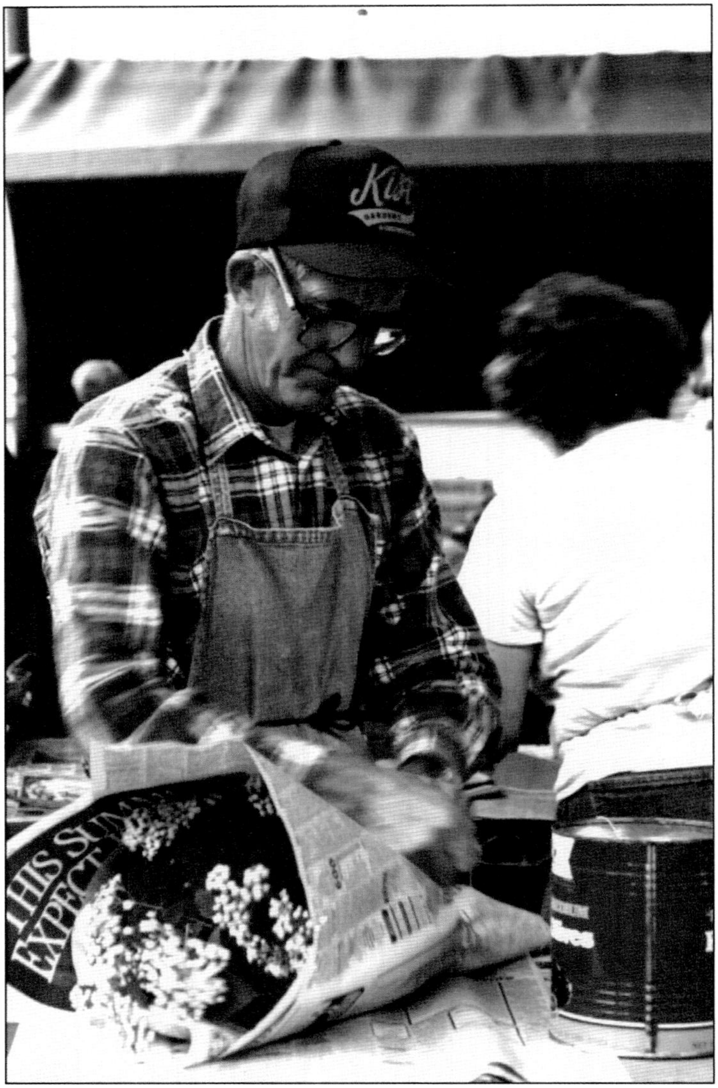

Both Cliff Kist (left and below, left) and his son Mark Kist (below, right) are market rats, and now Mark's daughter Sarah joins them on market on many Saturdays. Cliff's grandmother Rose Krismer reared her children on income generated by her bakery stand inside the market house, and Cliff has spent his lifetime on market. Below is the display of flowers and tomatoes raised in the Kists' greenhouses for sale on market. The truck in the background below hauls everything needed to operate their stand: the produce, the flowers, the string of lights, the hanging scale, the sawhorses, the newspapers, the signs, the bags, the string, the money drawer, the change box, their aprons. All these are packed up for market days ahead of time, hauled in each morning, and hauled out again each night. (Courtesy of the Kist family.)

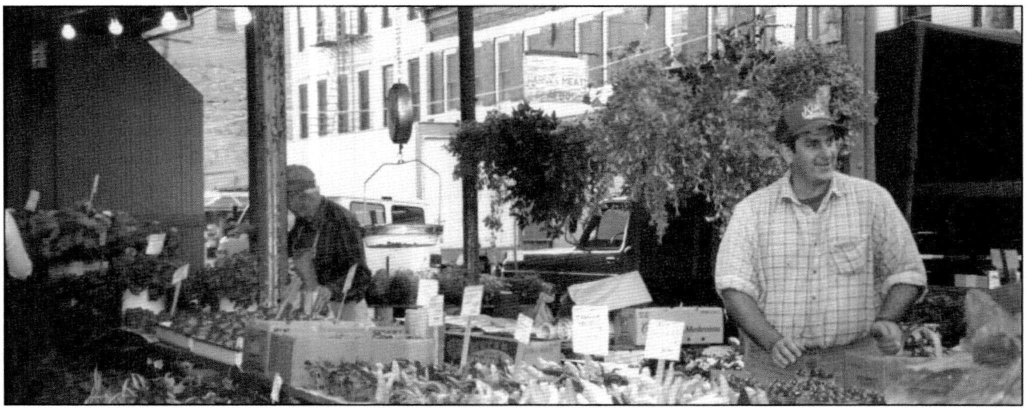

Silverglade's has had a Findlay Market presence since 1922. From the time he was eight years old and standing on a wooden Coke crate to help his parents at their outdoor stand, Al Silverglade Jr. has been on market. The portrait at right is that of Al Silverglade Sr., who began the business at Findlay Market. Below, and more than 50 years after the photograph at right, Al Silverglade Jr. is pictured at work in his stand in the market house. "I don't know if it's so much the building that makes the market or the way things are done," says Al Silverglade Jr. "All these are family businesses. We know the first names of the customers and they know us. They get personal attention." (Right, courtesy of Deborah Ooten; below, photograph by Dan Wheeler.)

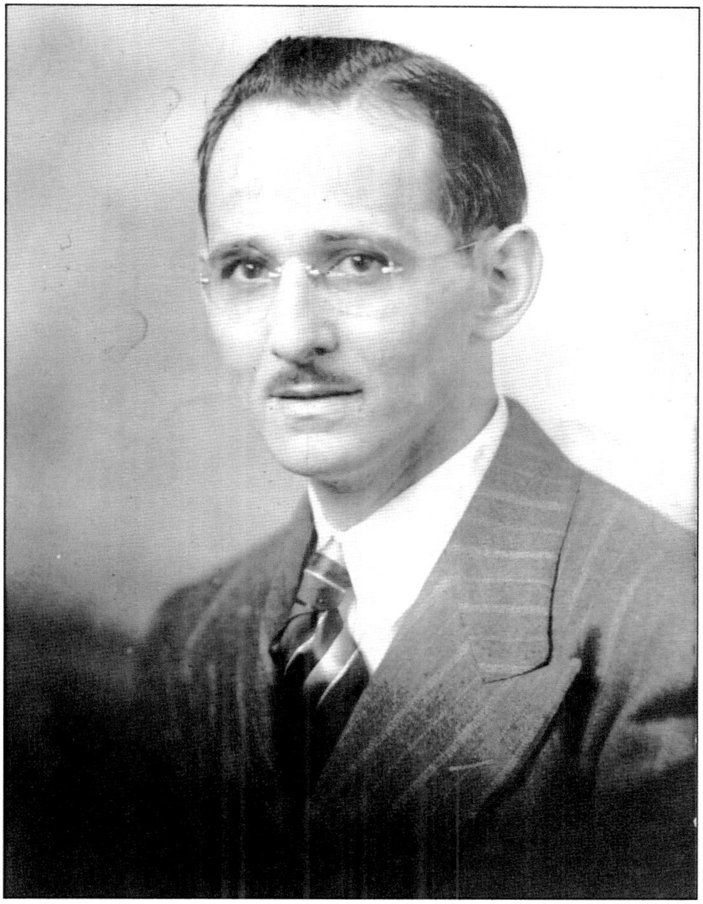

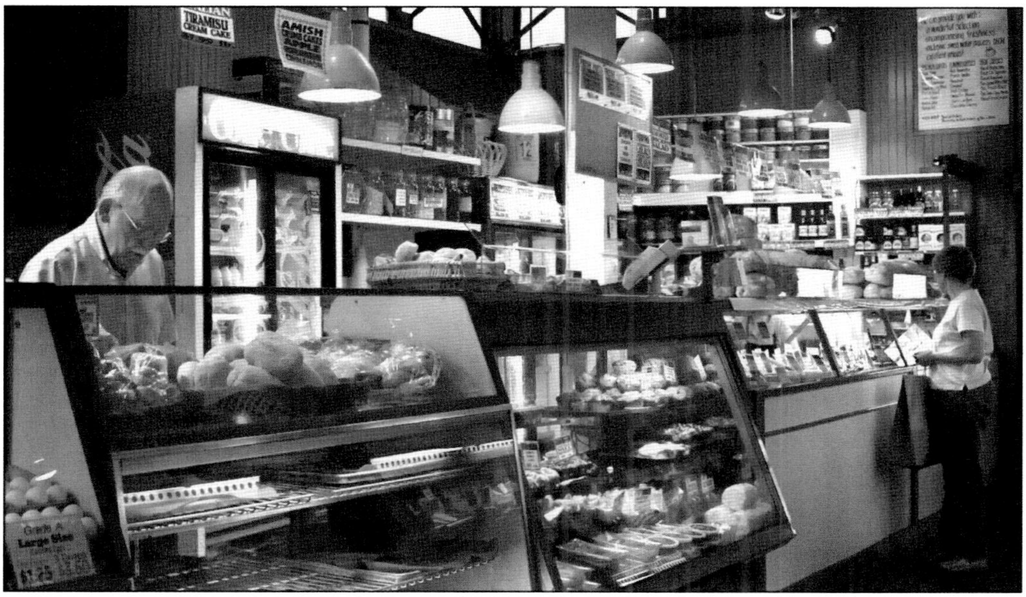

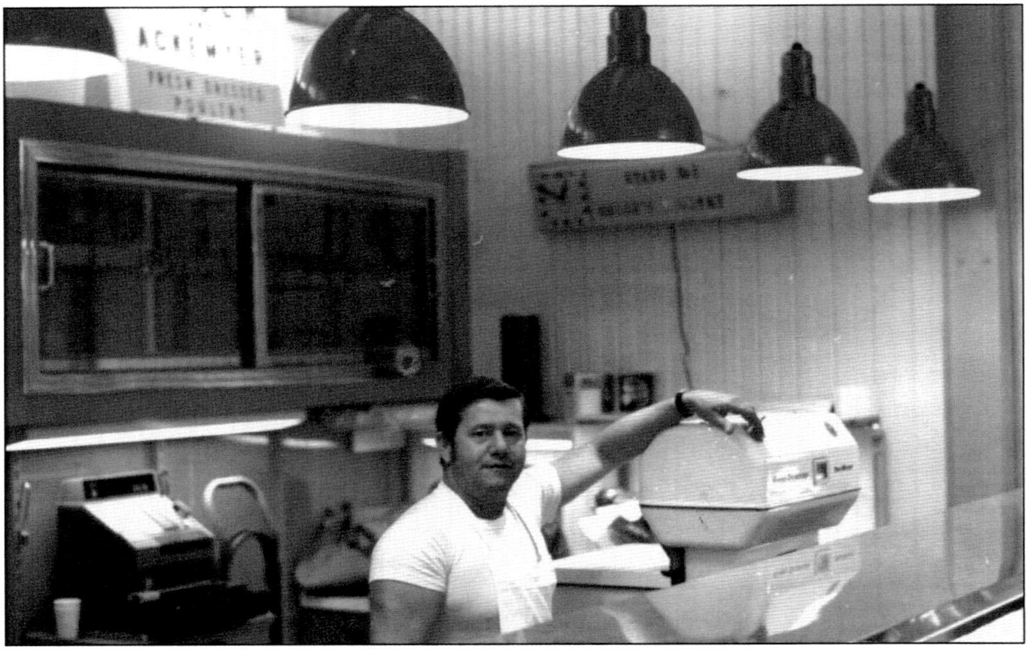

Eugene "Chink" Geiger and his wife, Alice, bought this Findlay Market stand from Lou Ackemyer. For many years, Geiger worked for Ackemyer at the old Sixth Street Market where, in addition to selling to their individual market customers, they killed, dressed, and delivered poultry to many well-known local restaurants. When Sixth Street Market was razed, Geiger moved his business to Findlay Market. In the photograph above and at his stand sometime after the 1974 renovation, Geiger holds a cigarette and rests his arm on his scale. Below, the playful Geiger shows off a freshly dressed rabbit. The Geigers' market rat daughter (and onetime president of the Findlay Market Association), Jean Bender, owned and operated Bender Meats, another Findlay Market business, until her son Tommy Bender assumed the responsibility in 2009. (Courtesy of the Geiger and Bender families.)

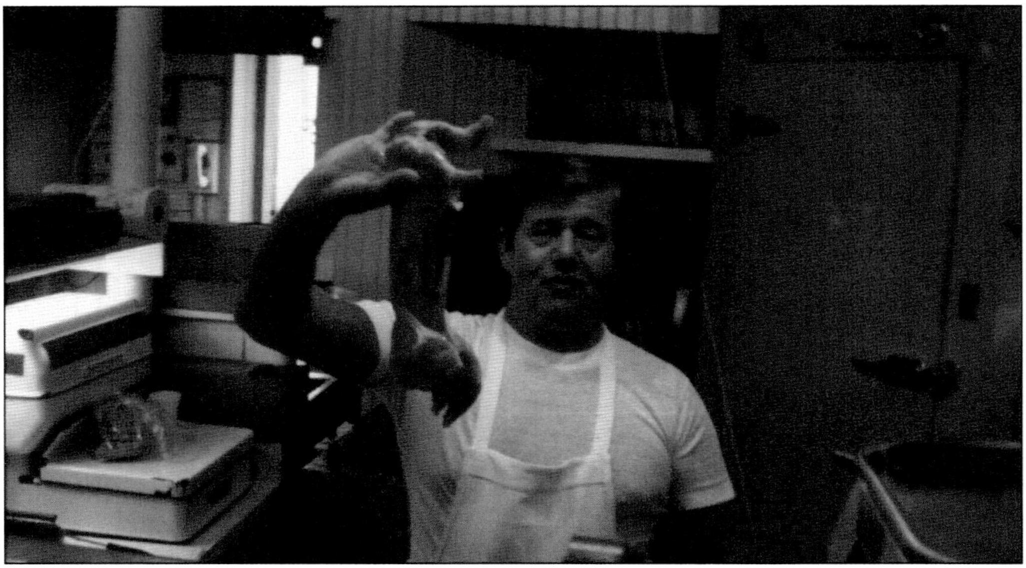

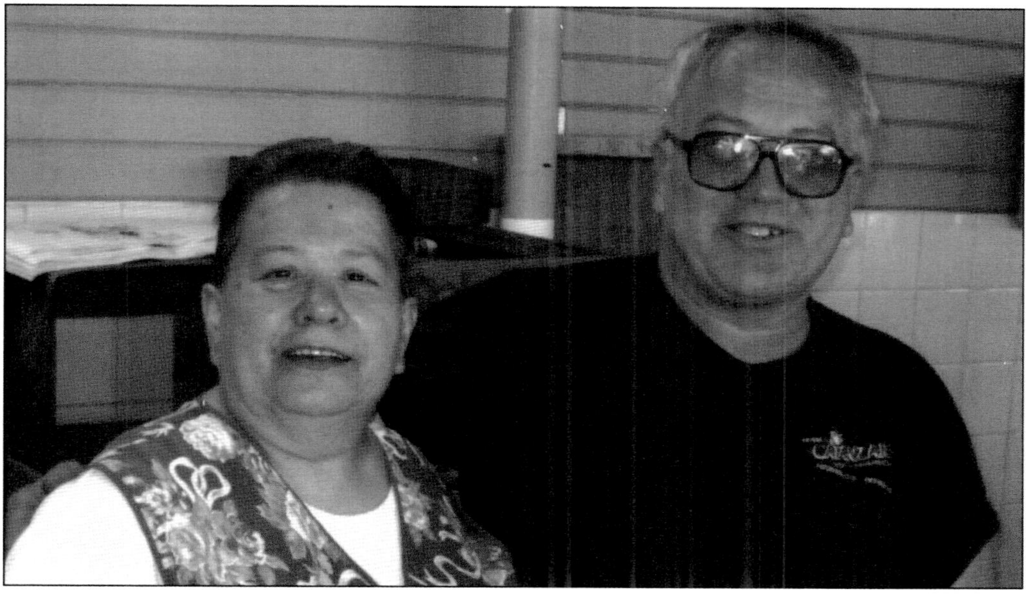

Above are siblings Judy Roth Gehrum and Ron Roth. Ron Roth owns and, with his sister Judy, continues to operate the produce stand started by his parents. Their siblings, George Roth and Debbie Roth Gates (below, center), work Elmer Simpson's stand beside Judy and Ron. This is the forever-interweaving story of families on Findlay Market; generations of brothers, sisters, mothers, fathers, daughters, sons, cousins, and families linked together by marriages work together, or they work side by side in competitive, cooperative, and supportive businesses. They know one another's produce, and they know one another's prices; if Ron has no cranberries this week, he points his customers to George. (Above, courtesy of the Roth family; below, photograph by Dan Wheeler.)

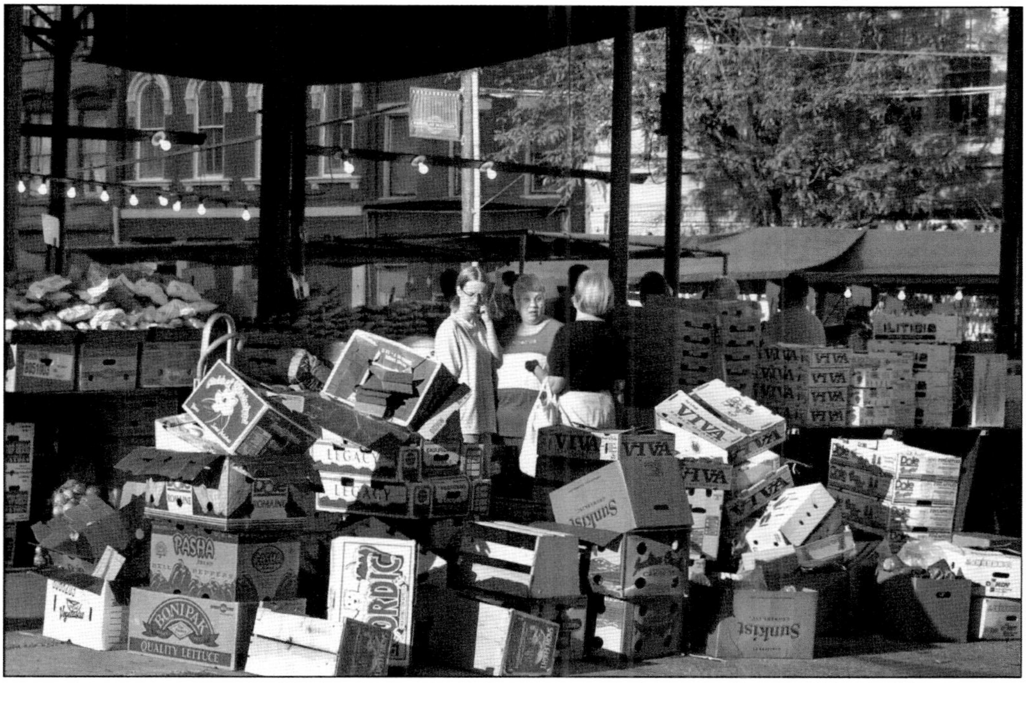

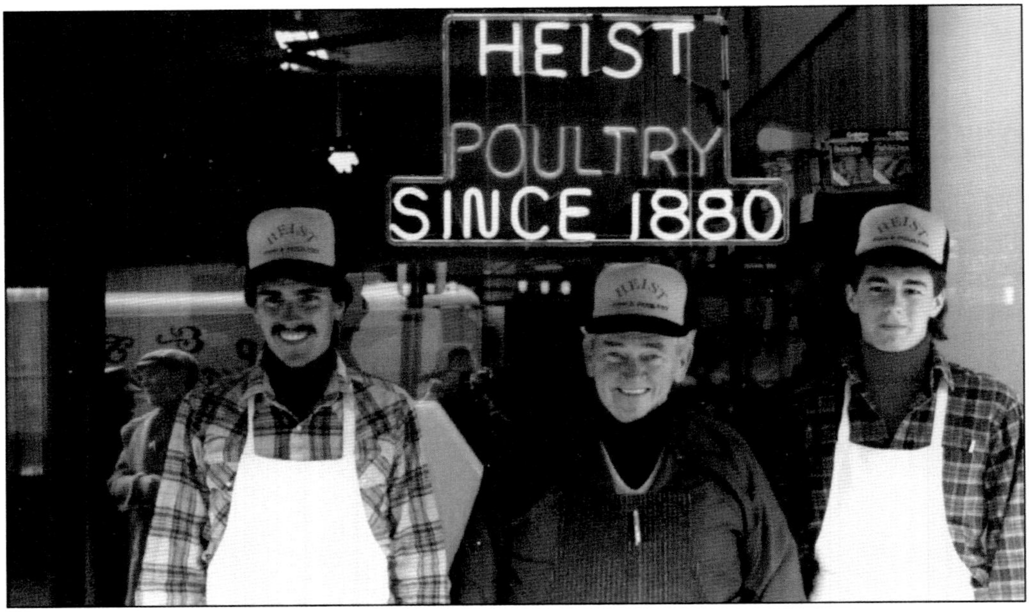

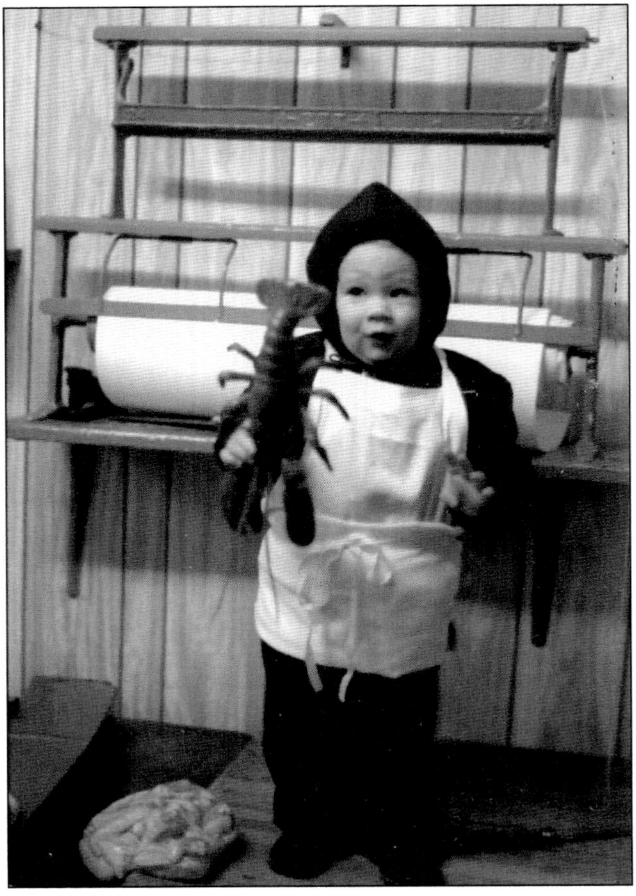

Timothy, Adam, and Michael Heist, pictured above from left to right, pose in front of the store the Heist family has operated at this location since 1938; at left, and after the business expanded to include fish and seafood, Timothy's aproned son, Adam Heist (named after his grandfather), stands on the Heists counter holding a live lobster with a bag of chicken wings at his feet. Until 2008, Adam continued to work in the family business currently owned and operated by his parents, Timothy and Barbara. (Courtesy of the Heist family.)

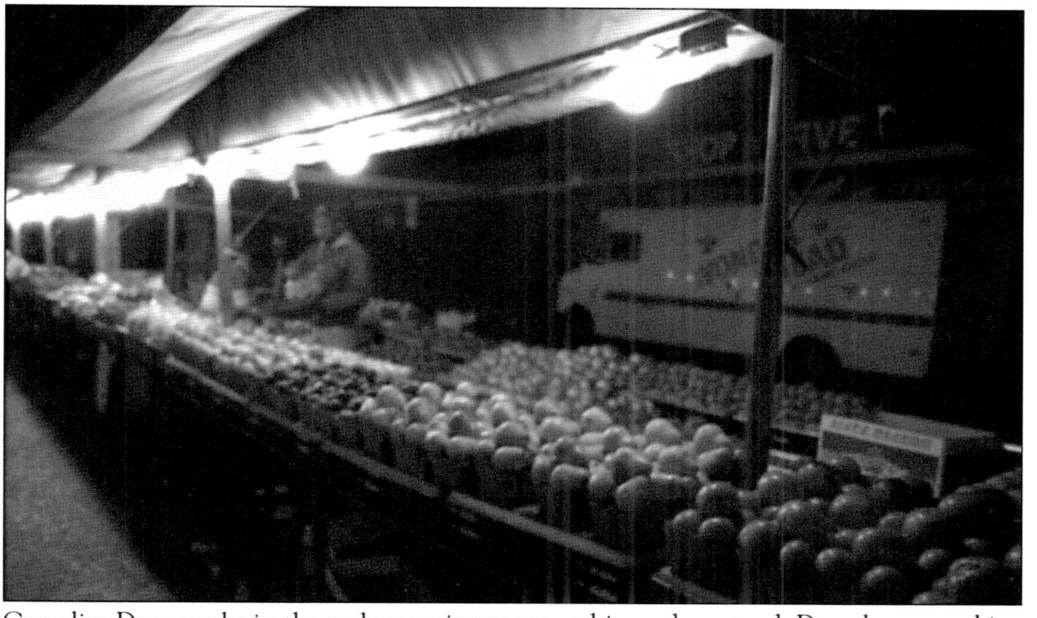

Cornelius Dean works in the early morning to set up his produce stand. Dean began working for Phil Sensio when he was in high school. From Sensio, Dean learned the value of good credit and how to operate a viable produce business, and he now owns and operates one of Cincinnati's few (and Findlay Market's only) black-owned produce businesses. He employs and teaches a next generation of nephews. (Courtesy of Marty Milligan.)

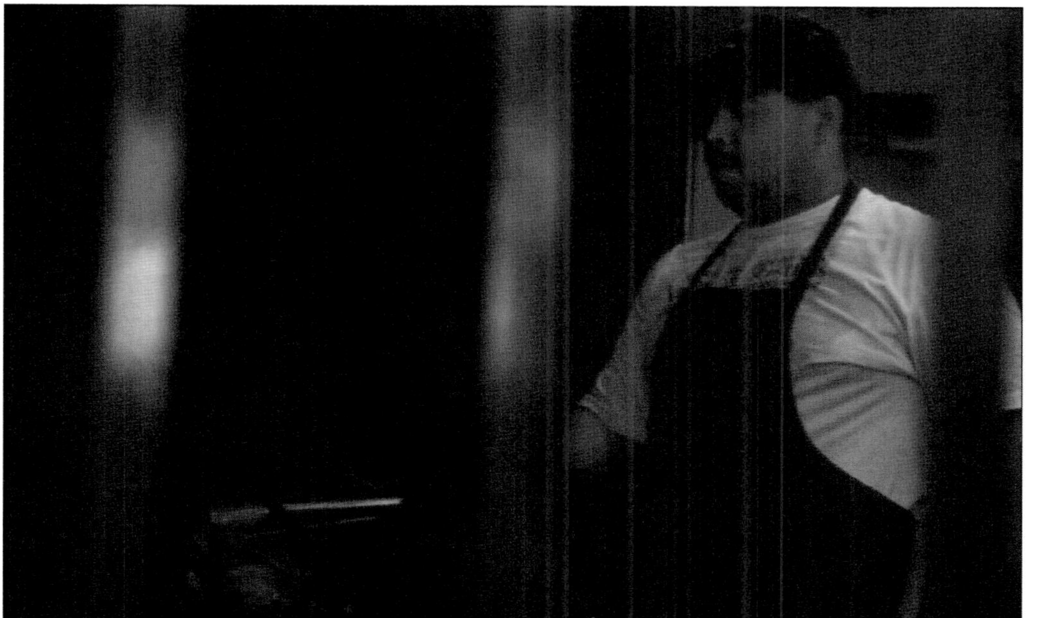

Mr. Pig founder Paul Sebron tends the grill that fills the air around Findlay Market with some of the best smells in the city. *Cincinnati* magazine readers have repeatedly recognized Mr. Pig for the magazine's "Best Barbeque" award. Sebron died in 2007, but in the tradition of families on market, Sebron's wife and son still keep the grill going. (Photograph by and courtesy of Jane Gahl.)

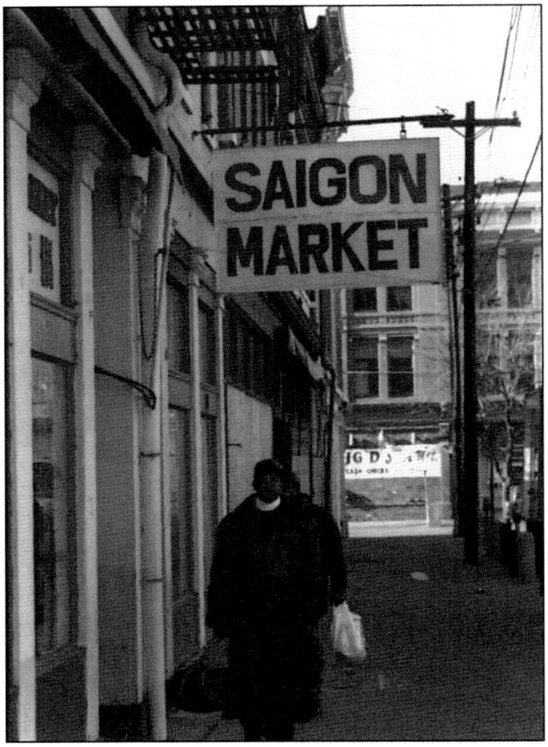

In 1975, and sponsored by a Jewish organization, Janet and Xu Ho arrived from Saigon, Vietnam, to Norwood, Ohio, a suburb of Cincinnati. They began saving money from their work at Ted's Market, and with the income also earned delivering the *Cincinnati Enquirer*, they were eventually able to purchase Saigon Market at Findlay Market with only about 10 items on their shelves. They made weekend driving trips to Chicago to buy more Asian foods and supplies. Today their son, Hgiep Ho (below), runs the very fully stocked and highly regarded Saigon Market. (Left, photograph by Marty Milligan; below, courtesy of the Ho family.)

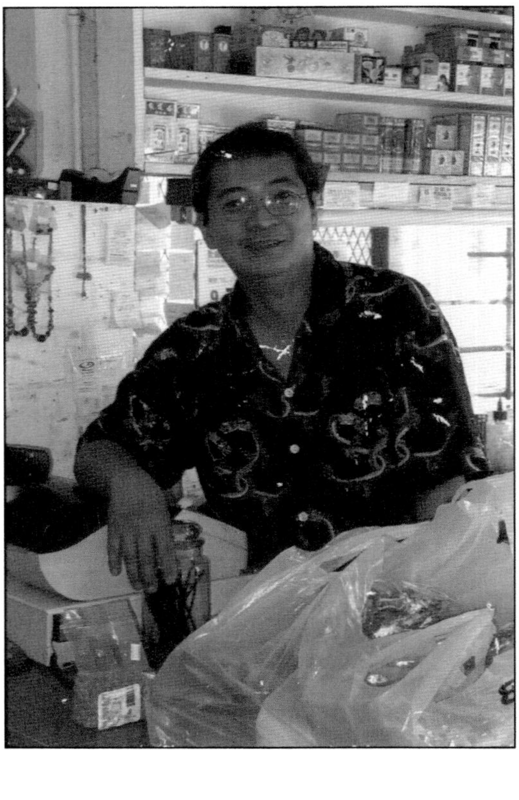

Two

Compliments of the Findlay Market Association

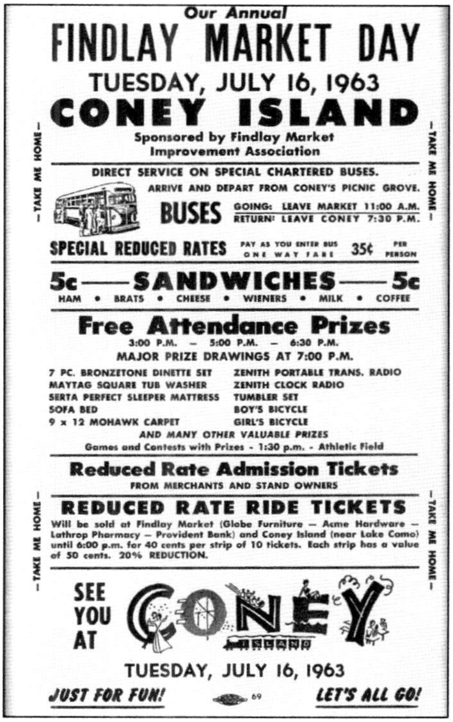

Each summer, the Findlay Market Association sponsored, organized, and hosted the annual Findlay Market Day at Coney Island. Thousands upon thousands of Cincinnatians attended these events; some were drawn by the door prizes and games, but more often remembered and most often talked about are the nickel sandwiches, hand assembled by long lines of Findlay Market family volunteers. (Courtesy of Elaine Kunkel Bourgraf.)

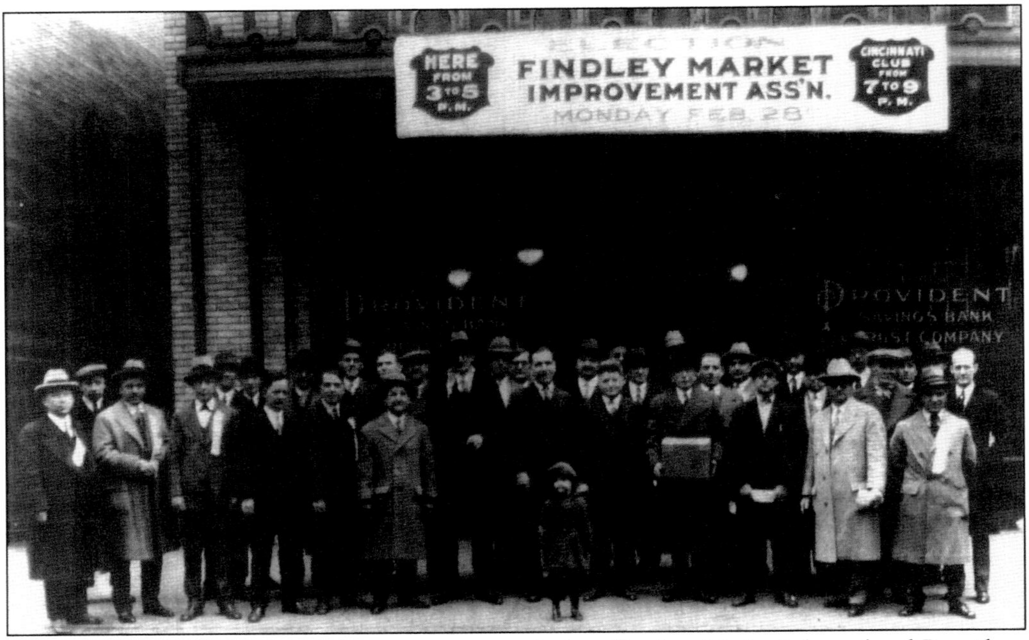

In 1927, the Findlay Market Association poses before Findlay Market's branch of Provident Savings Bank and Trust Company on officer election day. Indicating the group's importance to the city, voters could cast their ballots at this location from 3:00 to 5:00 p.m. or at the Cincinnati Club from 7:00 to 9:00 p.m. A front-row gentleman holds the box into which voters deposited their ballots. (Courtesy of Peggy Schmidt.)

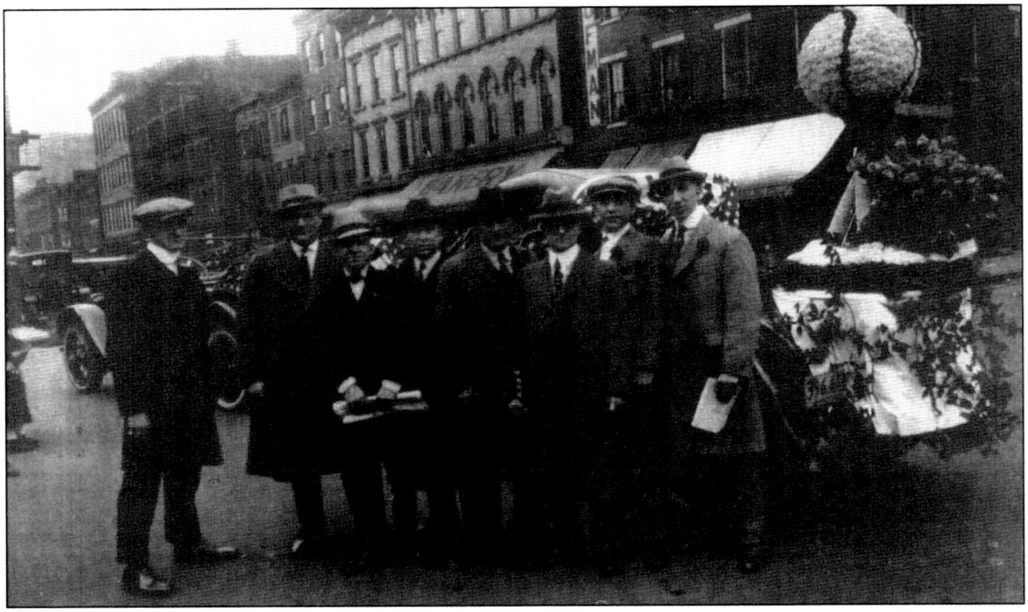

The first Findlay Market opening day parade took place in 1919 when the Findlay Market Association members decided to go as a group to the Cincinnati Reds' season-opening game at nearby Redland Field. Apparently, those first parades were nothing more than pub crawls to and from the game with many refreshment stops along the way. (Courtesy of Peggy Schmidt.)

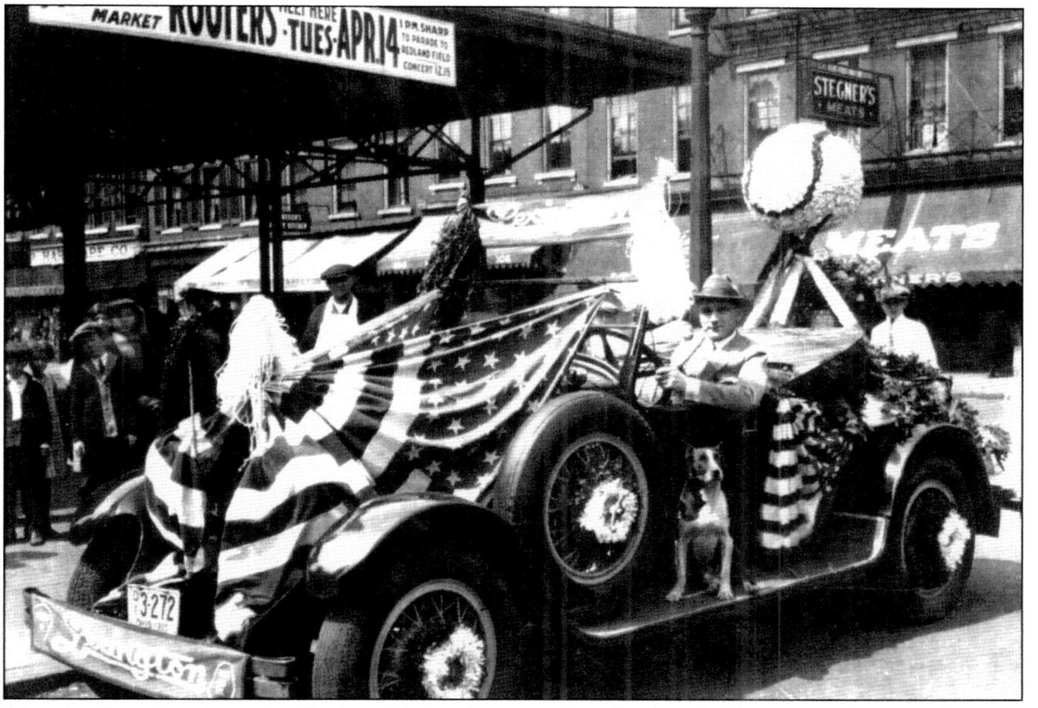

The sign hanging from the Findlay Market house rafters for the 1925 opening day parade reads, "Findlay Market Rooters Meet Here, Tues, April 14, 1 P.M. Sharp, to Parade to Redland Field, Concert 12:15." The decorated car parked before the market house quickly became a symbol of the Findlay Market opening day parade. (Courtesy of Peggy Schmidt.)

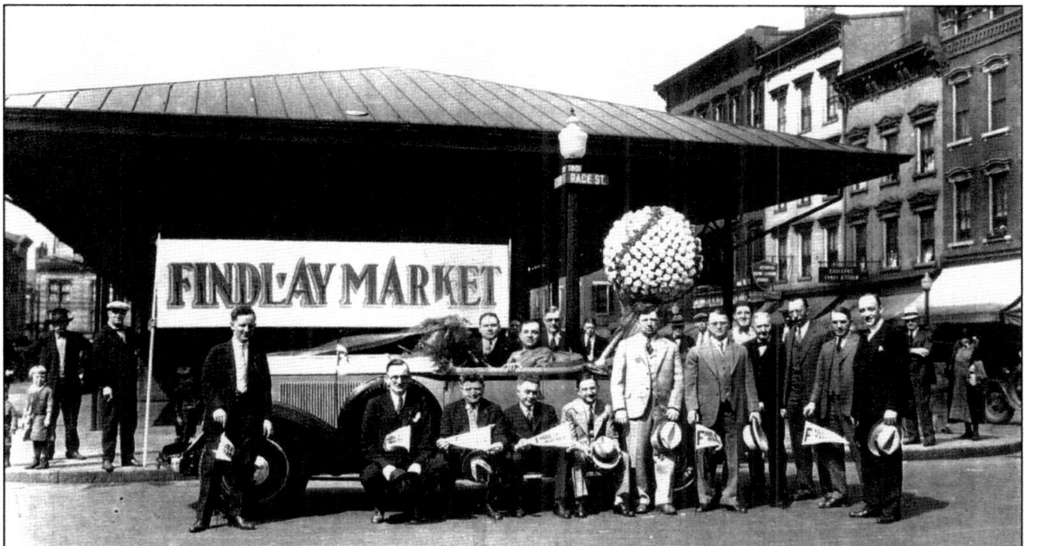

The Findlay Market opening day parade eventually became a huge and honored and exuberant Cincinnati tradition, but in the 1920s, the parade consisted of about 40 Findlay Market Association members dressed in their suits and ties and hats and waving these little banners. (Courtesy of Peggy Schmidt.)

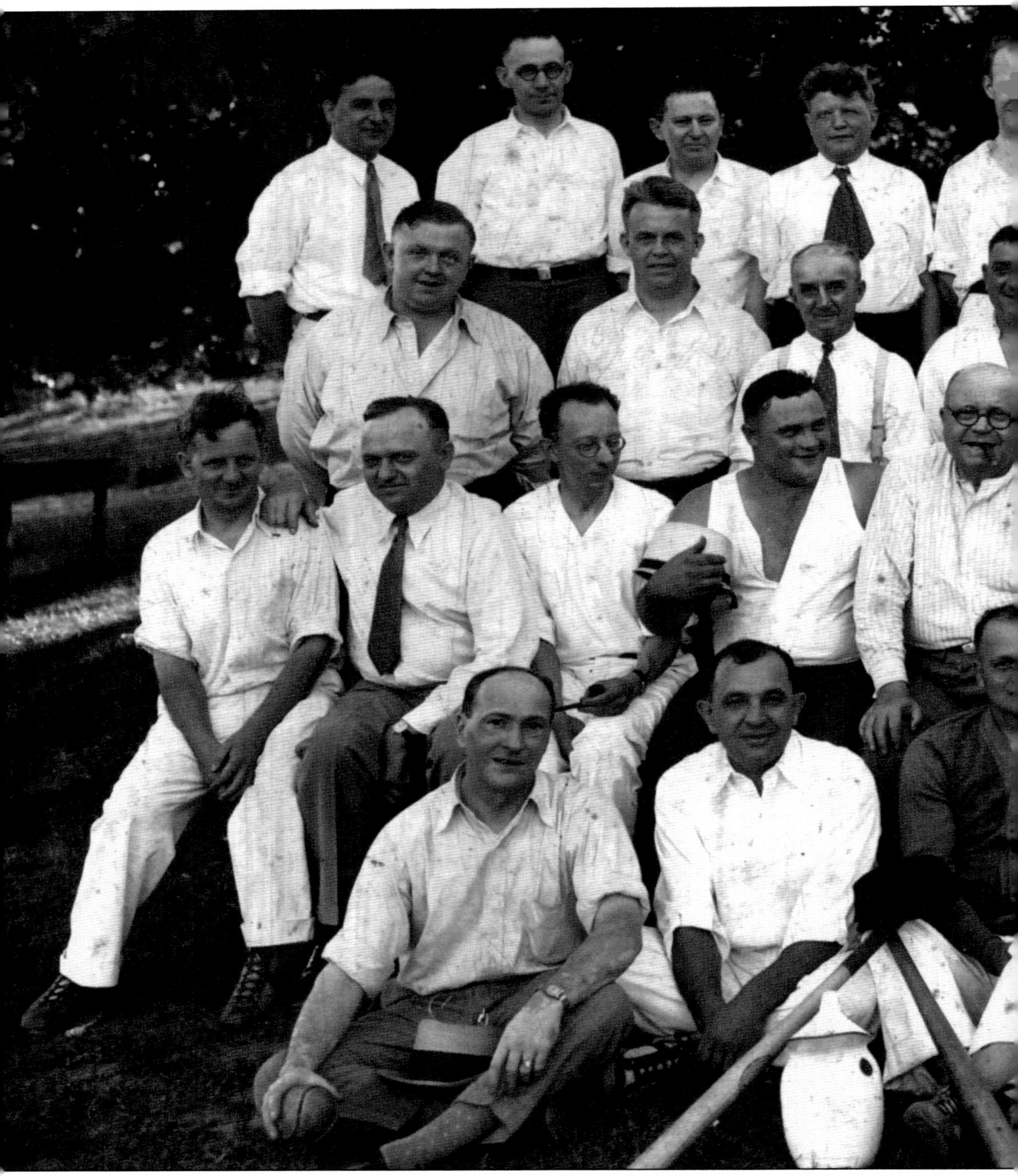

Gathered together off market in 1932, these Findlay Market Association members pose after a day of softball, games, and beer at the Pine Club. The very close and respectful brotherhood that existed between these men and their families is one aspect of the market about which people still speak and marvel. These close business and personal relationships rippled positive waves throughout Cincinnati; a whopping 30,000 people attended the 1924 annual Findlay

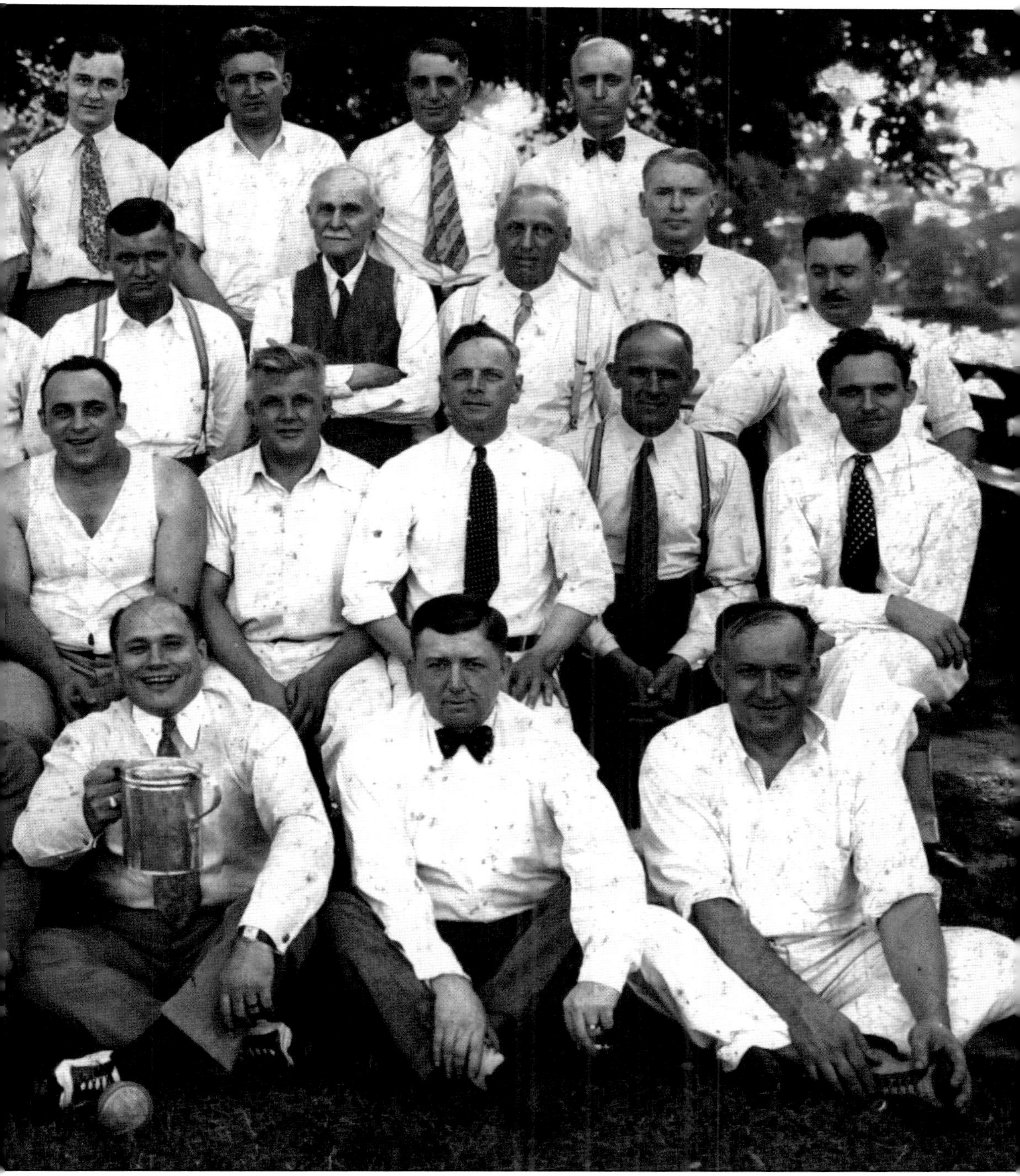

Market picnic at Coney Island, which was sponsored by the Findlay Market Association. The picnic lasted all day and included events like running races, wheelbarrow races, rabbit races, and a cracker-eating contest. Over 2,000 pounds of beef were consumed at the barbecue dinner. (Courtesy of Elaine Kunkel Bourgraf.)

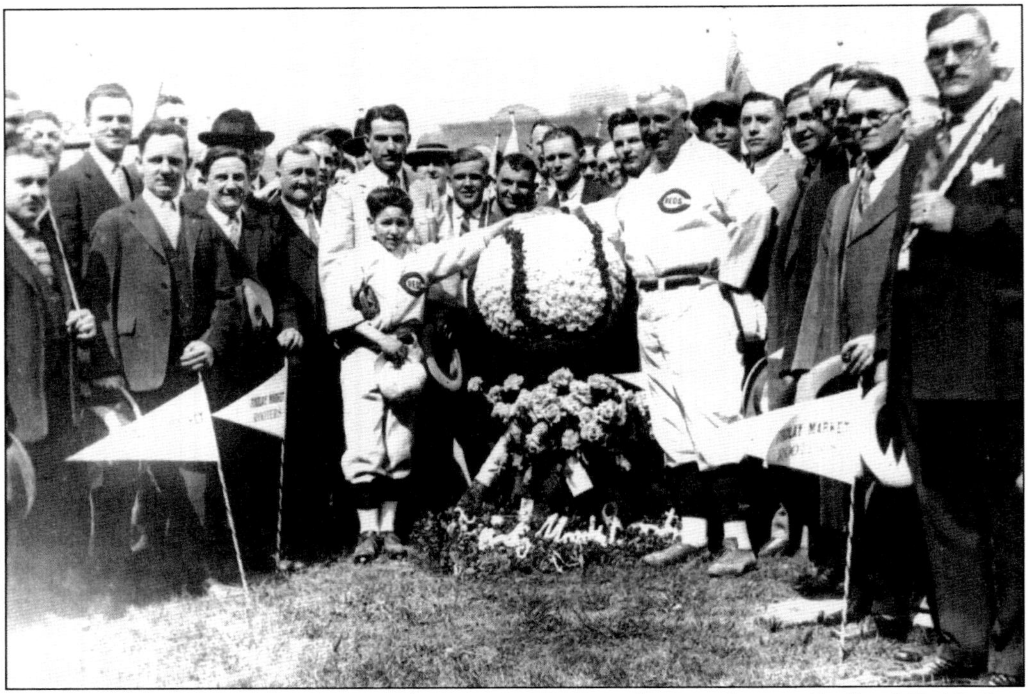

Once the small band of Findlay Market Association members made it to Redland Field, they marched right to home plate and presented the Reds' manager with a bouquet of flowers and the annual carnation baseball. Here Reds manager Jack Hendricks accepts the 1927 opening day bouquets. (Courtesy of Peggy Schmidt.)

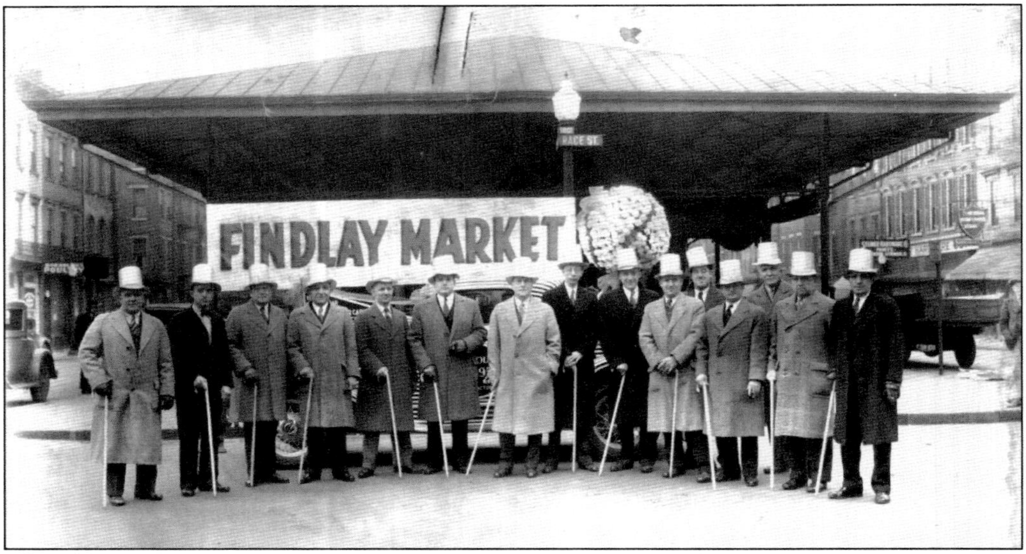

Dressed in topcoats and top hats and carrying canes, this dapper Findlay Market Association group poses before commencing the 1932 Findlay Market opening day parade. Behind the group are the three now-emblematic signatures for the early parades: the Findlay Market banner, the decorated car, and the baseball-shaped flower arrangement on a tripod of bats, all of which accompanied the group to Redland Field for the game. (Courtesy of Deborah Ooten.)

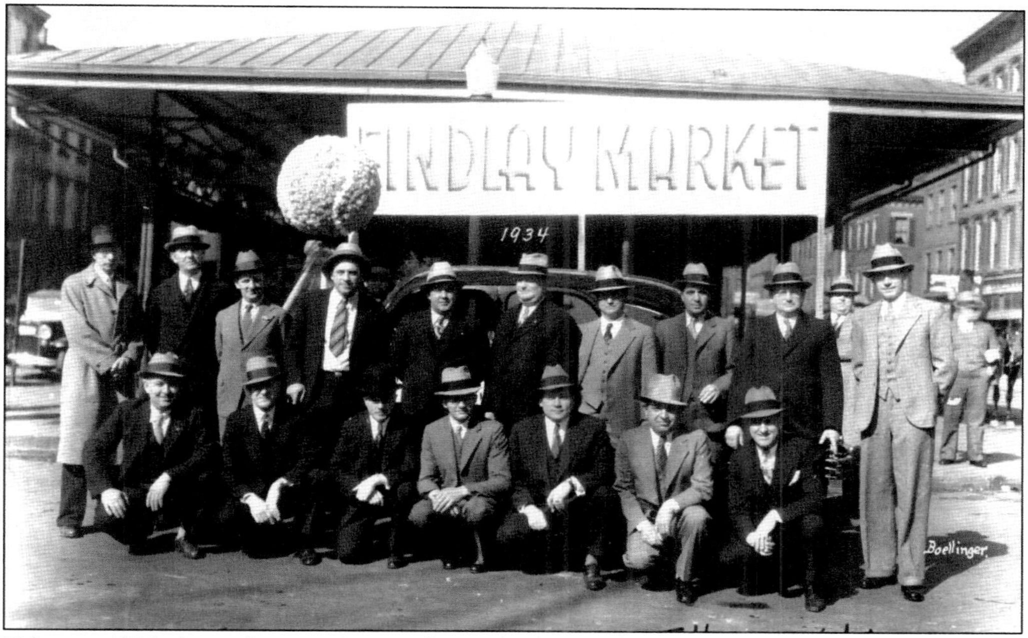

Taken in 1934, these photographs are almost the last in the series of official opening day group shots taken at the market's Race Street entrance. Within the next several years, Findlay Market druggist Chester A. Lathrop became parade chairperson, and for the more than 30 years he chaired the parade, future groups posed at the corner of Elm and Elder Streets in front of Lathrop's corner drugstore. Two slightly different poses are seen here: hats on and hats off. (Above, courtesy of Deborah Ooten; below, courtesy of Peggy Schmidt.)

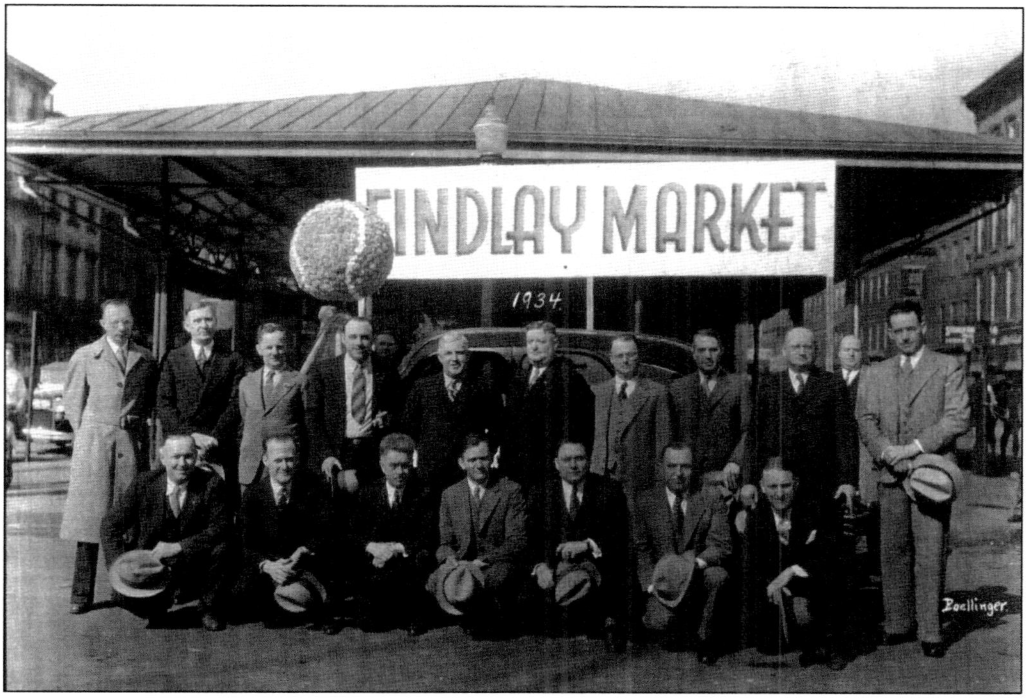

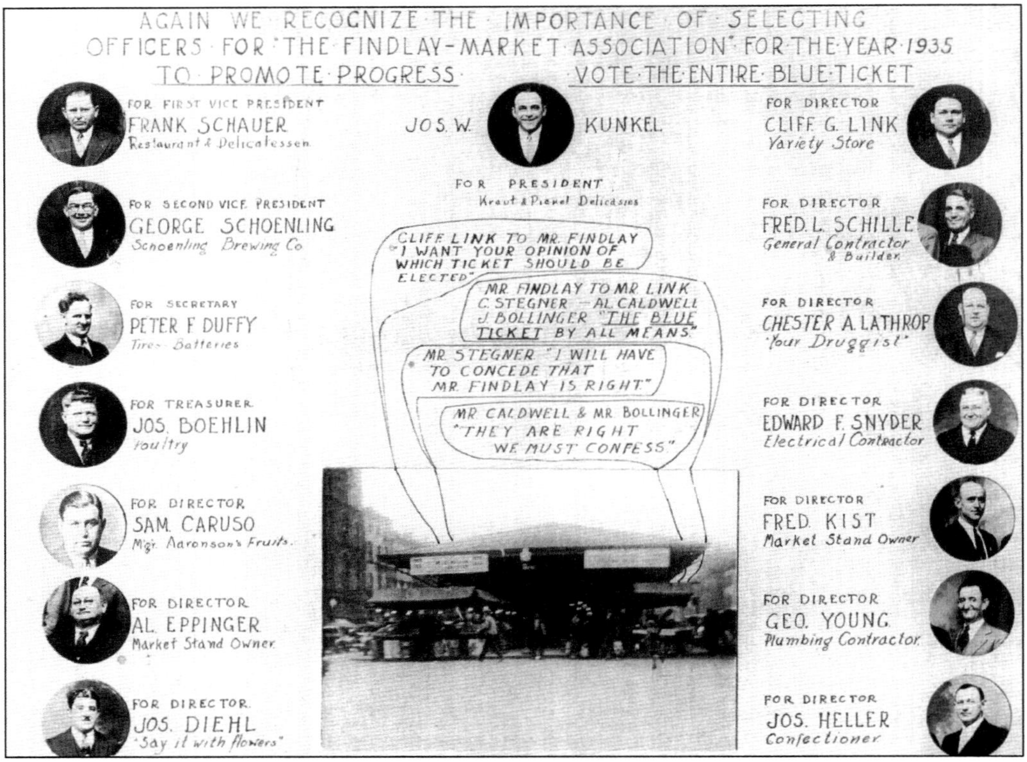

Officers for the Findlay Market Association were chosen from two distinct groups: the red ticket and the blue ticket. Red ticket candidates were chosen from those vendors with businesses inside the market house; blue ticket candidates represented vendors with outside stands or storefront businesses. Each year, these two groups determined their candidates, and a vigorous campaign and an election followed. The poster above, from the 1935 campaign, pokes some good-natured fun at red ticket candidates—notice the word balloons arising from red ticket candidates located inside the market house who agree with James Findlay in acknowledging the blue ticket should be elected. And because the portrait below lacks the accoutrements normally associated with the opening day parade, it may simply be a photograph of the 1936 Findlay Market Association officers posing beneath the market house roof. (Courtesy of Peggy Schmidt.)

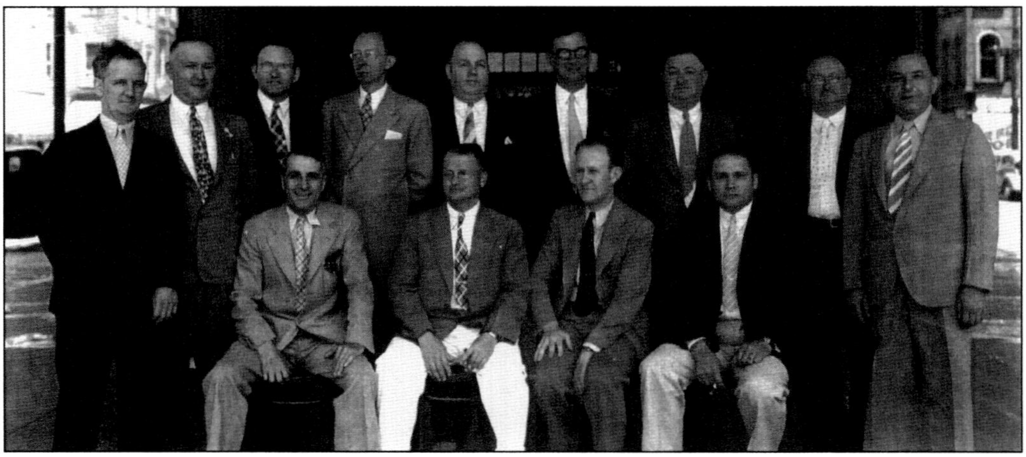

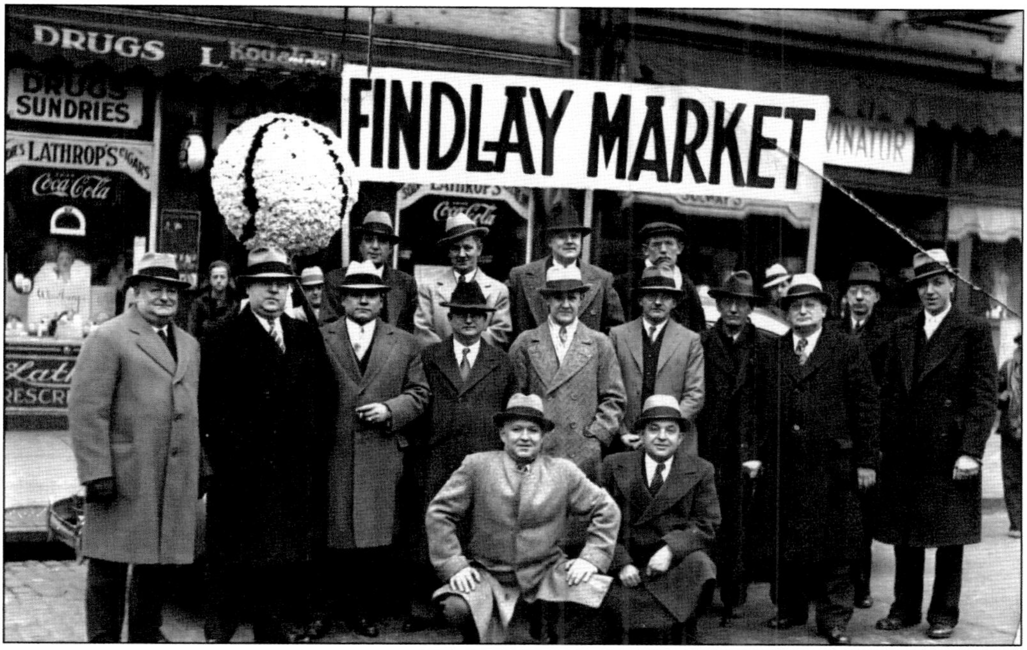

Here begins the series of official Findlay Market opening day parade photographs in front of Chester A. Lathrop's corner drugstore at Elm and Elder Streets; below is the 1937 portrait. These shots bring attention to the storefronts surrounding the Findlay Market house. The Findlay Market Association was composed of those business owners with stands inside the market, those with stands outside on the street and at the curbs, and those with storefront businesses in buildings surrounding the market. Even though the location of these portraits has moved, one can still see the Findlay Market banner, the mock-up baseball, and the car almost obscured behind the group. (Courtesy of Deborah Ooten.)

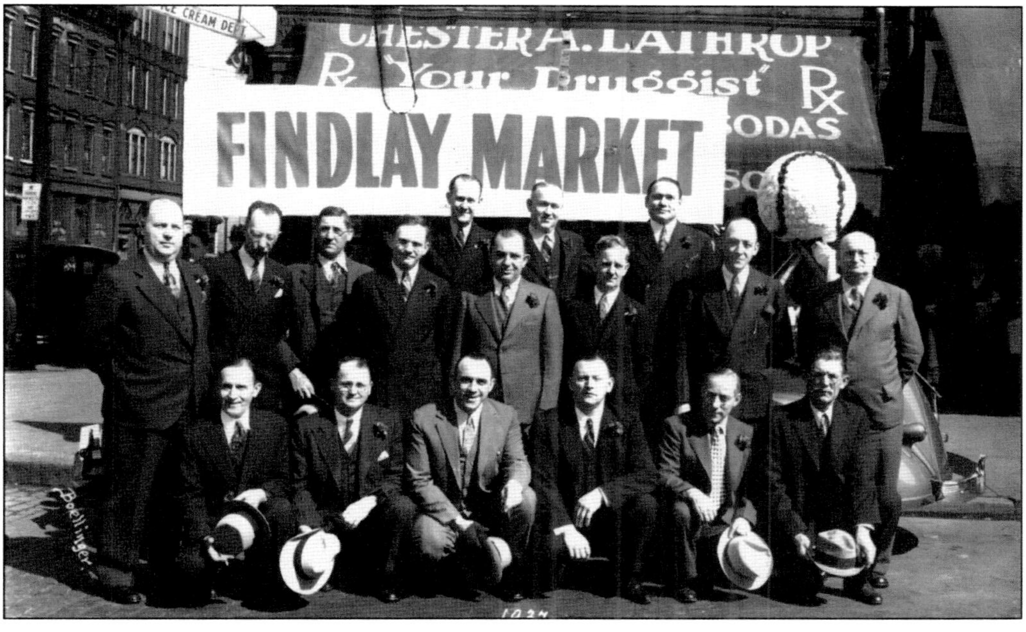

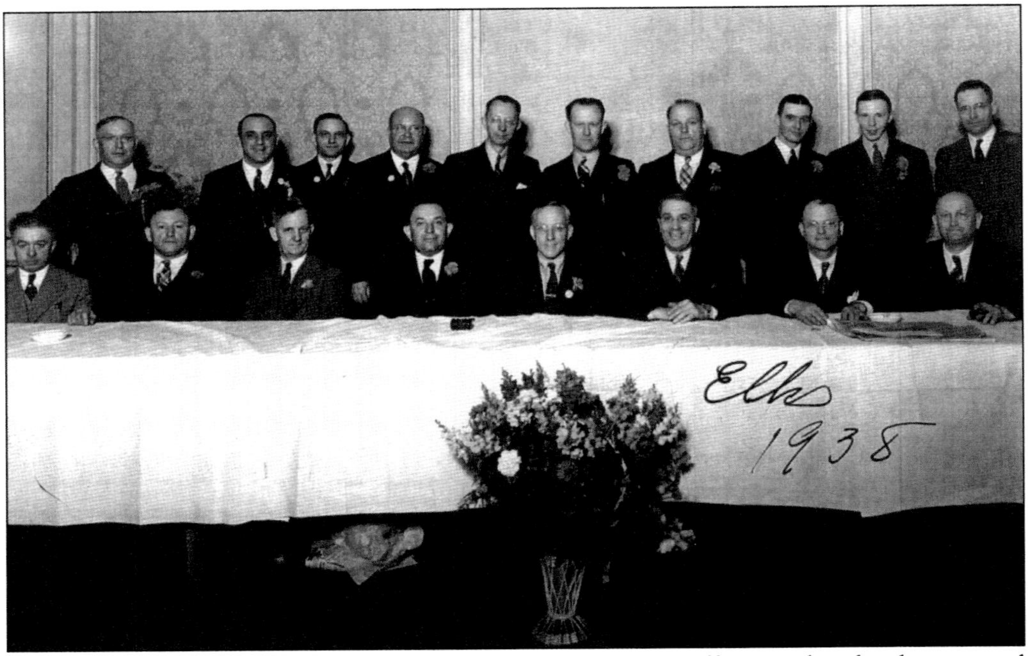

At the Elks Club above in 1938, Findlay Market Association officers gather for their annual installation banquet. At the opening day parade below, also in 1938, Findlay Market Association members pose with red carnations pined to their lapels, and several men in the front row hold their celebratory cigars. This portrait is the first of all previous Findlay Market opening day parade shots in which one cannot see a car parked behind the group. For years, these group portraits were signed "Boellinger." (Above, courtesy of Peggy Schmidt; below, courtesy of Deborah Ooten.)

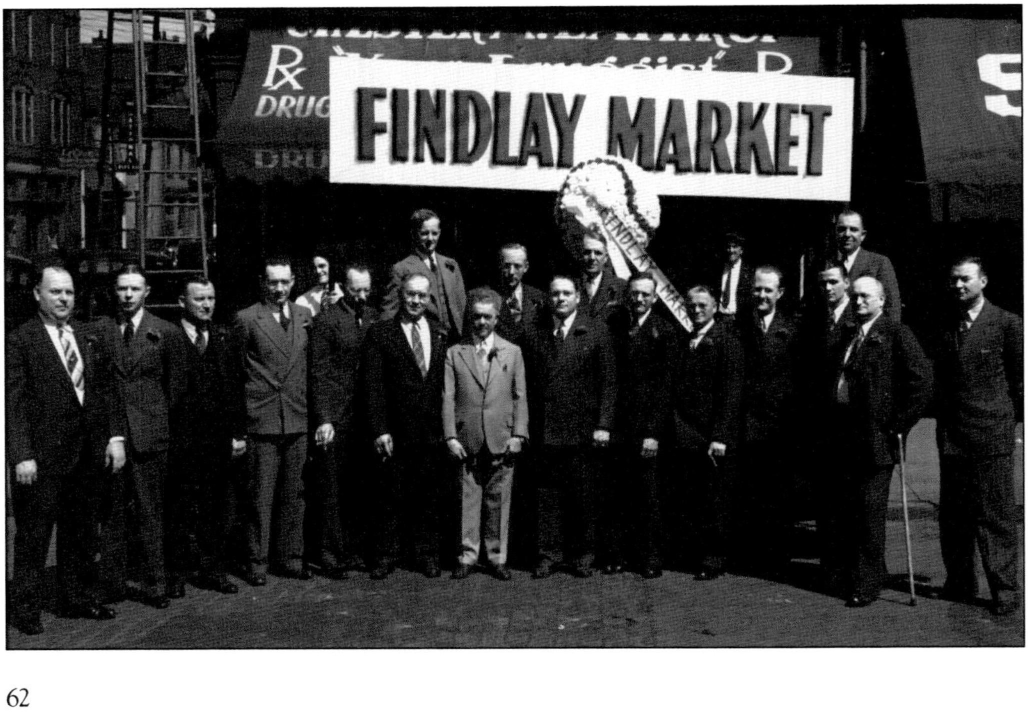

The Findlay Market opening day parade gained popularity and became a much more festive and citywide affair than in its early years. Eventually the Findlay Market Association added a grand marshal, usually a member of the association, to lead the parade. At right, grand marshal Russ Gibbs rides his beautifully saddled white horse beside the market house. Below, the parade crowd lines the street as the Gibbs' Butter and Eggs decorated car winds its way down Vine Street on its way to the opening game. (Courtesy of David Day.)

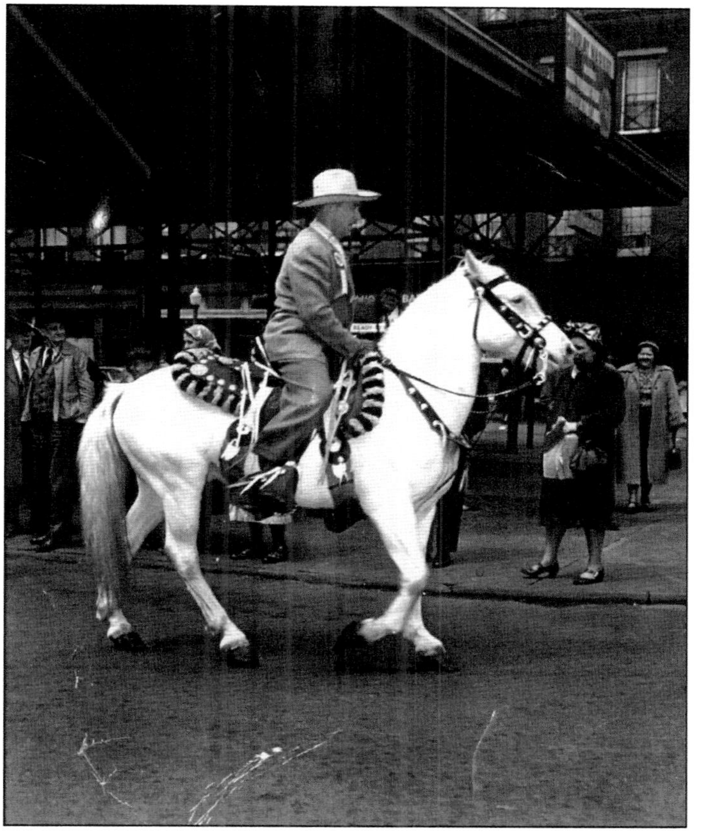

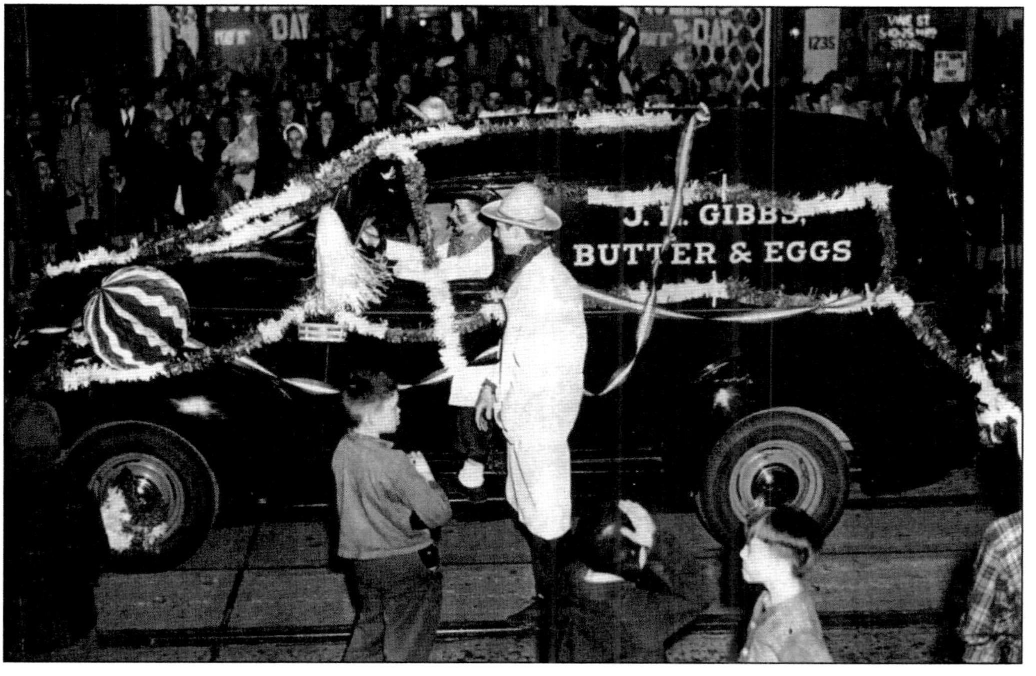

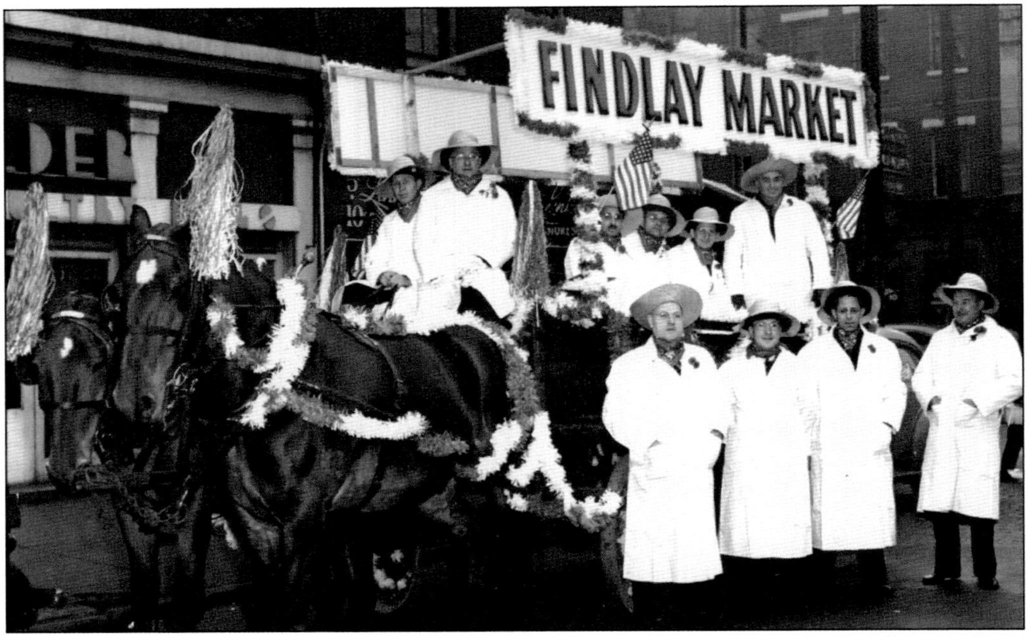

Each year, the Findlay Market Association's opening day parade committee tried to do something a little different. Above, members ride in a horse-drawn wagon and wear white butcher coats and hats; below, rodeo is the theme. One year, all members carried helium-filled balloons; another year, they all wore red carnations in their lapels. By the 1950s, the number of parade marchers had grown from 40 in its earliest years to approximately 200 people. Their trip began at the market at 12:30 p.m. and arrived about an hour later at Crosley Field (Redland Field was renamed Crosley Field in 1934, the year Powell Crosley bought the Cincinnati Reds baseball team). (Courtesy of Deborah Ooten.)

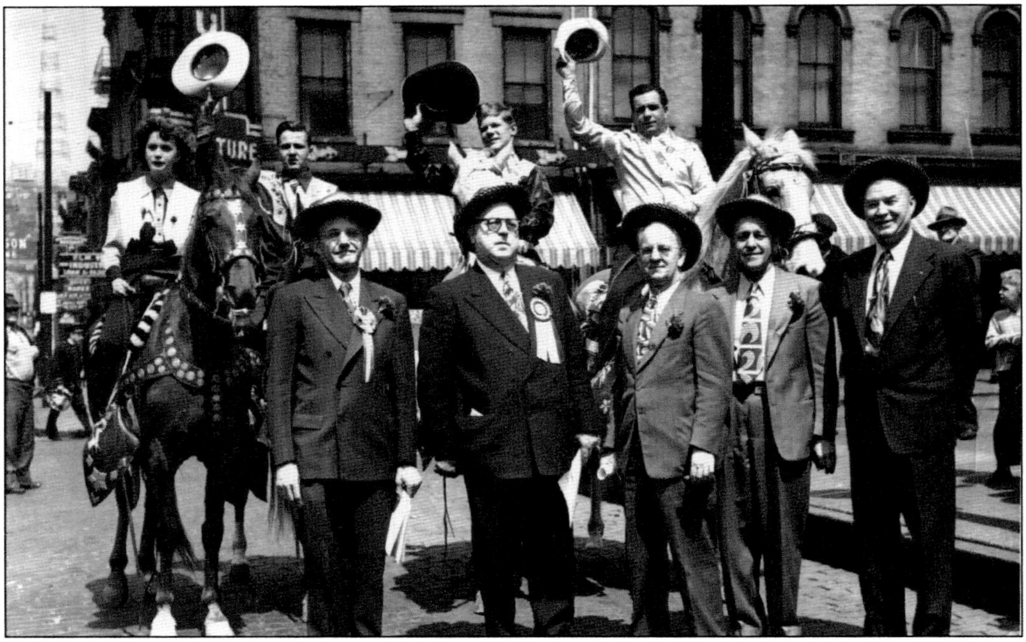

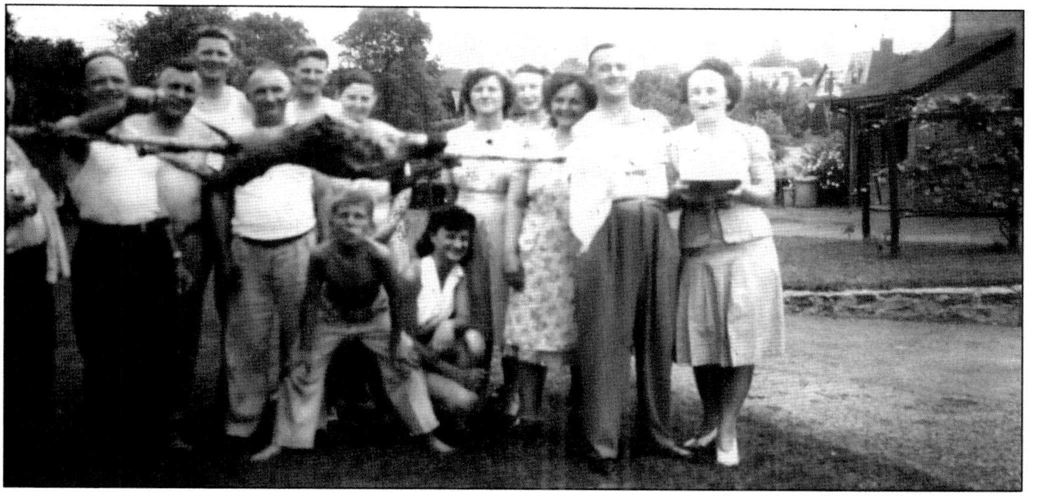

Members of the Findlay Market Association were close business associates on market, but they were friends away from market as well. In these photographs, several Findlay Market families gather for a pig roast at the northern Kentucky home of druggist Chester A. Lathrop. Included in the photograph above are members of the Yunger family, whose family-owned café was across the street from Lathrop's Elm and Elder Streets corner store and whose children still refer to Lathrop as "Uncle Chester." Even today, people refer to these Findlay Market relationships as extended families, and sometimes intermarriages make these "Findlay Market family" relationships quite literal. At right, one pig roast guest whips up some beer gravy for the crowd. If the gravy is too thick, add more beer; if the gravy is too thin, add more beer (and a touch of corn starch). (Courtesy of the Yunger family.)

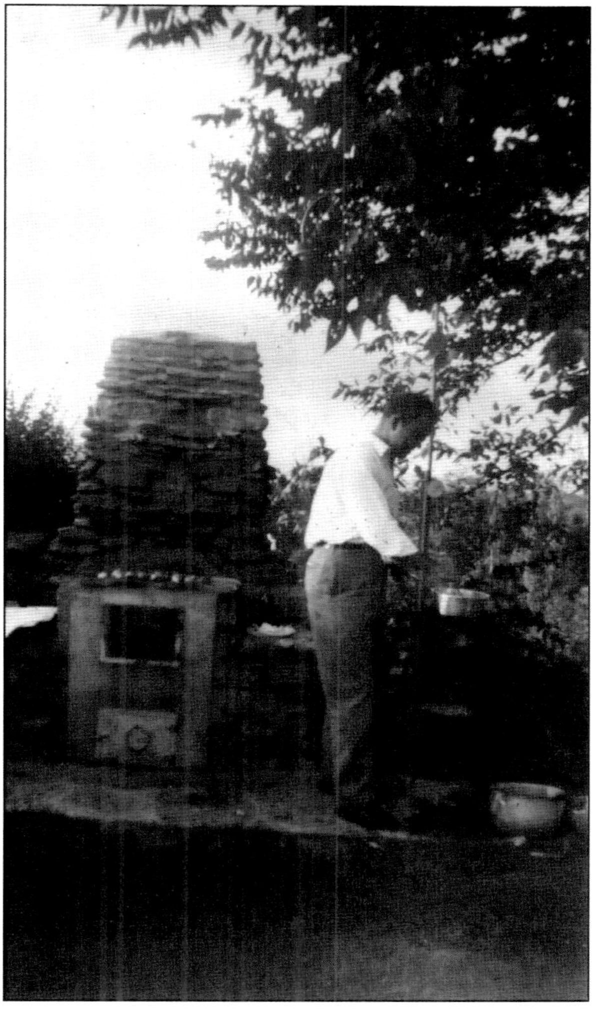

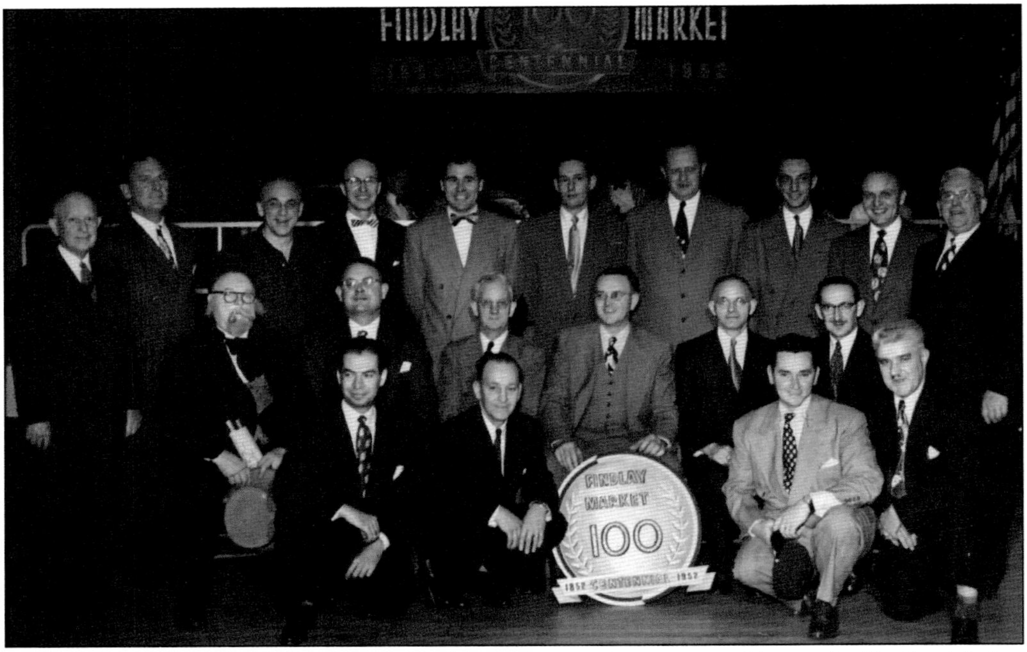

Findlay Market's 1852–1952 centennial celebration was a huge event. Above, the Findlay Market Association members pose at their centennial celebration banquet with signs and banners commemorating the market's 100th year. In the photograph above, centennial celebration chairperson Chester A. Lathrop (left, second row) is dressed in *c.* 1852 clothing, a fake mustache, and a beard; he holds a scroll. Below, and without his costume, Chester A. Lathrop proudly carries the centennial sign outside the market house and is surrounded by a few of his fellow vendors. (Courtesy of Deborah Ooten.)

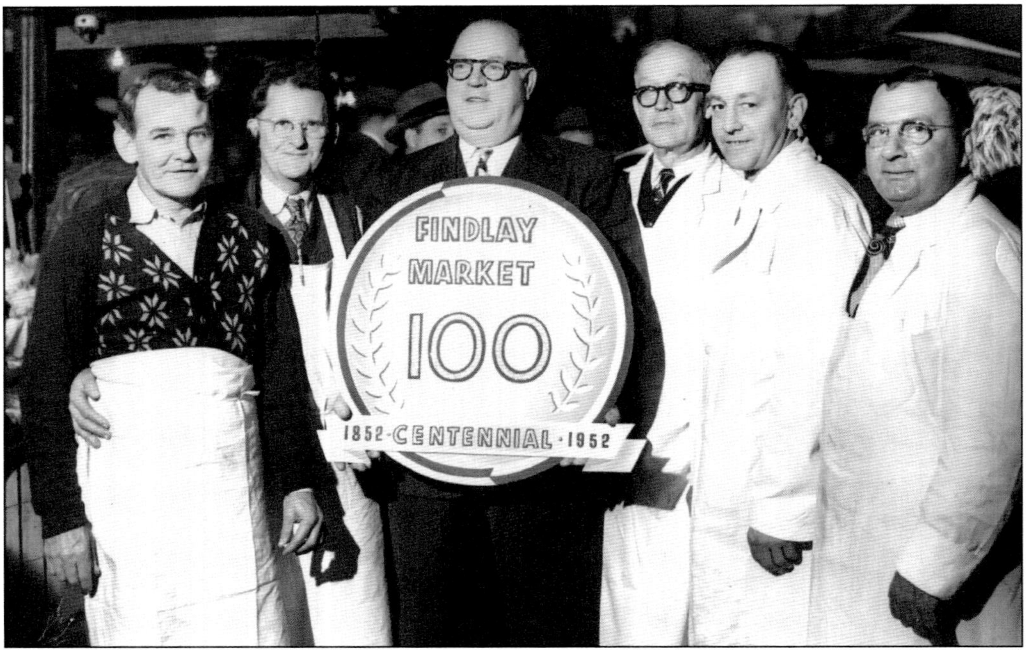

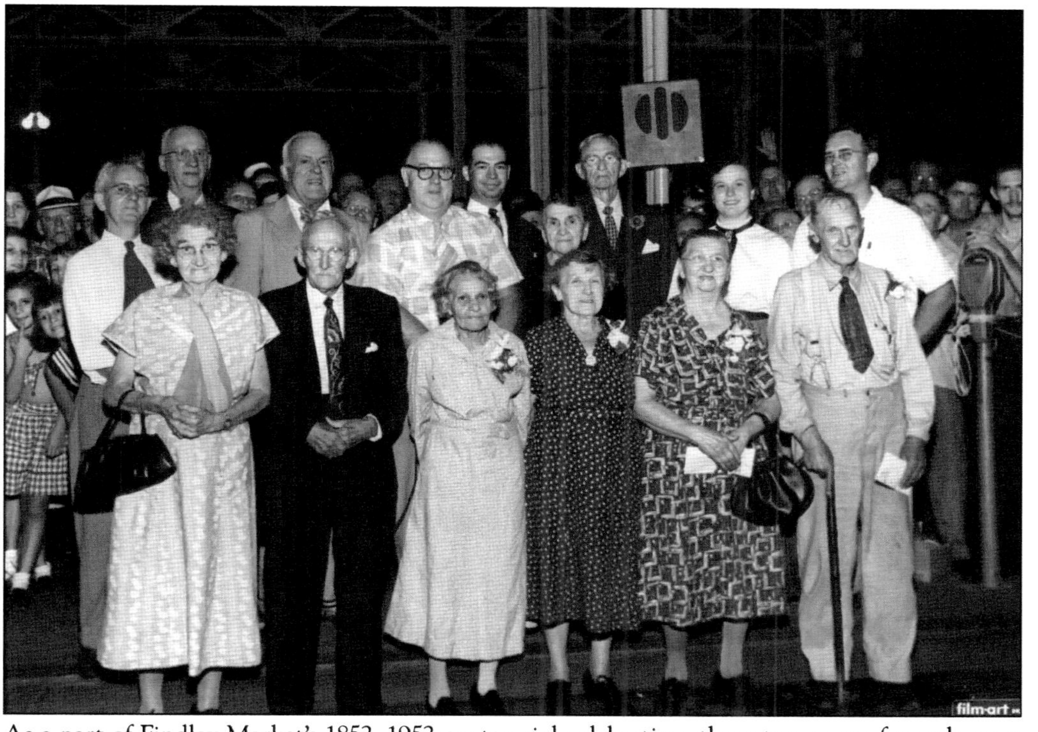

As a part of Findlay Market's 1852–1952 centennial celebration, these two rows of people were honored at Old-Timer's Night. Celebrants of all ages stand many rows deep under the market house roof; this night they were all on hand to celebrate Findlay Market's long history rather than to shop. (Courtesy of Deborah Ooten.)

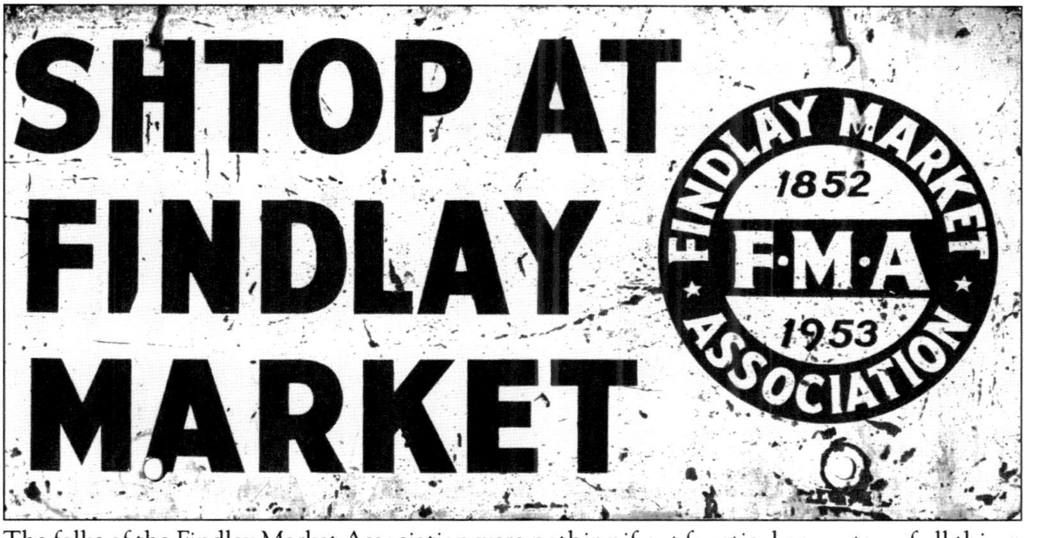

The folks of the Findlay Market Association were nothing if not fanatical promoters of all things market related, and Findlay Market's success can be traced to their unflagging efforts to build business. This 1953 steel plate was designed to fit on an automobile's license plate holder and encourages other driving Cincinnatians to "shtop" (*stop* and *shop* combined) at Findlay Market. (Courtesy of Jimmy Krismer.)

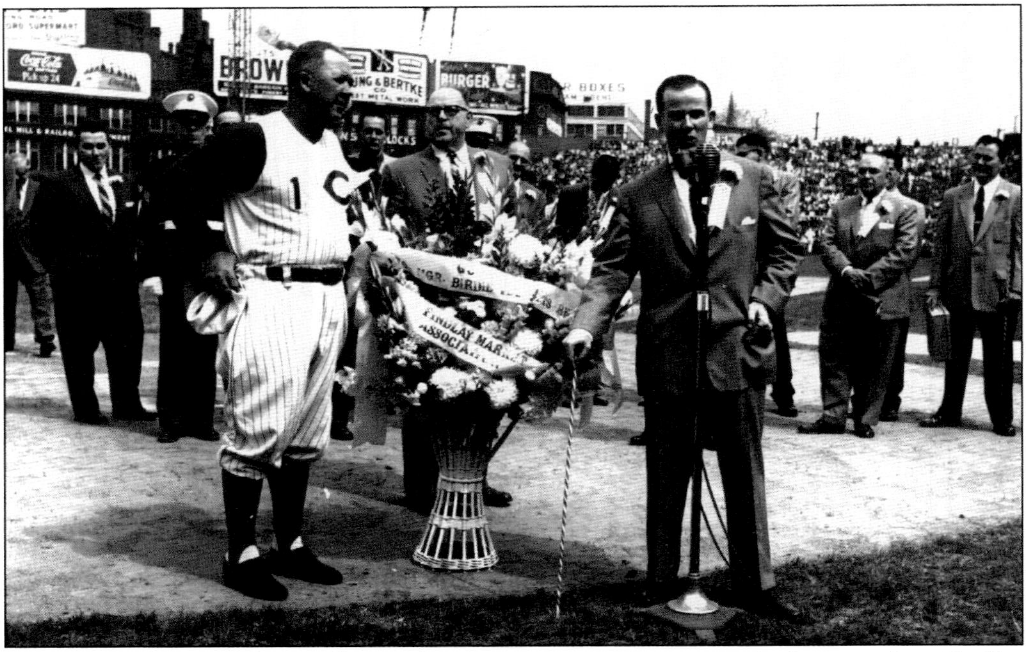

On opening day 1958, the Findlay Market Association made its annual pilgrimage from Findlay Market to the pitcher's mound at Crosley Field. There it made its traditional flower bouquet presentation to Cincinnati Reds manager Birdie Tebbets, above. Below, and with members of the Findlay Market Association looking on, Cincinnati Reds owner Powell Crosley (left) exchanges a folded American flag with Ohio governor C. William O'Neill. (Courtesy of Deborah Ooten.)

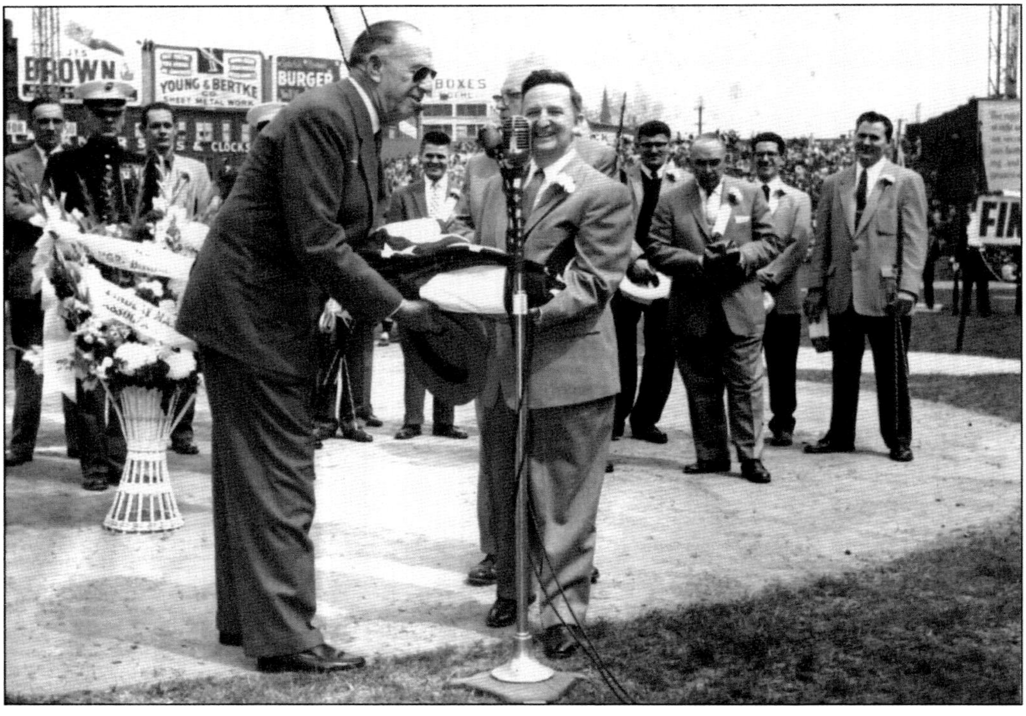

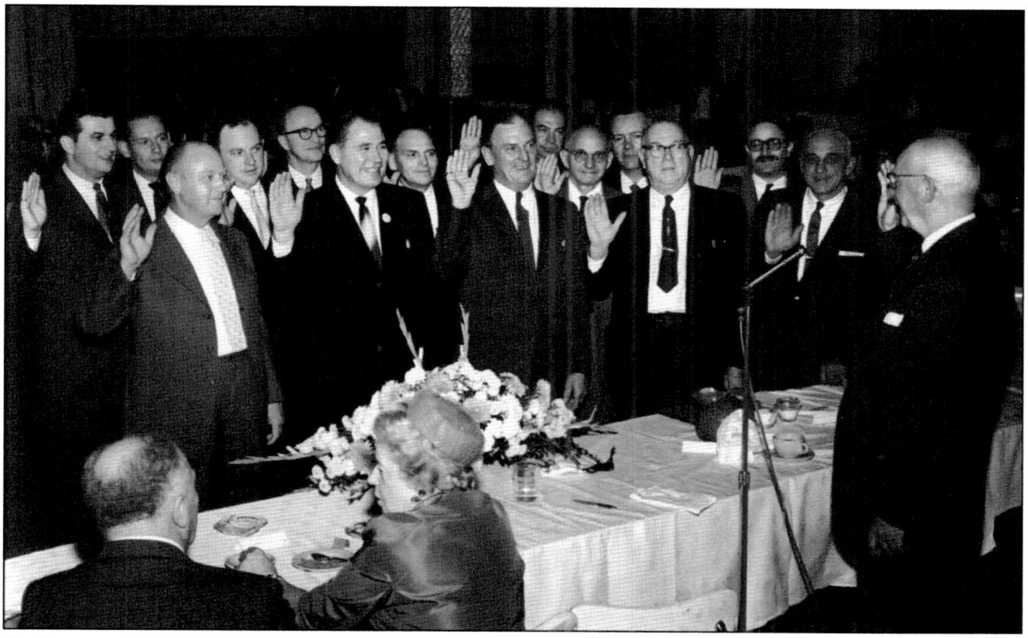

Each year, the Findlay Market Association rented a hall and hired a band for its annual induction banquet. Above, an official swearing-in ceremony is conducted by a local market-friendly judge. Local politicians, police officers, judges, and city administrators kept good and strong relationships with Findlay Market Association members because the association held quite a bit of influence when it came to city governing. The Findlay Market Association was a self-policing body, and if the association had a gripe with the city about anything affecting the market, it sent representatives straight to city hall. Below, at a local Knights of Columbus hall, the red ticket candidates wear matching paper top hats, and their ties all read, "Vote Red." (Courtesy of Deborah Ooten.)

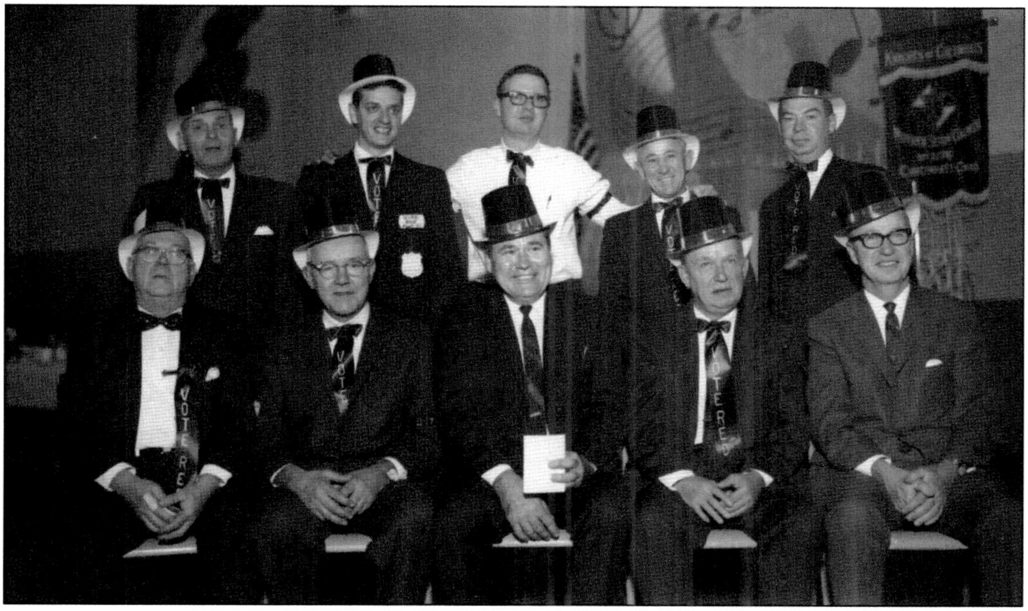

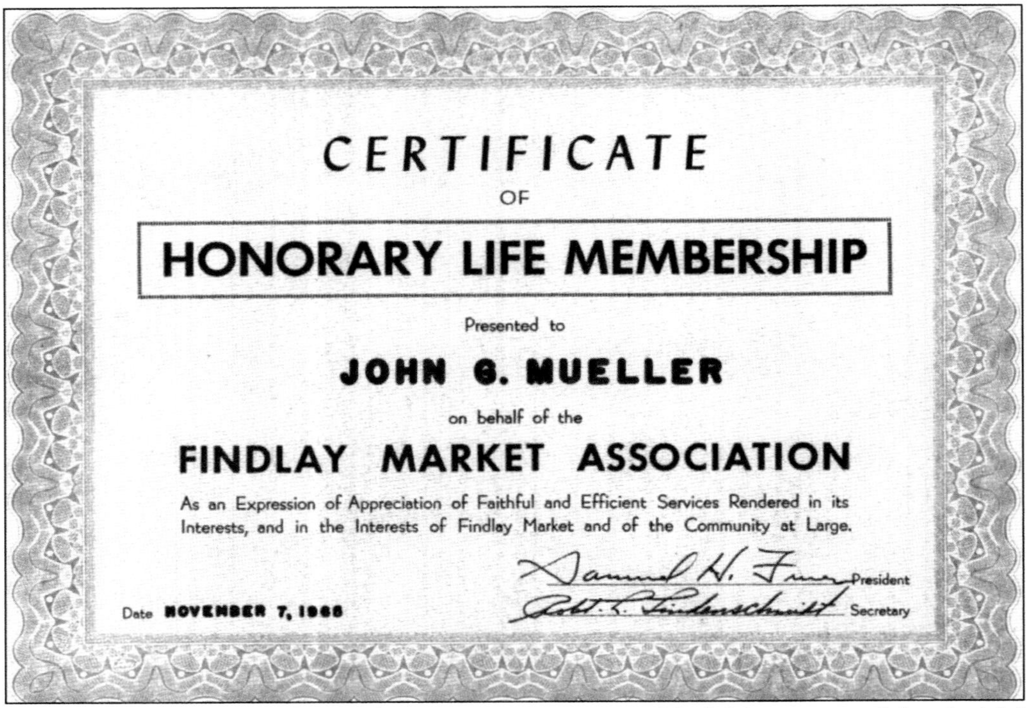

CERTIFICATE
OF
HONORARY LIFE MEMBERSHIP

Presented to

JOHN G. MUELLER

on behalf of the

FINDLAY MARKET ASSOCIATION

As an Expression of Appreciation of Faithful and Efficient Services Rendered in its Interests, and in the Interests of Findlay Market and of the Community at Large.

President

Date NOVEMBER 7, 1968 Secretary

Let it be said that the Findlay Market Association recognized faithful service, and that faithful service ran in more than one direction. The long and great success of the Findlay Market Association depended on faithful service to customers, to the association, to fellow association members, to other vendors, and to the City of Cincinnati. (Courtesy of Johanna Mueller Ritzi.)

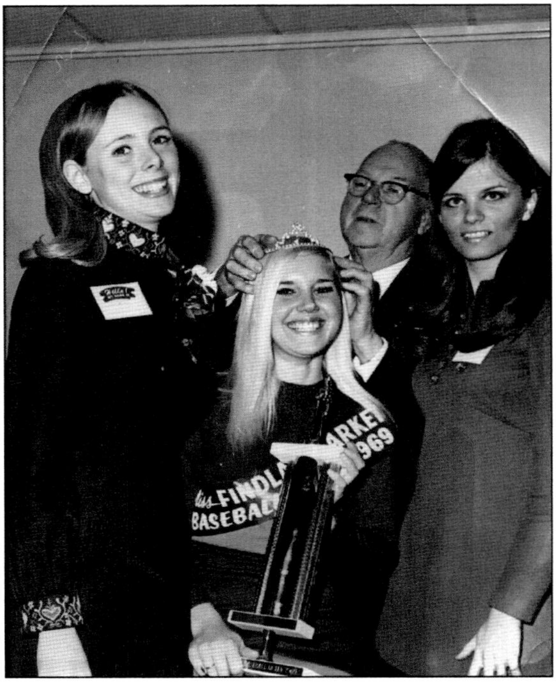

By 1969, the Findlay Market opening day parade had grown to include not only a parade grand marshal but also Miss Findlay Market Baseball Queen. Here Chester A. Lathrop, chairperson of the opening day committee for over 30 years, crowns Miss Findlay Market Baseball Queen 1969. She holds a trophy topped with a scepter-holding queen. (Courtesy of Deborah Ooten.)

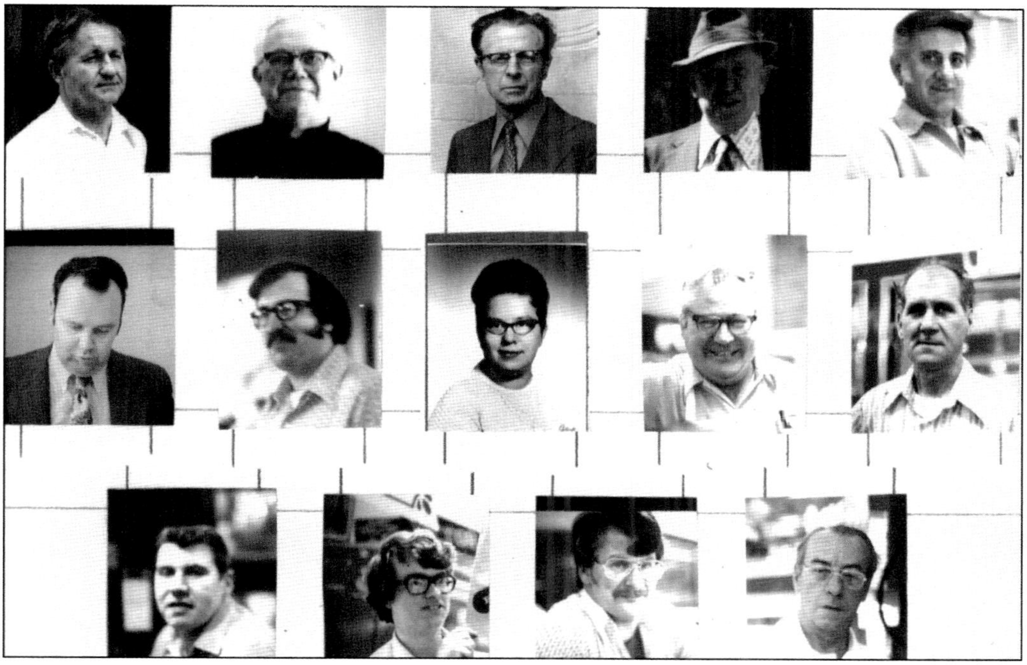

Rather than the usual lineup of white men in suits, above are the Findlay Market Association officers as they appear in the printer's dedication day book mock-up, a publication celebrating the market's 1974 renovation. In this array of photographs, one finally sees a woman's face in the mix. Judy Roth, who still maintains a produce stand on market, was one of the first women elected an association officer. At right is a sample of the Findley Market Association's official ballot (on which Judy Roth's name also appears). Further included on the sample ballot is the name of "Mrs. Curlen Hudson (cleaner)." Dorothy Hudson is African American, and her presence on the ballot indicates a broadening diversity of the Findlay Market Association. (Above, courtesy of Deborah Ooten; right, courtesy of the Catanzaro family.)

OFFICIAL BALLOT

FINDLAY MARKET ASSOCIATION ANNUAL ELECTION

Installation - Dinner at "The Farm" Anderson Ferry Road

Sunday, November 25, 1979

READ CAREFULLY

ase mark the ballot and return in the special envelope enclosed, as soon as possible. Ballots must be mailed no later n Wednesday, November 21, 1979. All ballots must be mailed in order to be valid and counted. It is not necessary to e straight red or straight blue tickets.

RED TICKET	BLUE TICKET
HENRY J. GERBUS (Contractor) President	JIM ZARNOWIECKI (Grocer) President
JOE BARE (Butcher) Vice-President	MIKE LUKEN (Retail Fish) Vice-President
LARRY HATFIELD (Banker) Secretary	LARRY HATFIELD (Banker) Secretary
ROBERT GEISS (Barber) Treasurer	ROBERT GEISS (Barber) Treasurer

DIRECTORS

Vote for not more than five (5).

JUDY ROTH (Produce)	EVELYN MANIS (Produce)
FRANK C. CATANZARO (Produce)	G. MALLARD (Furniture)
RUTH SHERLOCK (Grocery)	KEN WASSLER (Butcher)
CHIP BARE (Butcher)	PAT RUSS (Pickels)
TONY BARE (Butcher)	ELMER SIMPSON (Producer)

This space for write-in votes if any, for Directors.

Vote for not more than two (2) in this group

MIKE CUNDY (Variety Store)	JOHN MIRLISENA (Plumber)
MRS. CURLEN HUDSON (Cleaner)	FR. KREMP (Priest)

his space for write-in votes if any, for Directors.

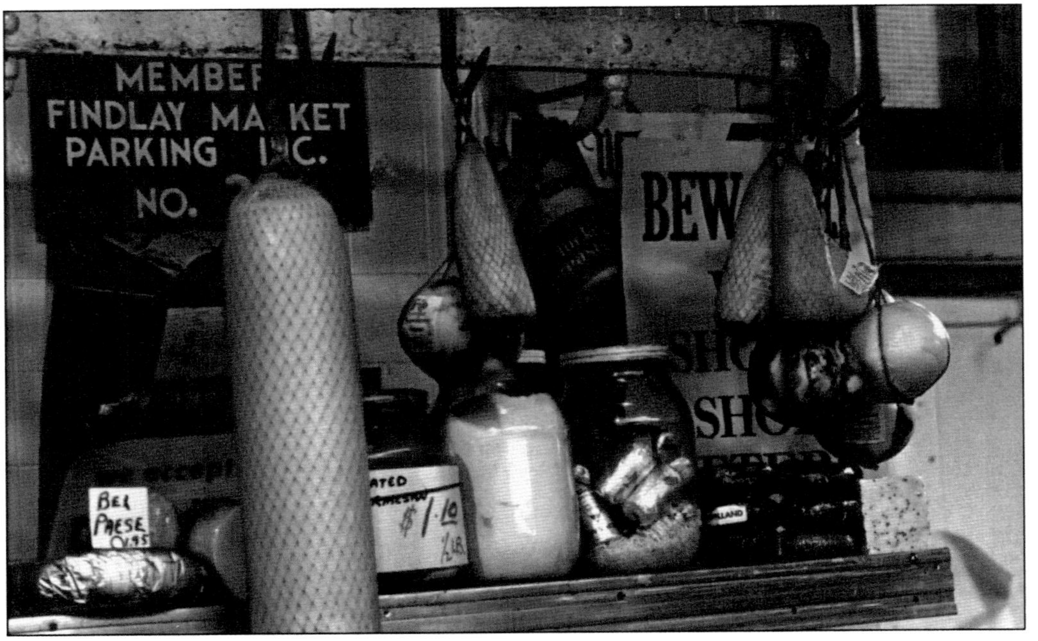

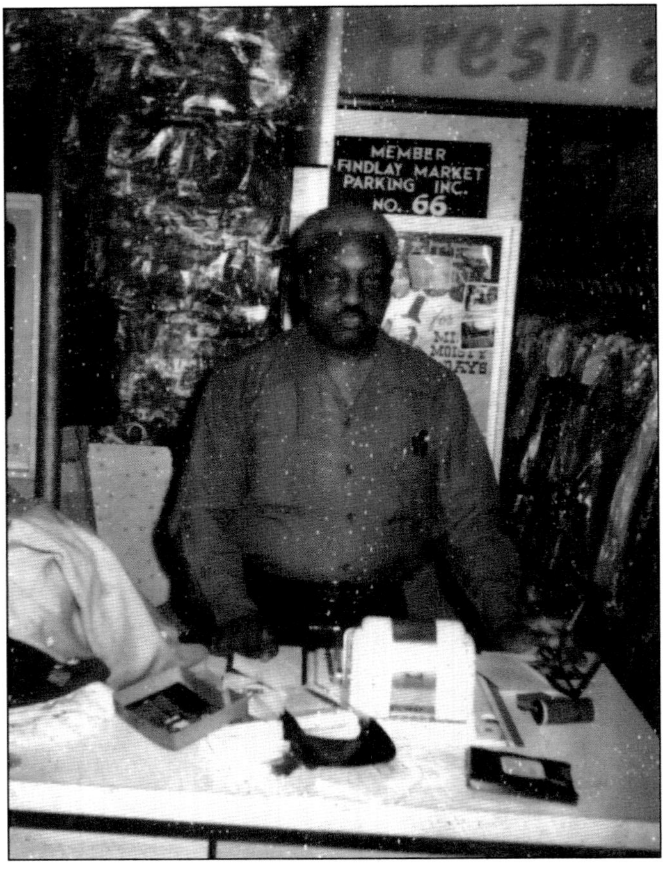

Consistently dogging the market has been the issue of parking space. Behind the cheeses above hangs a sign indicating this stand's participation in Findlay Market Parking Inc. Customers parking in designated lots could park for free if they purchased something from participating vendors who would then stamp their parking receipts. "We take care of our customers, and our customers take care of us" is a refrain often repeated among Findlay Market vendors. At left, although Hudson Brothers Dry Cleaning was located around the corner from the Findlay Market house, Curlen Hudson and his wife, Dorothy, actively participated in the Findlay Market Association. Behind Hudson hangs the sign indicating his membership in Findlay Market Parking Inc. (Above, courtesy of Elaine Kunkel Bourgraf; left, courtesy of the Hudson family.)

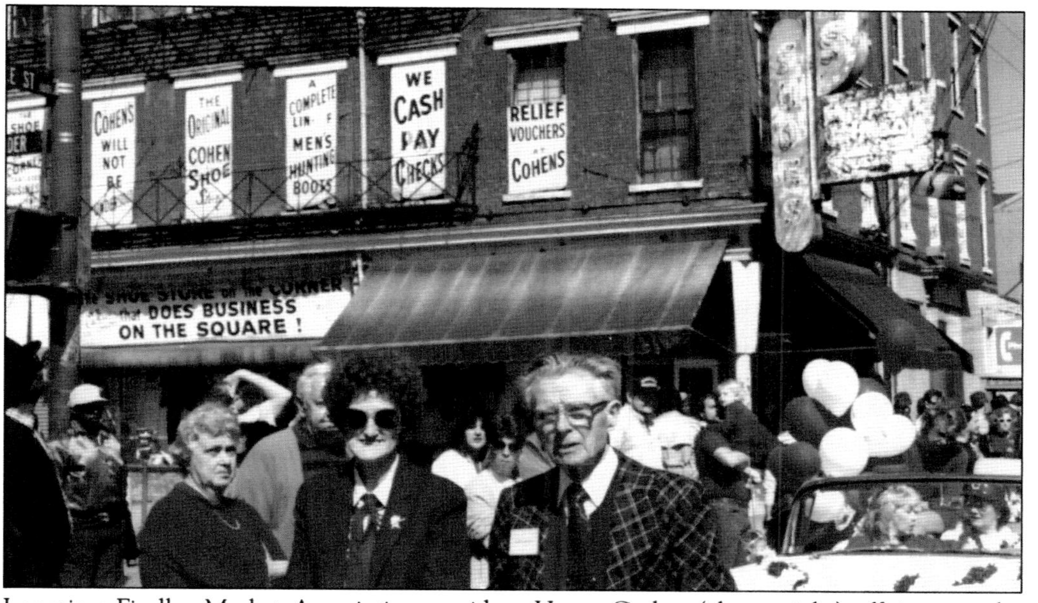

Longtime Findlay Market Association president Henry Gerbus (above, right) officiates as the opening day parade grand marshal. Behind Gerbus is Cohen Shoes; the signs over Cohen's upper windows read, "Relief Vouchers at Cohen's" and "We Cash Pay Checks" and attest to an income decline in the market's Over-the-Rhine neighborhood. Below, with throngs of parade watchers gathered, the Findlay Market opening day parade winds to Fountain Square. Once the Cincinnati Reds left Crosley Field for their new home at Riverfront Stadium, the parade that once culminated on Crosley Field's pitcher's mound now ends at Fountain Square, site of the old Fifth Street Market. (Courtesy of the Catanzaro family.)

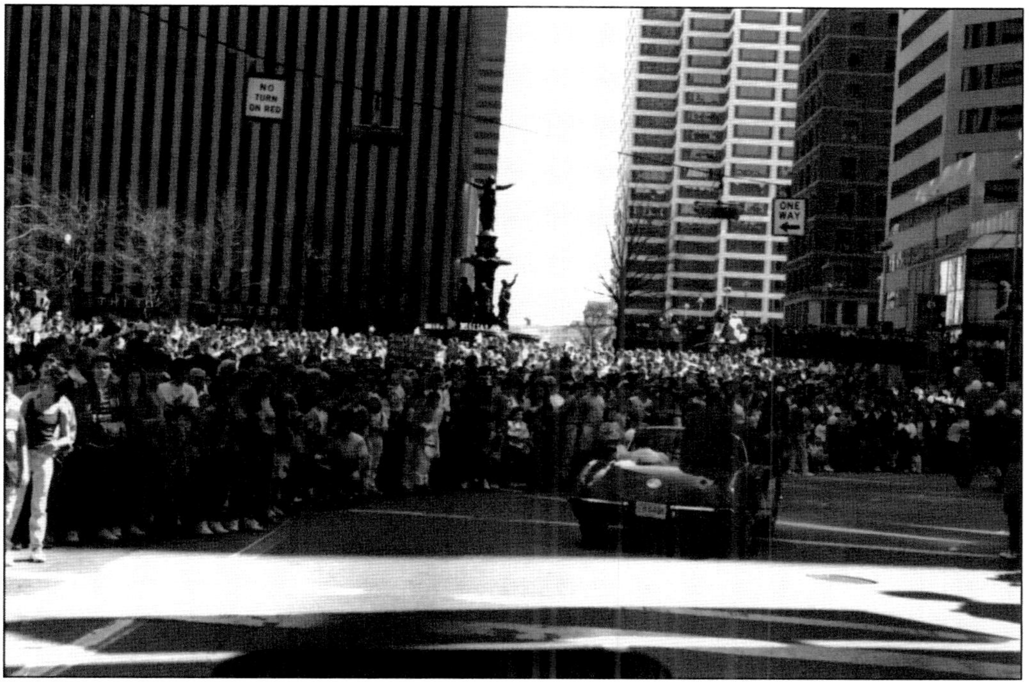

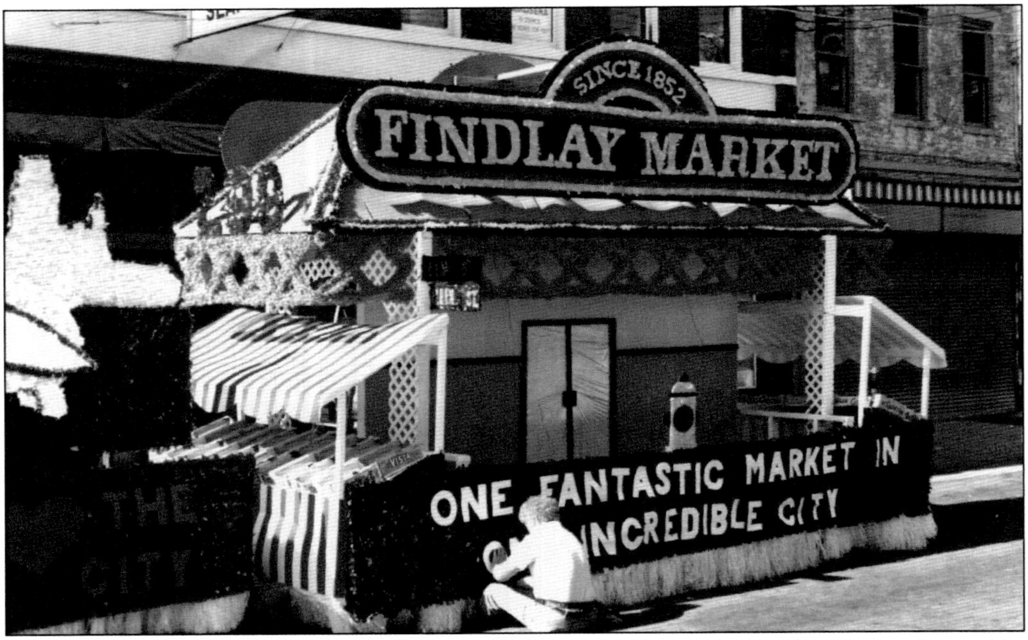

The two Findlay Market opening day parade floats above signal the close-knit relationship established over more than 150 years between the market and the City of Cincinnati. One float reads, "One Fantastic Market in One Incredible City," and the other announces, "Heart the City." The most visible float above is a wonderful mock-up of the market house, including the Elm and Elder Streets signs, the fire hydrant, and the produce stands that have become so recognizable in all these photographs. Below are Jean Bender (left, owner of Bender Meats and active Findlay Market Association member) and country western singer Jo Dee Messina, the year's parade grand marshal. Messina signs a sweatshirt autographed by many previous grand marshals and owned by Tom Bender. (Courtesy of the Bender Geiger family.)

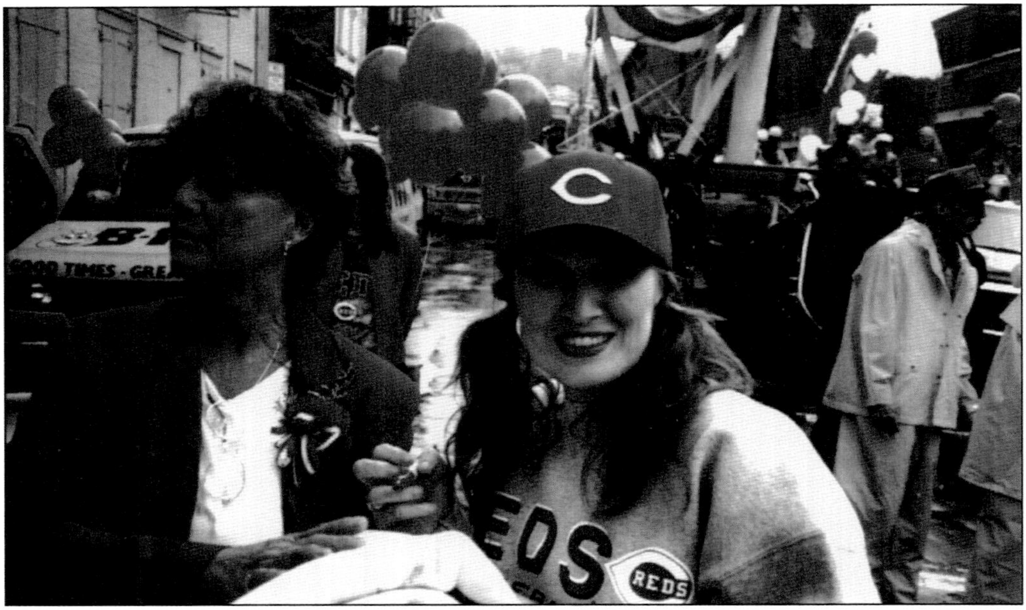

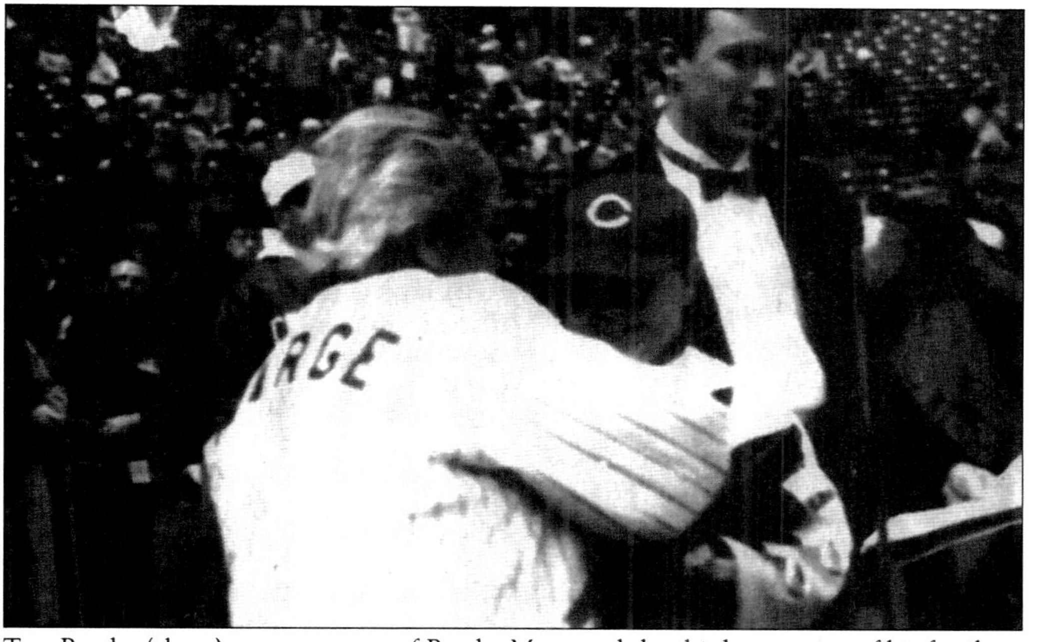

Tom Bender (above), current owner of Bender Meats and the third generation of his family to work on market, presents then Cincinnati Reds owner Marge Schott with the traditional opening day flower arrangement at Riverfront Stadium. Below in 1996, Tom's sister, Jamie (right), pins a carnation on the lapel of Sparky Anderson, manager of the Cincinnati Reds and legendary Big Red Machine member from 1970 to 1978. Anderson returned to Cincinnati in 1996 at the invitation to serve as grand marshal of the Findlay Market opening day parade. (Courtesy of the Bender Geiger family.)

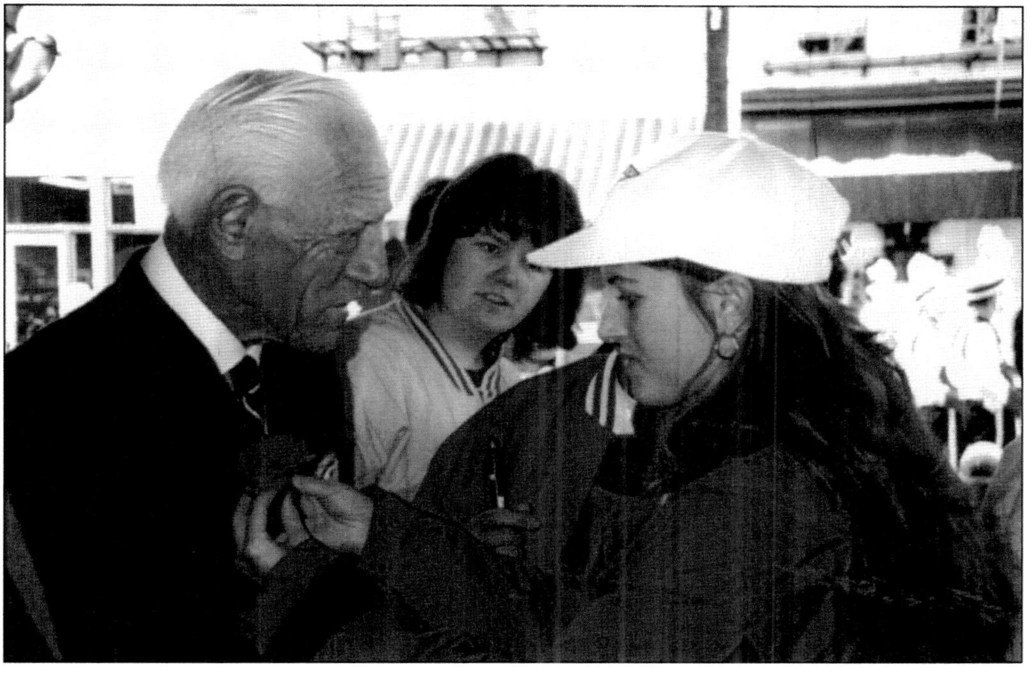

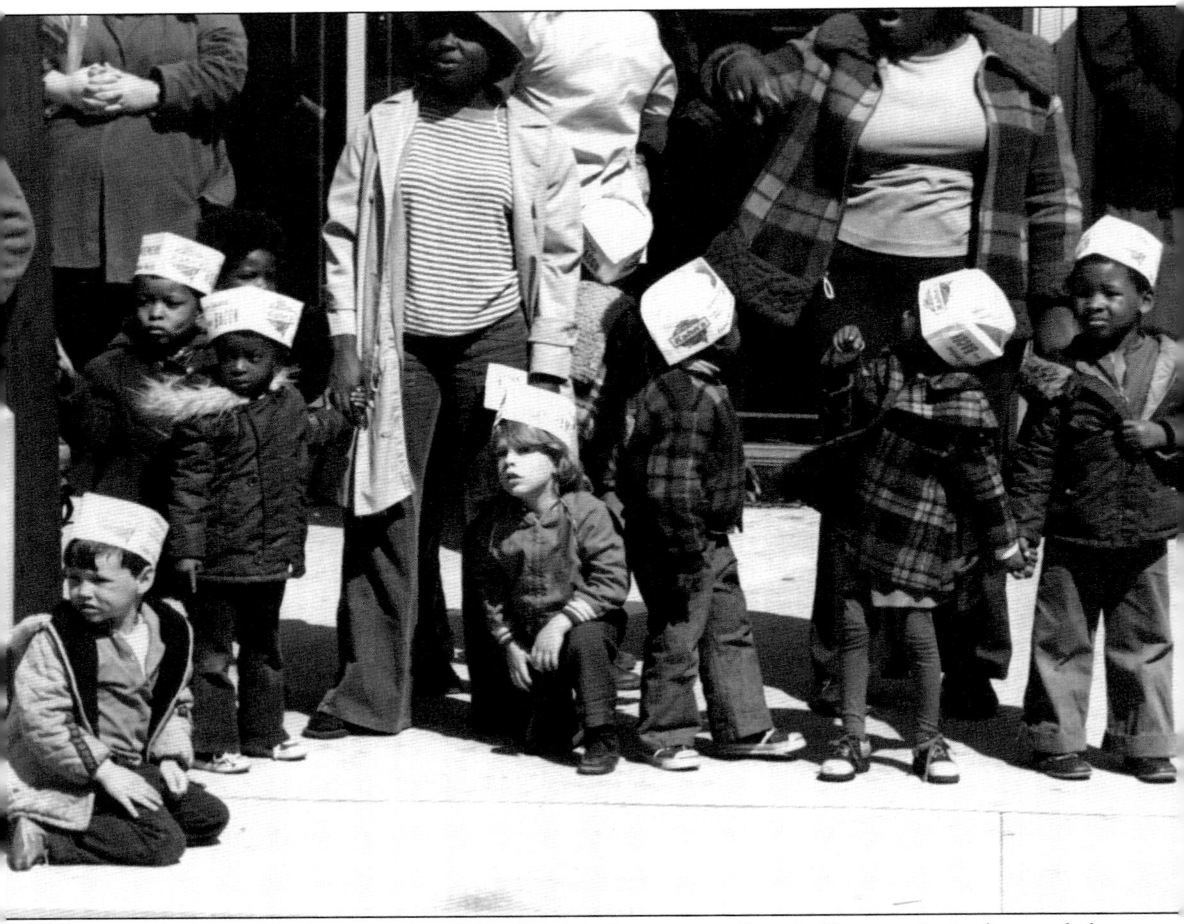

"They can't start the game until Findlay Market appears," said Chester A. Lathrop of the Cincinnati Reds in 1960. By the 1970s, the Findlay Market opening day parade had become a huge event; businesses close, kids and their parents both play hooky, and one local barbershop hangs its annual sign in the window, "Gone to the Funeral: Grandma Died Again." Grade schools all along the parade route let out so the kids can watch as the parade passes by. The students pictured here in their Kahn's Meat butcher hats indicate the ethnic change in Findlay Market's Over-the-Rhine neighborhood and customer base. What began as a primarily German population shifted over the years to a majority Appalachian heritage and most recently to predominantly African American. But just as people of diverse ethnic and cultural backgrounds, socioeconomic levels, gender, age, and sexual preference rub shoulders watching their now-beloved parade, so do the same diverse populations continue to exchange recipes at Cincinnati's beloved market. (Courtesy of Deborah Ooten.)

Three

THE FINDLAY MARKET HOUSE

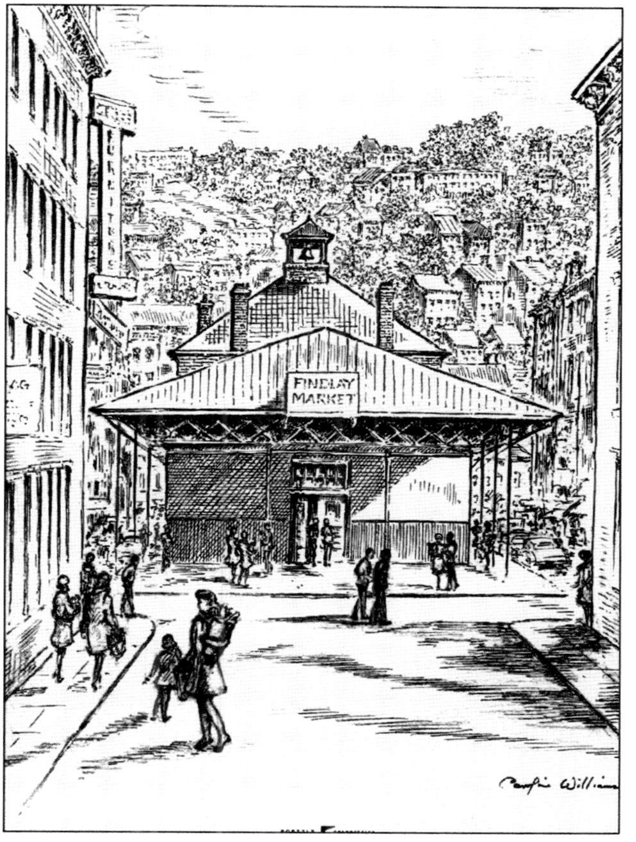

Cincinnati artist Carolyn Williams sketched this Elm Street entrance of the 1960s Findlay Market house; behind the market, Williams highlights the looming Cincinnati hillsides. Although Elder Street around the market is packed with cars, and although Williams indicates that this was a market day, she sketches no vendor stands at the market entrance and no cars in the Elder Street foreground where the woman crosses. (Courtesy of the Geiger Bender family.)

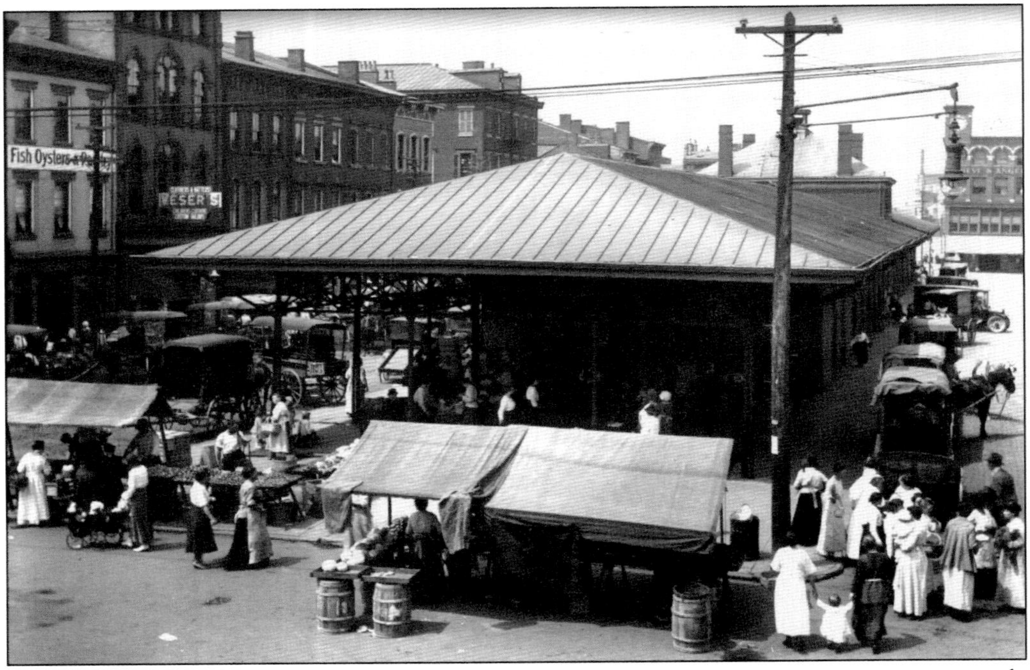

These images show the Findlay Market house from the same vantage point approximately 25 years apart. Above is the oldest known photograph of the market house; horses and buggies line both sides of Elder Street, and one vendor on the left stands with the stump of his amputated leg propped through his crutch. The buzz around the market shows a busy market day. Below, children work and play on the Elder and Race Streets corner in 1935; because this photograph was taken on a nonmarket day, one has a clear view of the cast-iron structure so familiar to Findlay Market lovers. Business signs on Elder Street show two poultry stores, a clothing store, a dry goods store, and a furniture store. (Above, courtesy of Elaine Kunkel Bourgraf; below, courtesy of the Cincinnati Historical Society.)

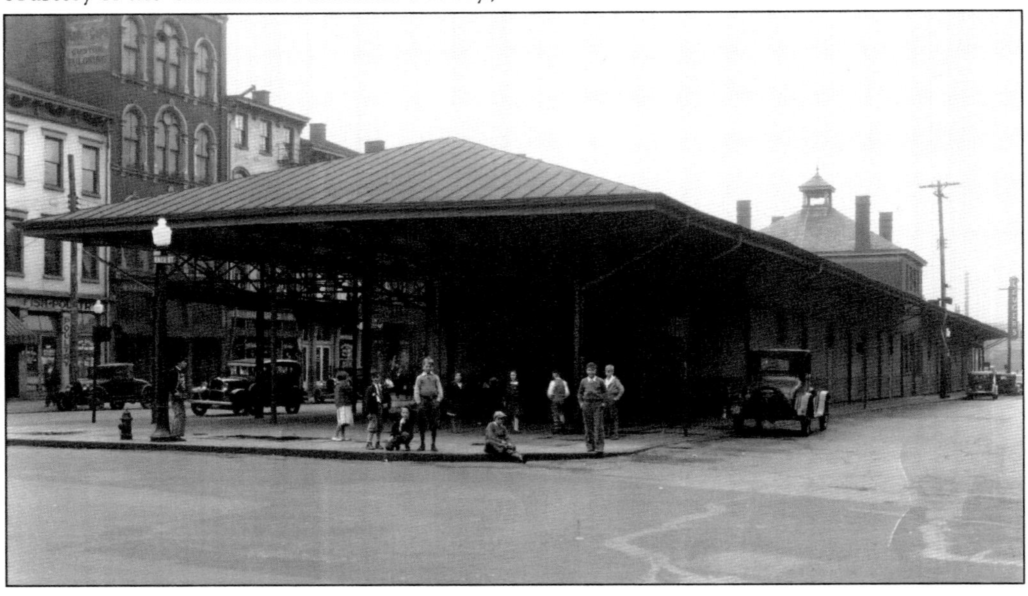

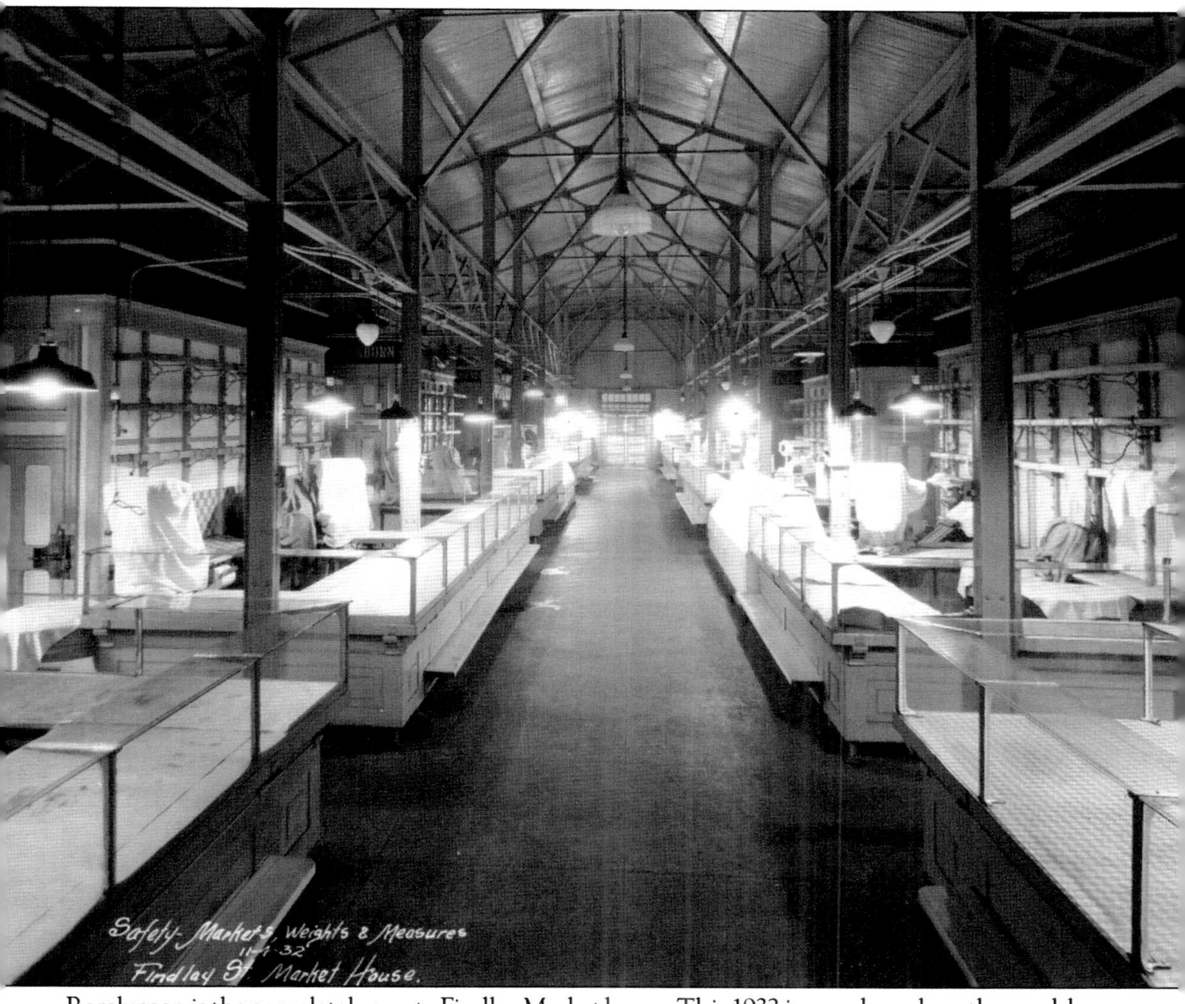

Rarely seen is the completely empty Findlay Market house. This 1932 image shows how thoroughly the indoor merchants cleaned and cleared their stands each night. Because the market house had no refrigeration other than ice, all unsold meat was removed from the counters and from the hooks at the end of the market day; hooks and counters were restocked again each market morning. To keep it clean, these counters are covered with butcher paper, and almost every piece of equipment and every scale is draped in cloth and secured with string. The German heritage of these merchants translates into a pristine market house. This photograph also draws attention to the open cast- and wrought-iron structure that could almost serve as a metaphor for Findlay Market's endurance. Because of its iron construction, Findlay Market was not so easily razed as the other wood- or brick-framed markets. (Courtesy of the Cincinnati Historical Society.)

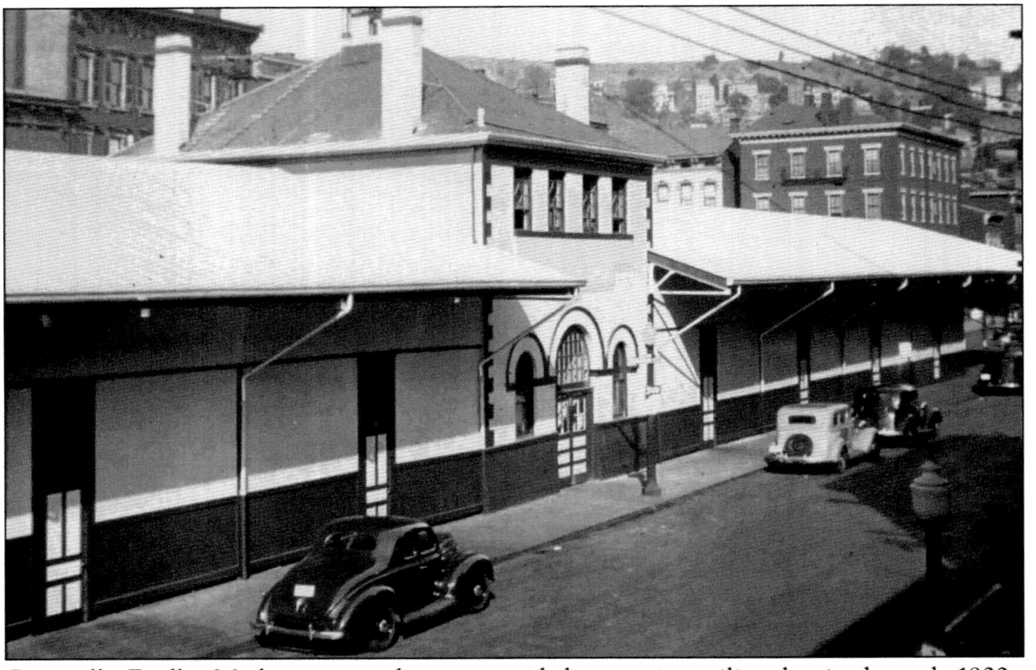

Originally, Findlay Market was simply an open-sided, open-air pavilion, but in the early 1900s, public health concerns regarding pollution and the exposure of food to the elements prompted the addition of plumbing, refrigeration, and the walls seen here. Adding the walls made the interior market darker, an issue future renovations would try to address. This image shows another nonmarket day around 1935. (Courtesy of the Corporation for Findlay Market.)

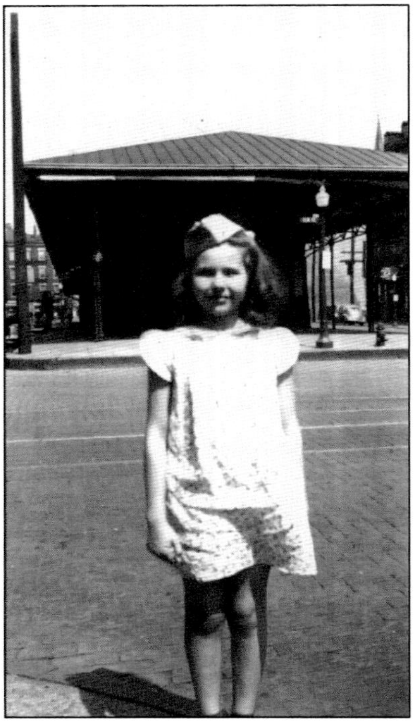

At left, and in her brother's army hat, Mary Ann Yunger stands in front of the Findlay Market house on a Sunday. Notice the clean streets; the German-heritage women of Findlay Market (who were known for their cleanliness) not only swept but scrubbed these streets, curbs, sidewalks, and stoops on their hands and knees. (Courtesy of the Yunger family.)

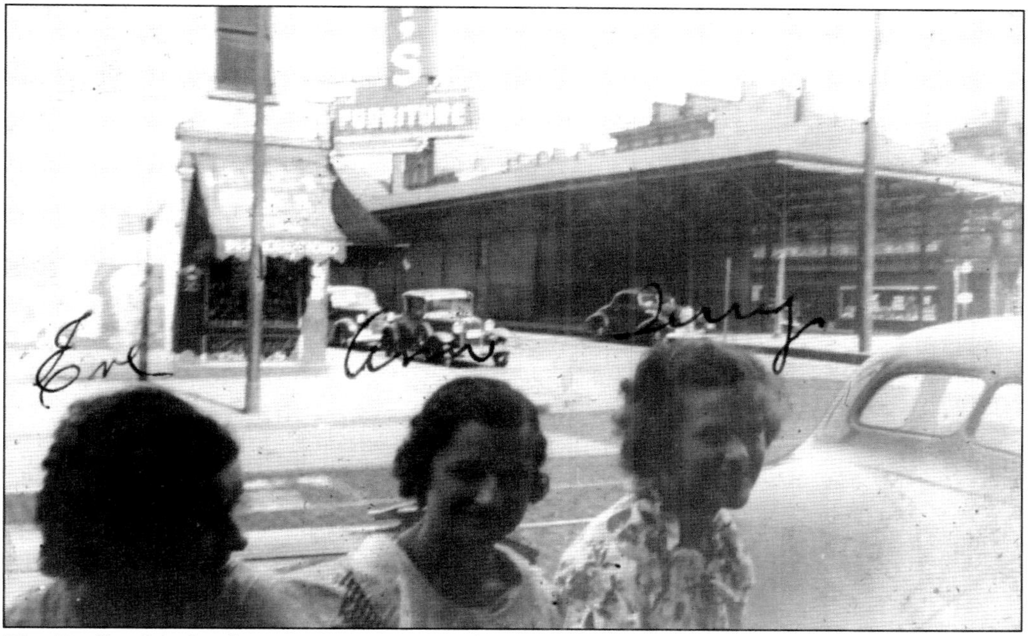

The Findlay Market house on a quiet Sunday is the backdrop of the 1937 image above, from the Yunger family collection. The Yungers lived above their Elm Street café in front of which these women pose, and the market house appears in many of their family photographs the way an old oak tree in a yard may appear in photographs of other families. Below, and again on a Sunday, the Yunger family poses for a group shot; the Findlay Market house is simply part of the background. (Courtesy of the Yunger family.)

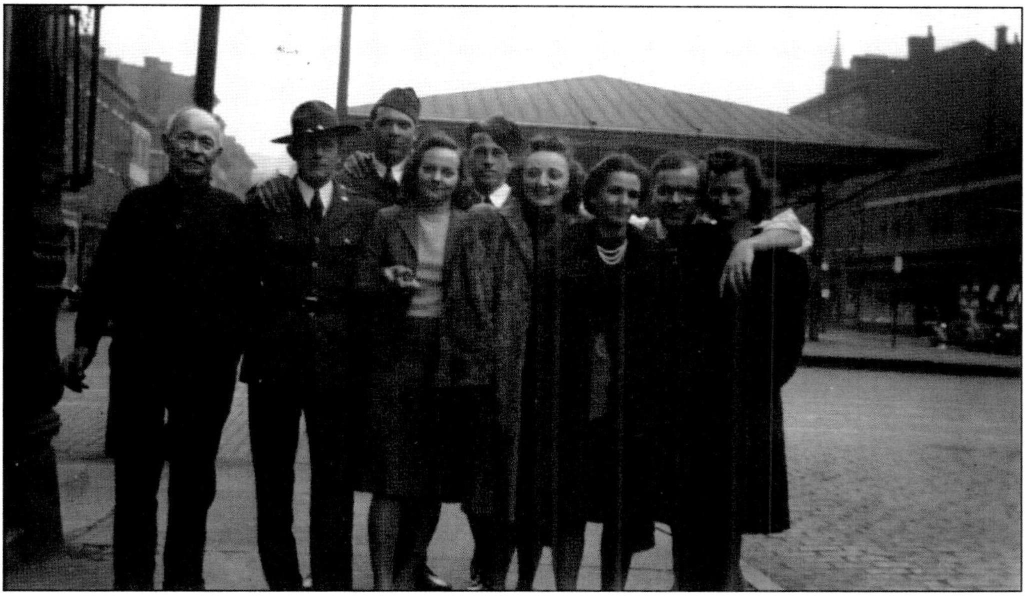

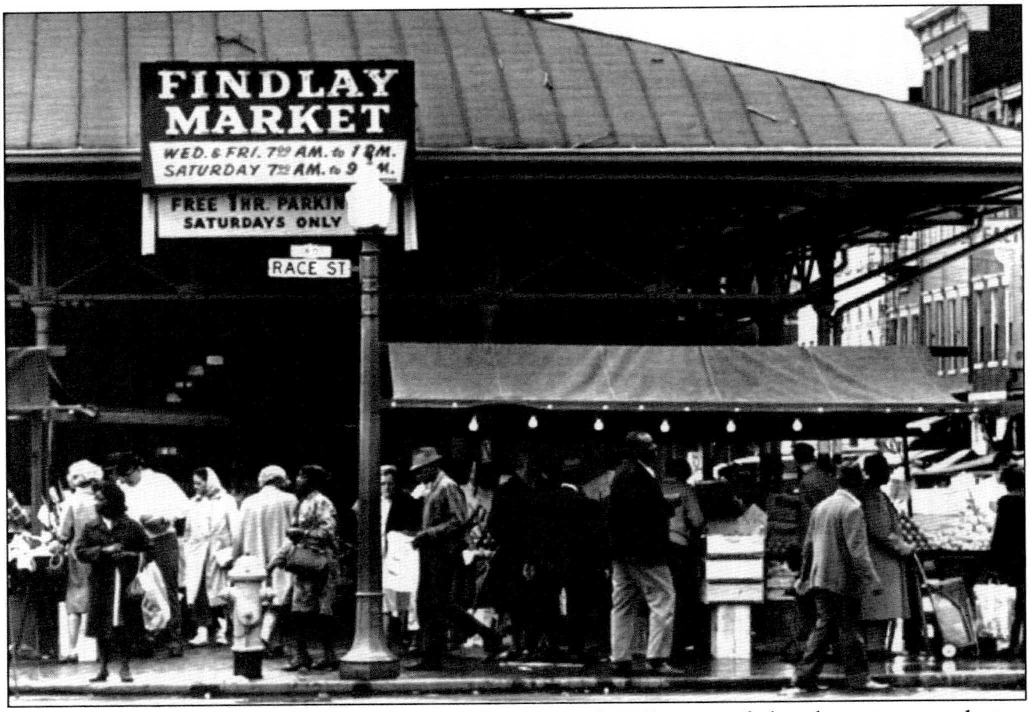

The 1960s brought an increase of skin colors to Over-the-Rhine, and the changing population shopping the market is captured here around 1965. The Findlay Market sign above the pavilion is neon lit because so much of the market's business is conducted before dawn and after dusk. What have not changed are the gas lamp, the 1801 Race Street sign, and the fire hydrant. (Photograph by Don Nesbitt, courtesy of the Corporation for Findlay Market.)

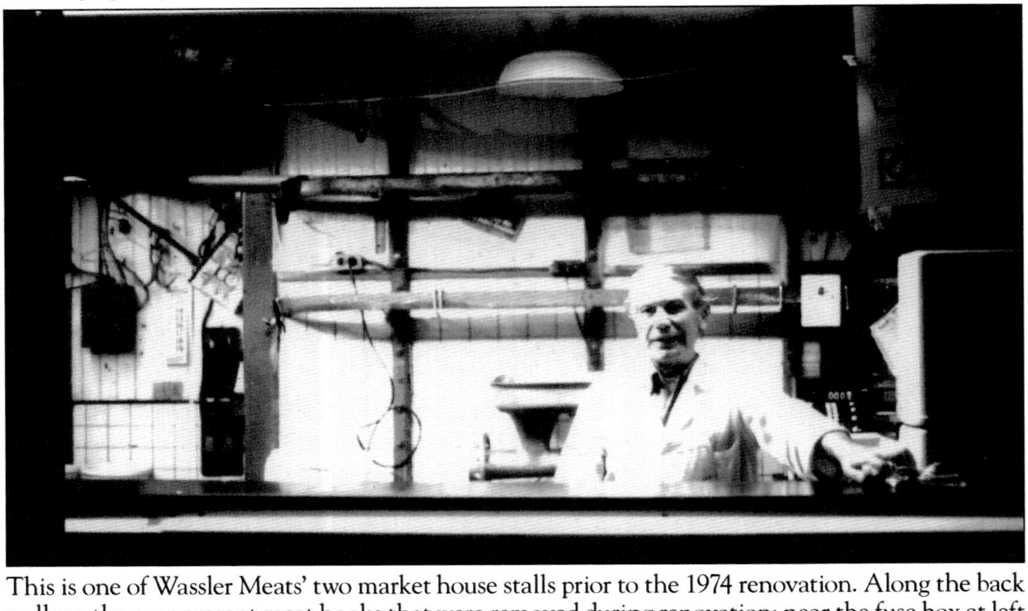

This is one of Wassler Meats' two market house stalls prior to the 1974 renovation. Along the back wall are the ever-present meat hooks that were removed during renovation; near the fuse box at left is a double hook used for weighing beef on hanging scales. (Courtesy of the Wassler family.)

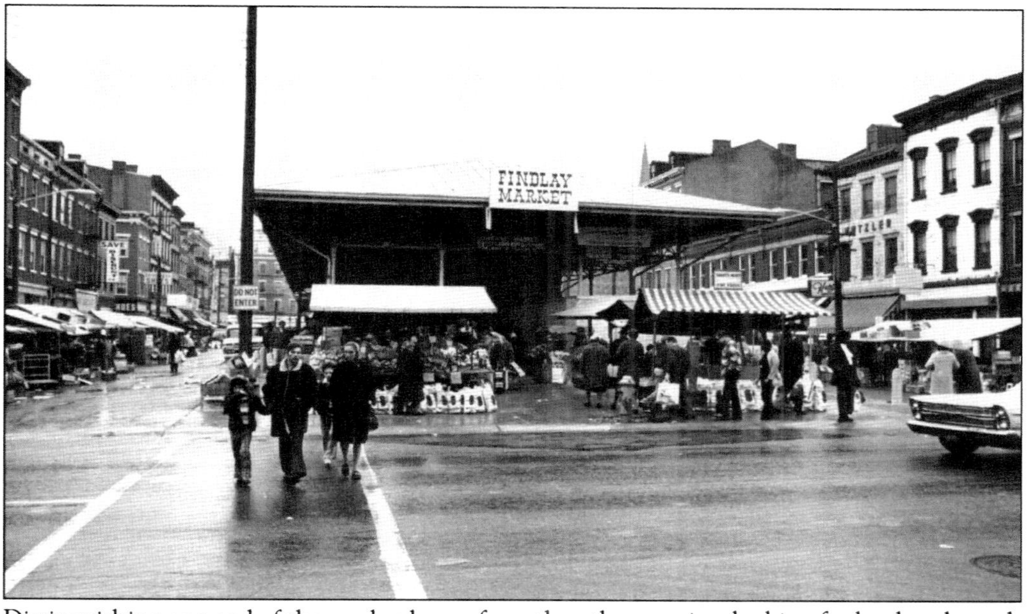

Distinguishing one end of the market house from the other requires looking for landmarks such as a lamppost, a street sign, or the shape of a neighboring building. This is the Elm Street end of the market house before the renovation of the 1970s. The sign hanging from the iron rafters announces the renovation project. (Courtesy of Elaine Kunkel Bourgraf.)

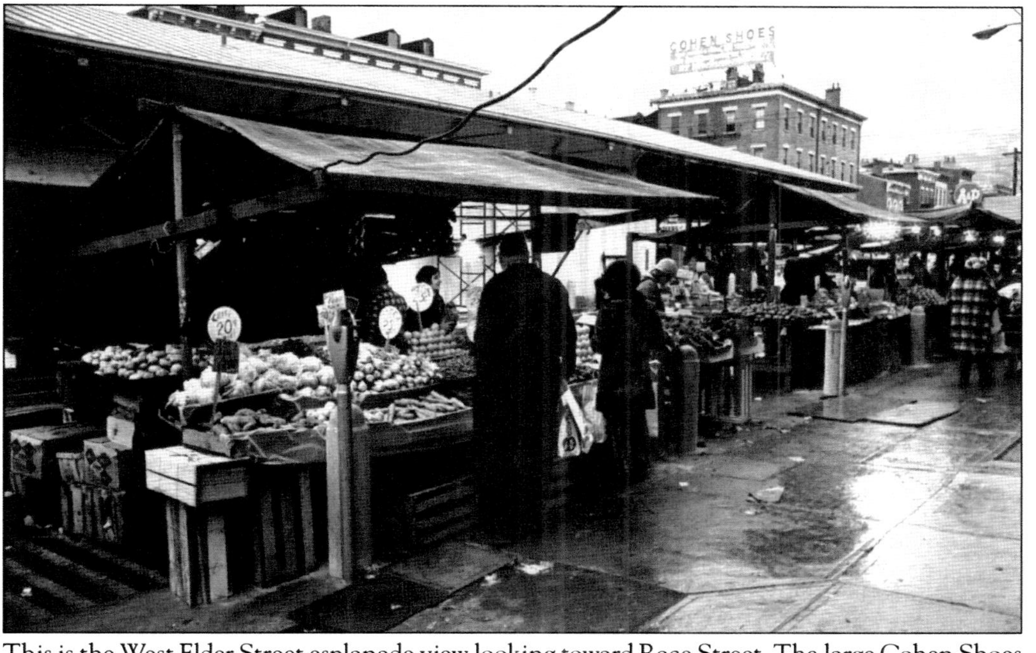

This is the West Elder Street esplanade view looking toward Race Street. The large Cohen Shoes letters have fallen from the sign in the background, but the ghost of the words "We undersell them all!" below it remain today. Every market day, vendors set up and remove everything from the melon boxes supporting their shelves to the lights strung above their stands. This is labor-intensive and detailed work. (Courtesy of Deborah Ooten.)

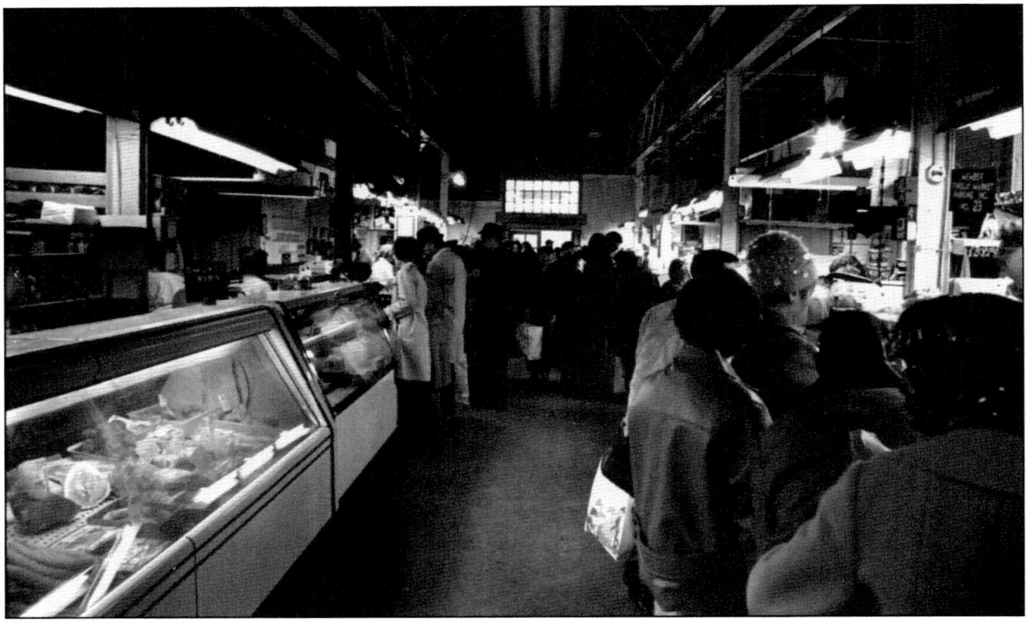

These photographs show the market interior before its 1974 renovation. The aisle was wider in the old market, the floor was concrete, and fluorescent lights lit the stands. Some shoppers and some vendors strongly prefer the atmosphere of the old market to that of the new one. But before renovation, the temperature inside the building on a busy summer Saturday could reach 110–117 degrees; it was cold in the winter, and vendors lacked running water to their stands. Renovations were necessary to bring the market up to board of health standards, and without significant changes, the city would have closed the market. (Courtesy of Deborah Ooten.)

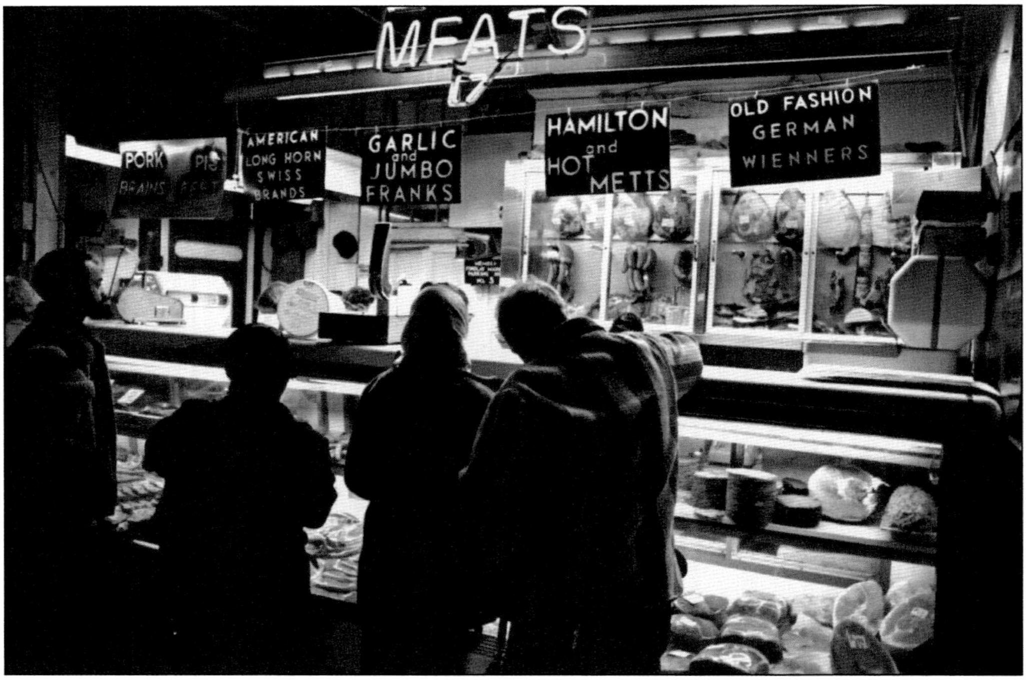

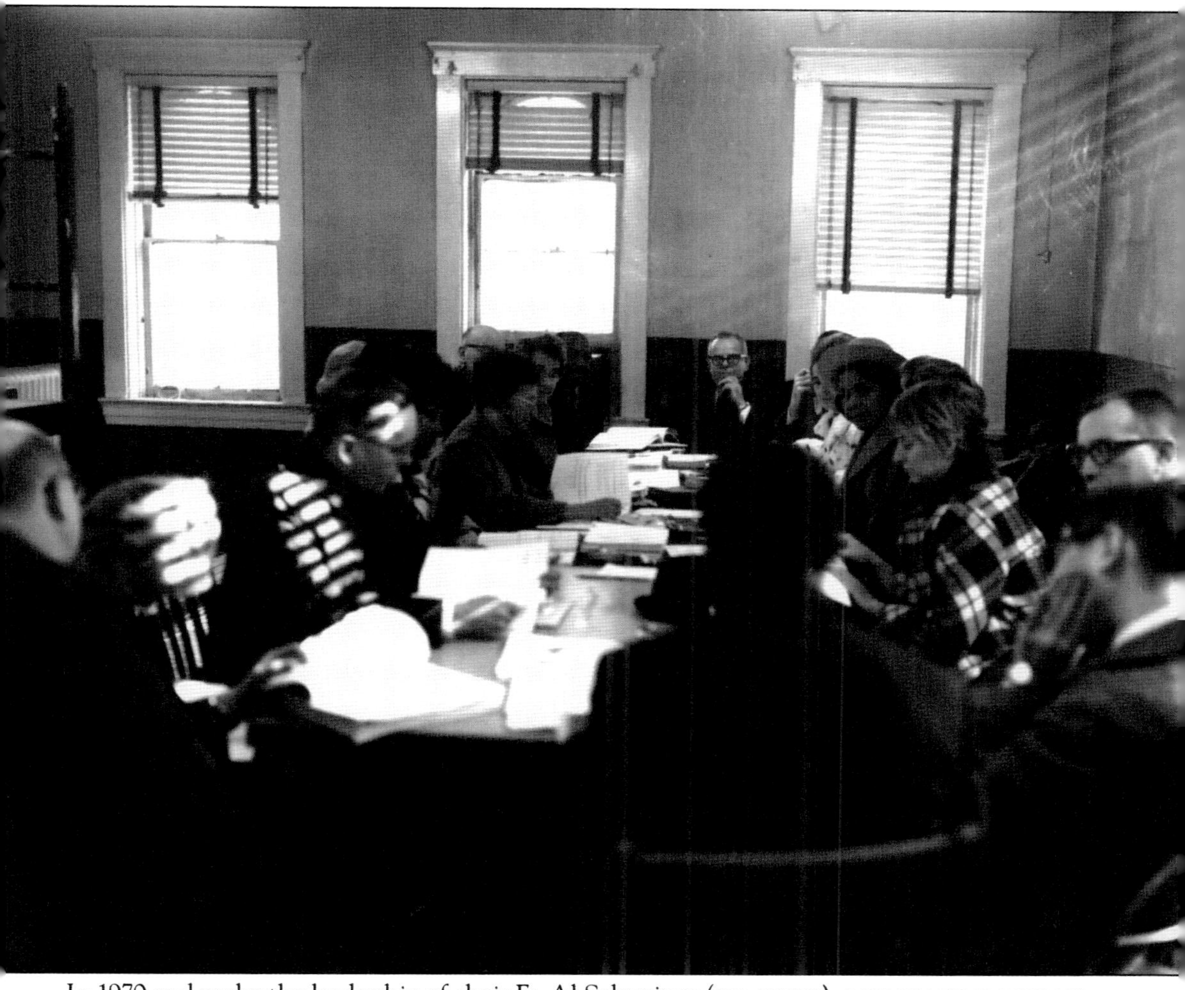

In 1970 and under the leadership of chair Fr. Al Schweitzer (top center), a grassroots movement resulted in forming the Findlay Market/Pilot Center Board to revitalize Over-the-Rhine and rejuvenate the market area. In the century since the market opened, the character of the Over-the-Rhine neighborhood had changed, and the board took action to address the needs of those living near and shopping at Findlay Market. Led by a dedication to preserving the market house and its surrounding neighborhood, the group shown here was charged with weaving new standards and technology into the old building. Improvements from this renovation included widened stands (and reduced aisle space) to make room for larger walk-in iceboxes, installing air-conditioning and central heating, and running hot water to each stand. (Courtesy of Deborah Ooten.)

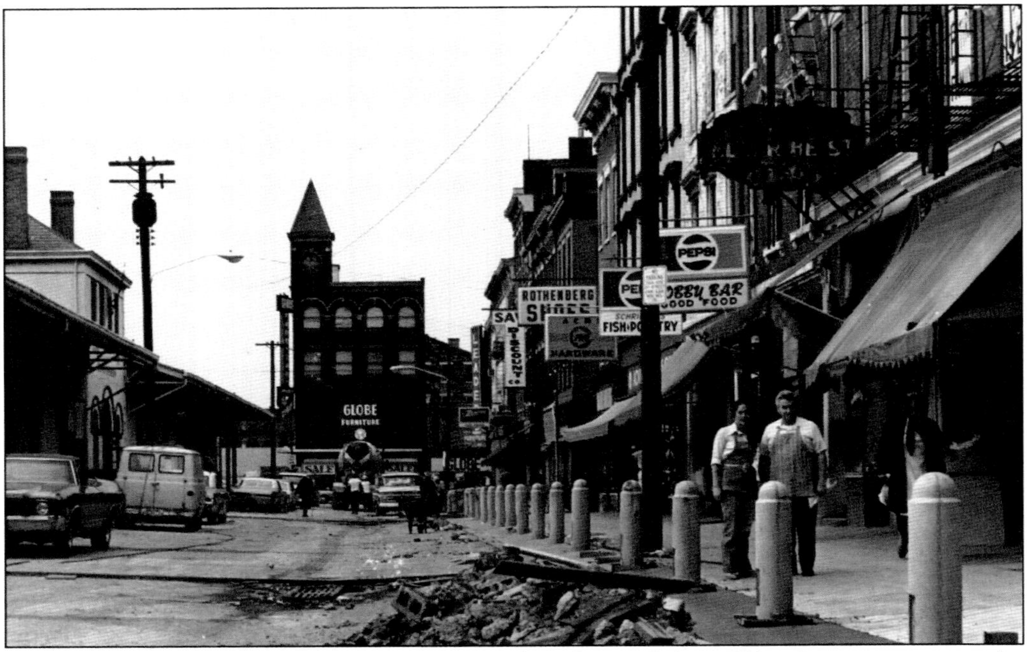

Ray Heist and his daughter Cindy Heist stand in front of their Elder Street store near the beginning of the 1974 renovation project. The faded sign above them indicates a time when Elmer Heist owned the store and advertises both poultry and fish. The concrete barriers being installed controlled curb traffic, and the market house exterior remains in its pre-renovation state. (Courtesy of the Heist family.)

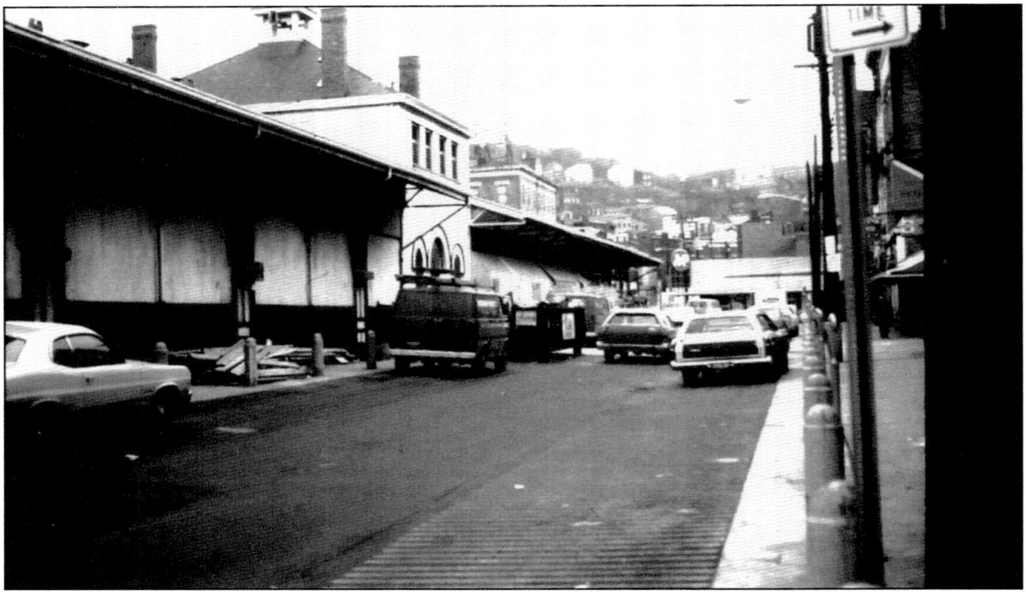

This image, taken on Elder Street and facing Race Street, captures the market house mid-renovation. At the Race Street end of the photograph, one sees the stalls have been expanded. The part of the market pictured in the foreground shows the part of it not yet renovated. (Courtesy of the Wassler family.)

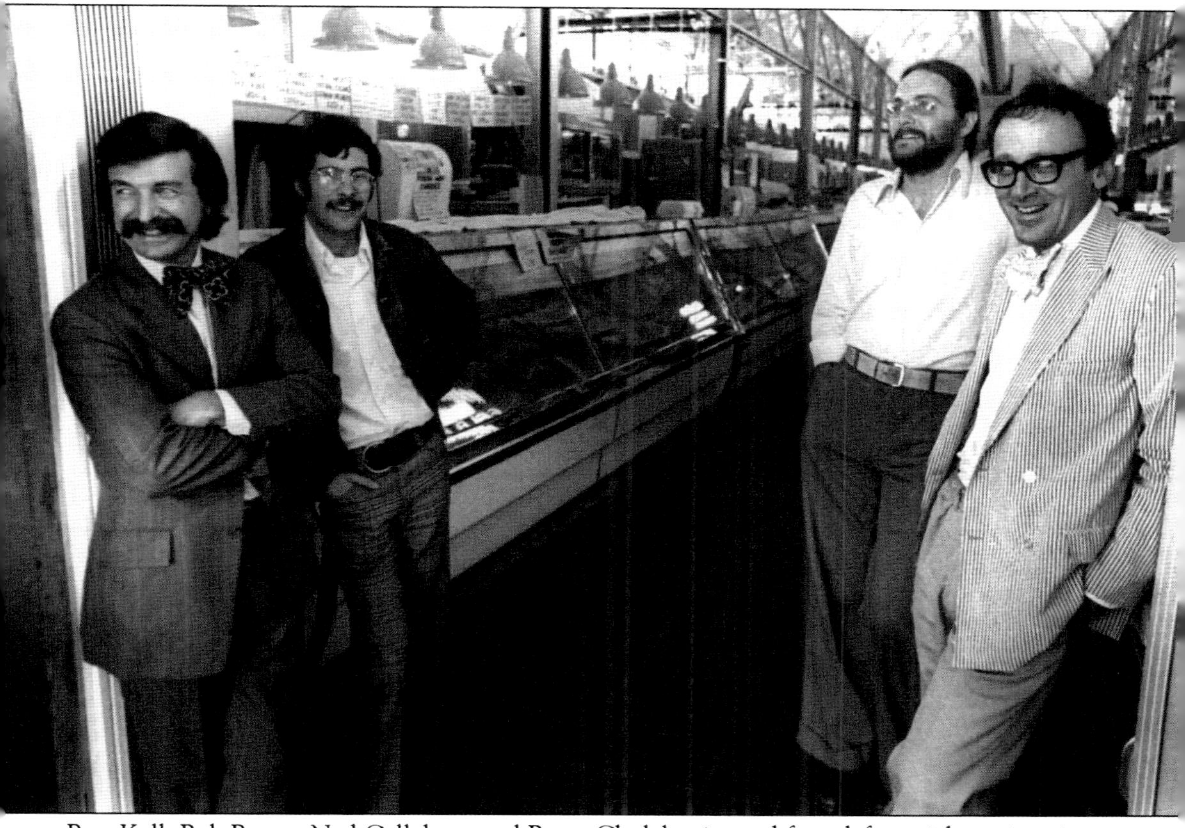

Ron Kull, Bob Rosen, Ned Callahan, and Barry Cholak, pictured from left to right, epitomize the "grassrootsy dreamers" of the city's Department of Urban Development who helped the Findlay Market/Pilot Center Board work toward the successful 1974 Findlay Market renovation. The Findlay Market and community center dedication book author records, in that wonderful language of the 1970s, "Nobody in Findlay Market will ever think again of agencies of the 'establishment' as cold bureaucracy—for all of us together in teamwork dreamed a dream together, and the Department of Urban Development was an indispensable, warm-hearted part of the Dream." Behind the team is the new market interior; the long, low-hanging fluorescent lights have been replaced with individual incandescent ones, and the old concrete floor is now tiled. Not visible in this shot are the expanded refrigeration space and the installation of plumbing running to each stall. At the market dedication ceremony, rather than cutting a ribbon, officials cut through a string of sausages. (Courtesy of Deborah Ooten.)

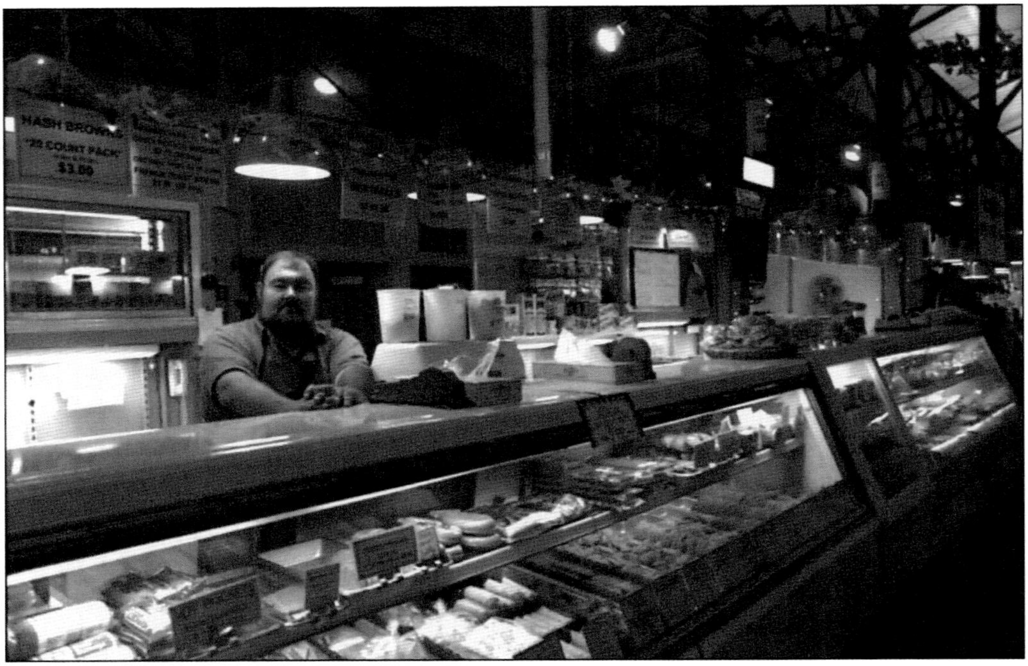

Shown here are the public and the private sides of Mike Bender's Mike's Meats stand. These photographs were taken after the 1974 renovation and just prior to the 2000–2004 renovation. Before 1974, vendors hauled water from a centrally located, shared water source; the sink shown below indicates a market improvement that meant a lot less work and hassle for inside vendors. For a long time, the lack of refrigeration in the stands meant much physical labor for the vendors. Below is a collection of the refrigerators and freezers necessary to keep today's customers' meat fresh. (Photographs by Marty Milligan.)

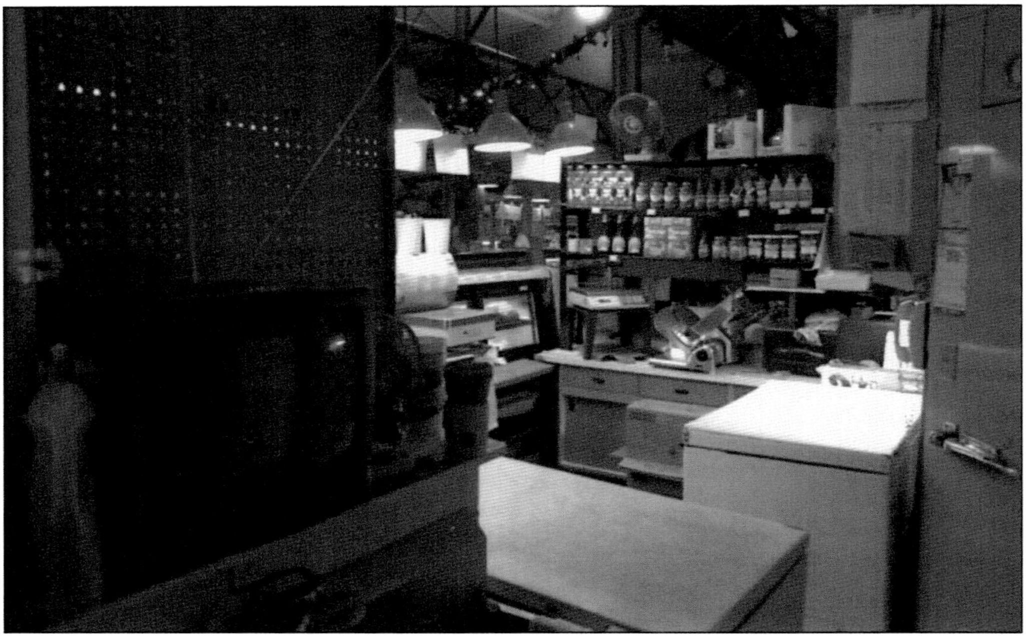

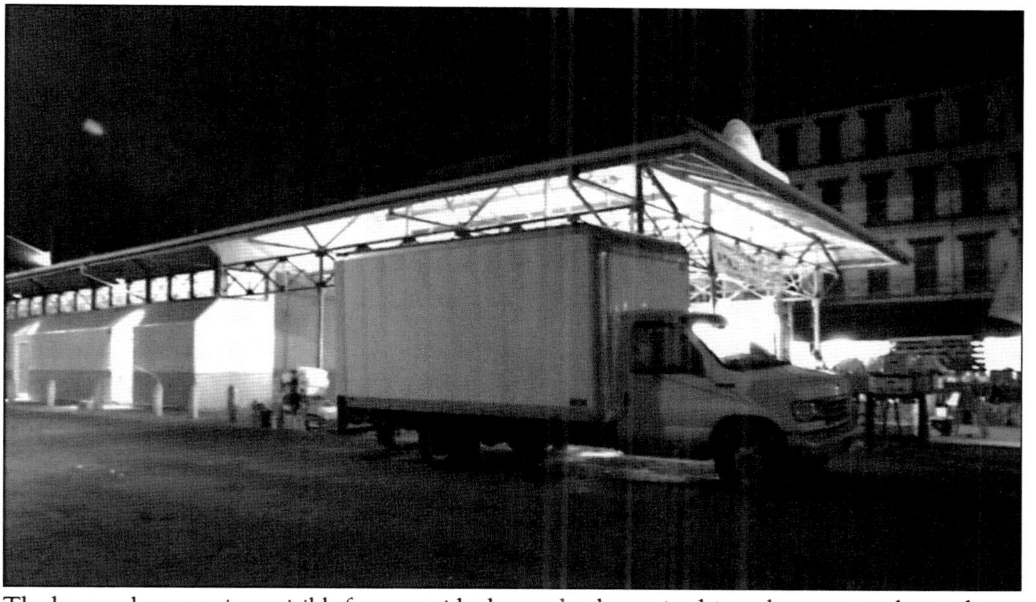

The bumped-out sections visible from outside the market house in this early-morning shot indicate one way stand space was increased for refrigeration, plumbing, and storage in 1974. Instead of simply taking away inside aisle space to enlarge the stands, the stands expanded to the outside. These extensions disappeared in the 2000–2004 renovation. (Photograph by Marty Milligan.)

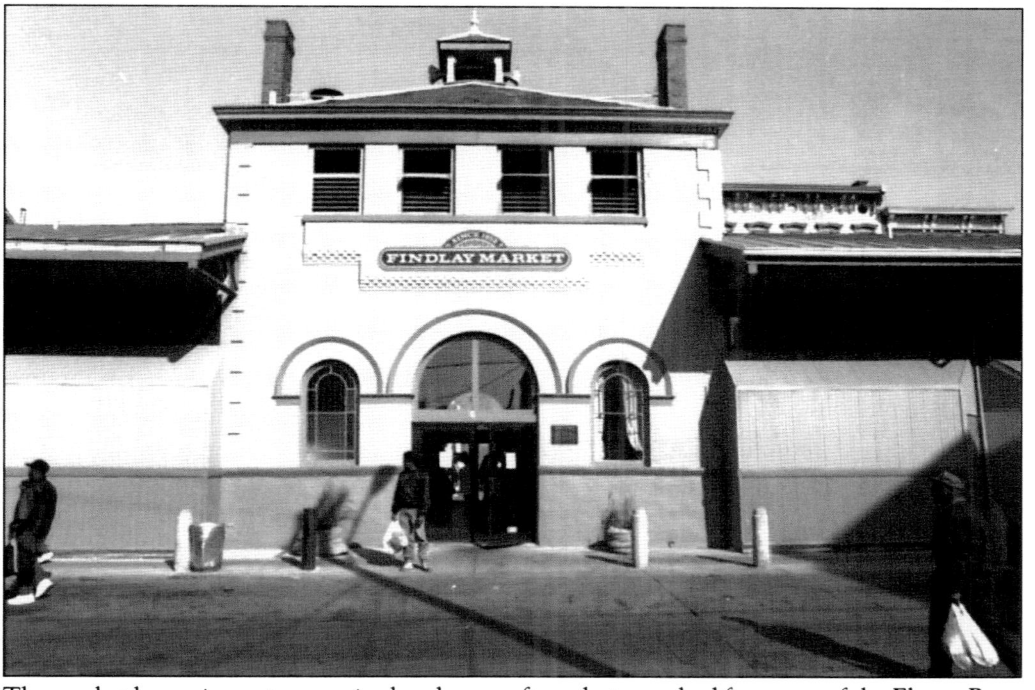

The market house is most recognized and more often photographed from one of the Elm or Race Street ends. There are two main entrances from Elder Street as well, and this photograph shows one of those entrances before the most recent renovation in the early 21st century. (Photograph by Marty Milligan.)

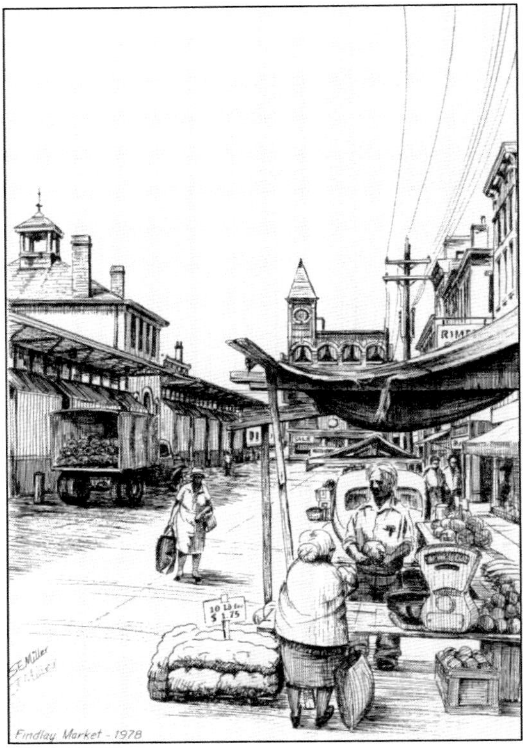

This drawing by S. E. Miller captures a number of notable Findlay Market details before the 2000–2004 renovation: the market's recognizable bell tower, the Elder Street entrance, the bumped-out back of the interior stands, the truck loaded with produce, the Globe Furniture tower in the background, the produce vendor and his oilcloth tarp, the ever-present scales, and the stocky women shoppers carrying their heavy bags. (Courtesy of Elaine Kunkel Bourgraf.)

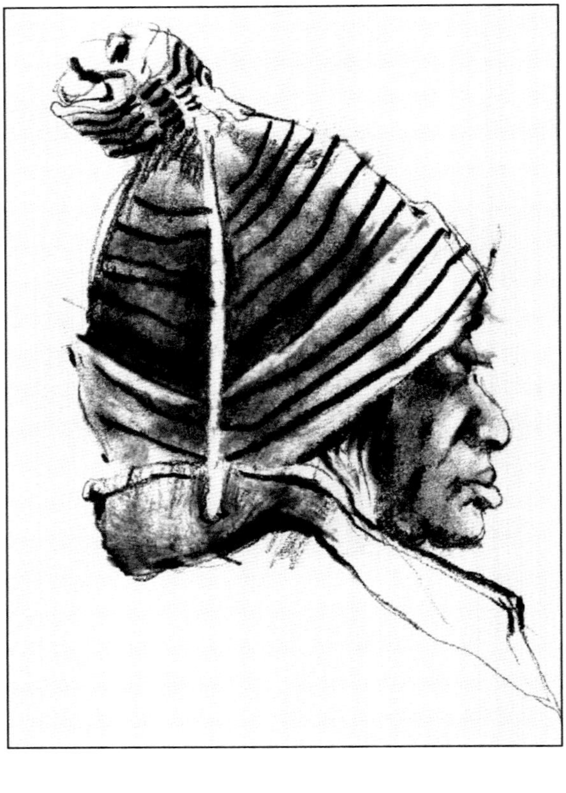

Artist Don Marsh spent many Saturdays over many years sketching Findlay Market shoppers, and his work captures the diverse array of Cincinnatians who rub shoulders and exchange recipes with one another there. (Courtesy of Don Marsh.)

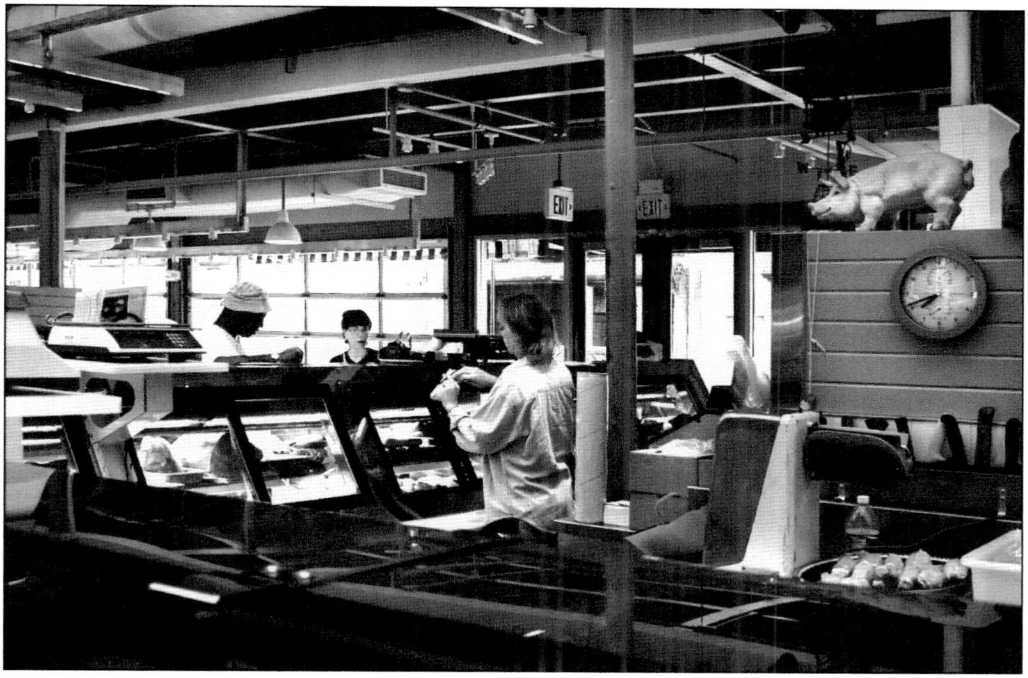

Four years of extensive renovations from 2000 through 2004 resulted in a brighter, more open market. Sunlight pours indoors where no windows previously existed, and on the outside, glass, garagelike doors can now be pulled down to protect full-time produce vendors from extreme temperatures. In nice weather, the garage doors open and the vendors once again contribute to the busy market's street scene. (Above, photograph by Dan Wheeler; below, courtesy of the Madison family.)

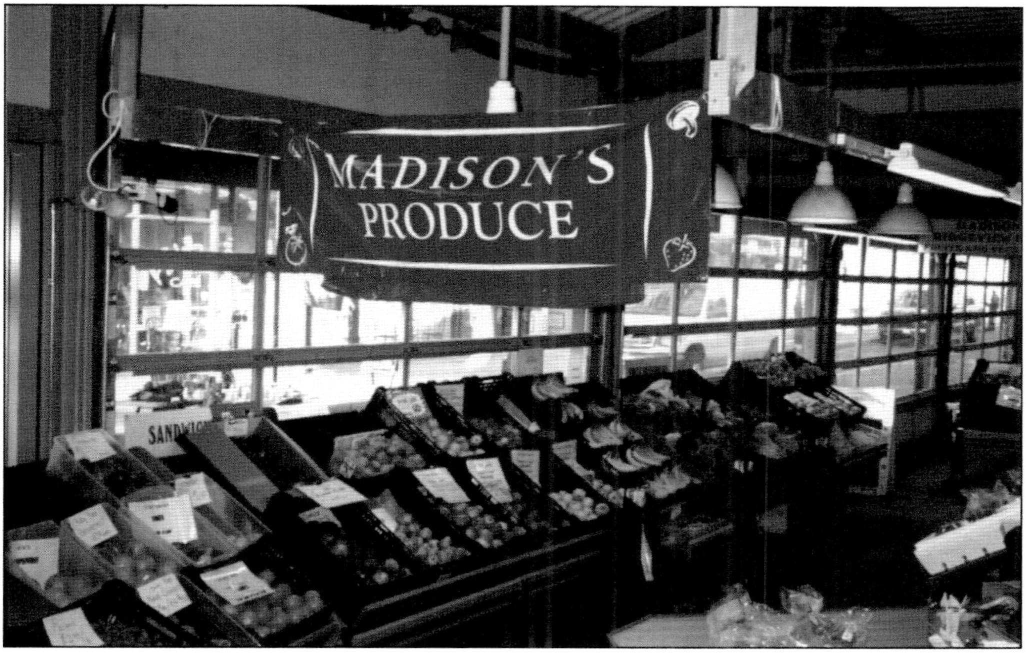

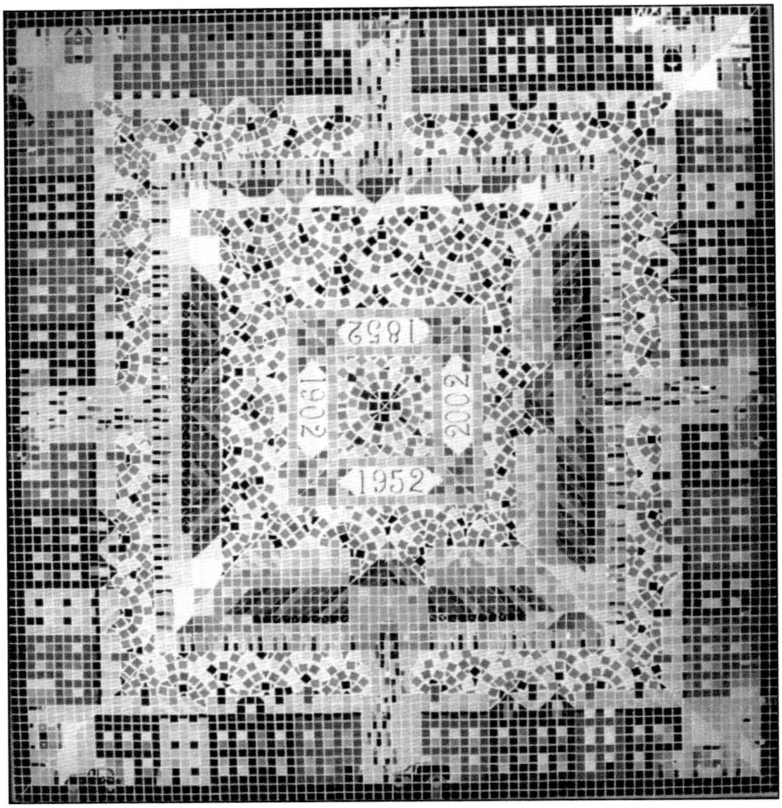

To commemorate Findlay Market's 150th year, market lovers David and Barbara Day designed this "market carpet," a colorfully tiled mosaic installed in the exact center of the market beneath the bell tower. The mosaic depicts the market as it appeared in 1852, 1902, 1952, and 2002. The dates appear in brass numbers that are shined by the feet walking over them. (Courtesy of David and Barbara Day.)

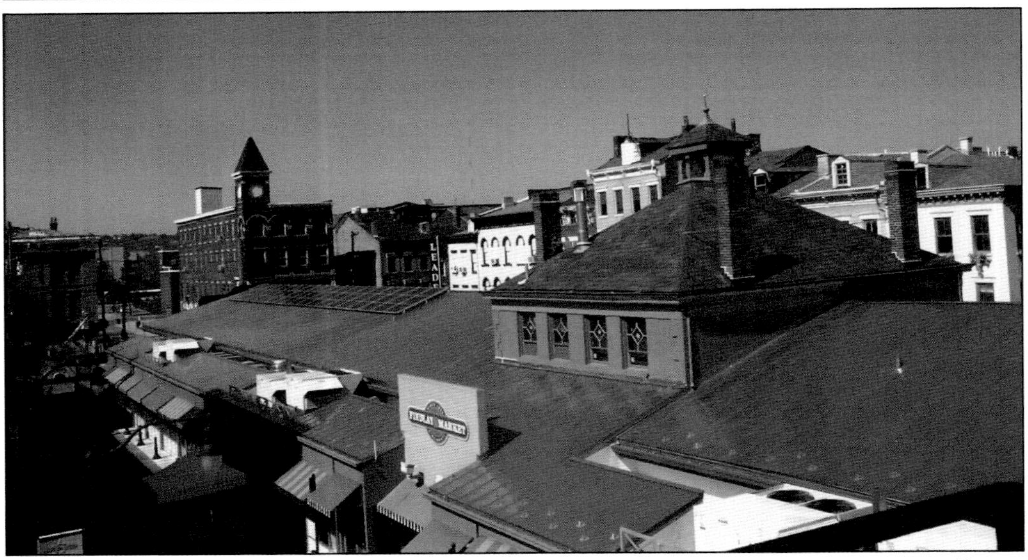

With funds from gifts and grants, the Corporation for Findlay Market oversaw installation of 114 solar panels on the market's locally iconic tin roof in 2008. Not only will these panels reduce the market's electric bill and carbon dioxide emissions, the panels help underscore Findlay Market's ongoing role as a community leader and educator in recycling, composting, tree planting, and local food sourcing. (Courtesy of the Corporation for Findlay Market.)

Four

Cincinnati's Other Public Markets

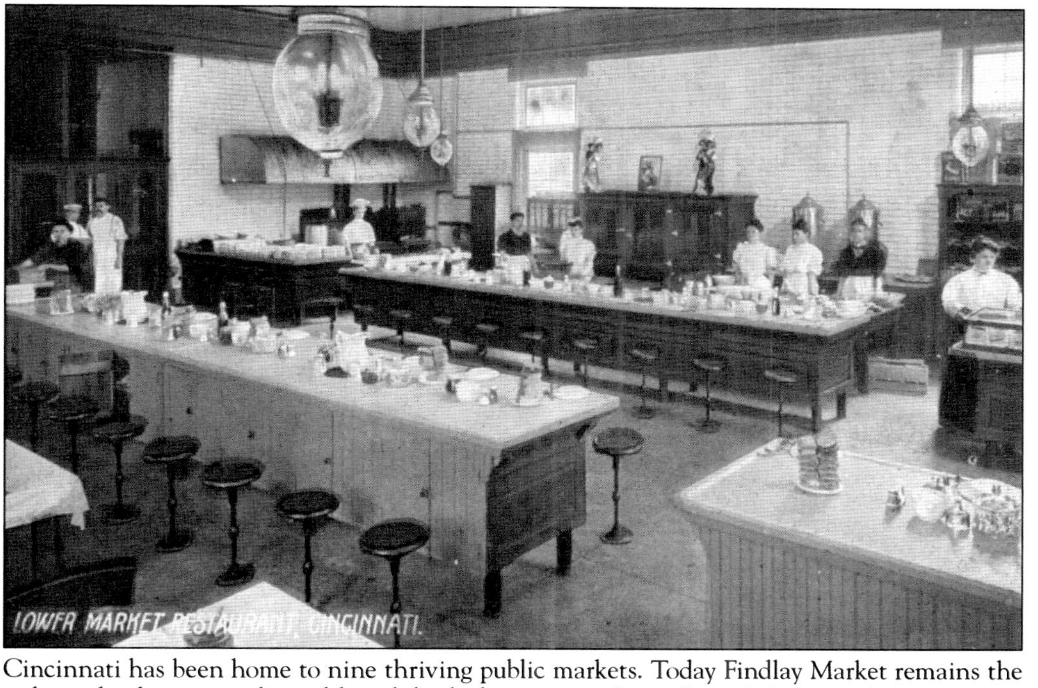

Cincinnati has been home to nine thriving public markets. Today Findlay Market remains the only market house standing, although both the open-air Court Street Market and an increasing number of new seasonal farmers' markets continue to provide Cincinnatians with fresh produce. (Courtesy of the Cincinnati Public Library.)

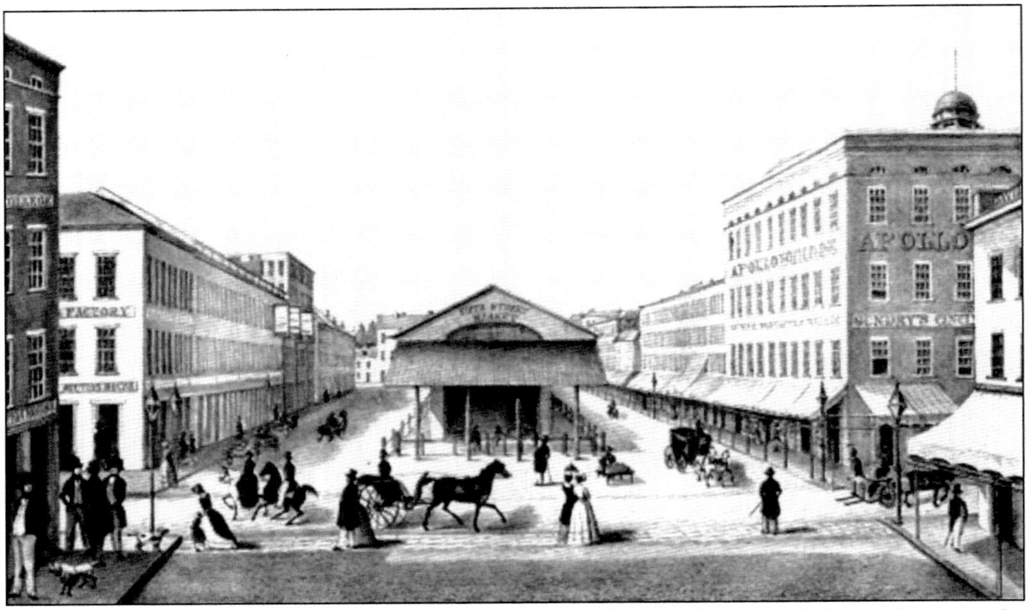

Fifth Street Market was established in 1829 and demolished by force in 1870 to make room for the Tyler Davidson Fountain. When threatened by an 1862 Civil War siege (that never took place), martial law ordered a civilian militia formed of all able-bodied men. Cincinnati women united too and employed the Fifth Street Market house to cook for and feed between 7,000 and 10,000 men daily. (Courtesy of the Cincinnati Historical Society.)

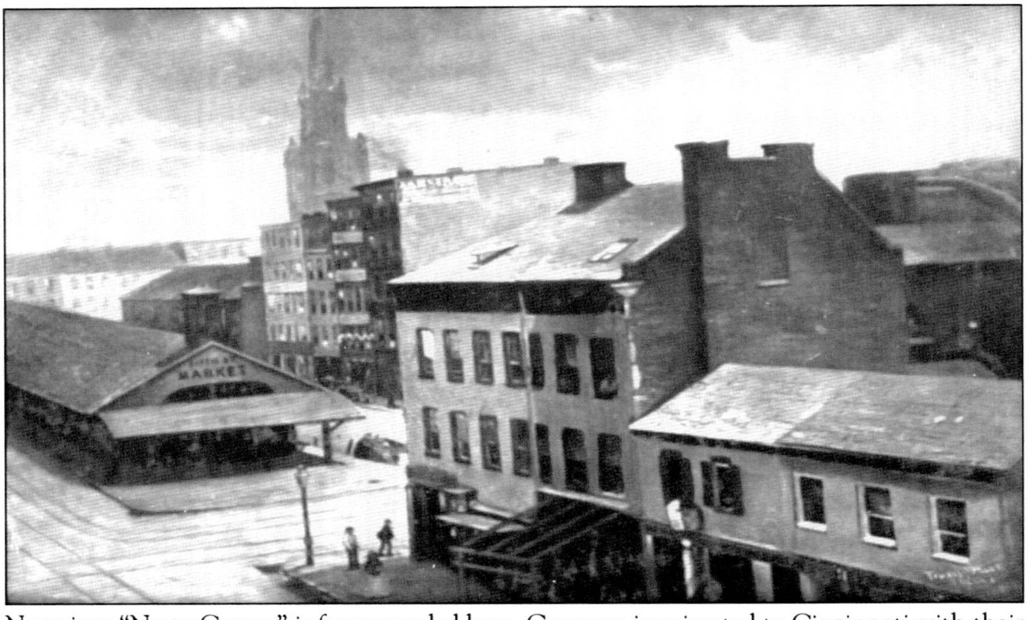

Notorious "Nasty Corner" is foregrounded here. Germans immigrated to Cincinnati with their treasured beer, and by 1880, 1,837 taverns had spawned. At the time depicted in this painting, 113 saloons operated near the Fifth Street Market at Fifth and Vine Streets. Looming in the background is the First Presbyterian Church steeple. Salvaged wood from the demolished church was eventually used to construct Wade Street Market. (Courtesy of Cheryl Eagelson.)

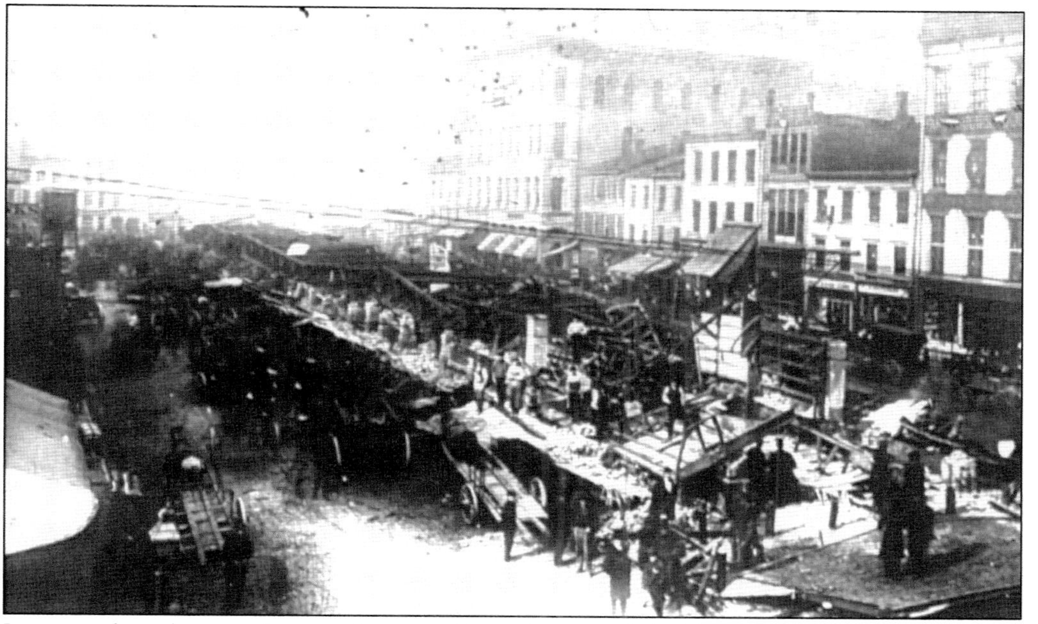

In a secretly orchestrated move, city council voted to demolish Fifth Street Market and deployed street cleaners armed with axes, picks, and crowbars to dismantle the building. The demolition team surprised the 54 meat merchants cleaning up from the previous day's market, and although the butchers resisted, within an hour the market roof was gone. By day's end, rubble had replaced Fifth Street Market. (Courtesy of the Cincinnati Public Library.)

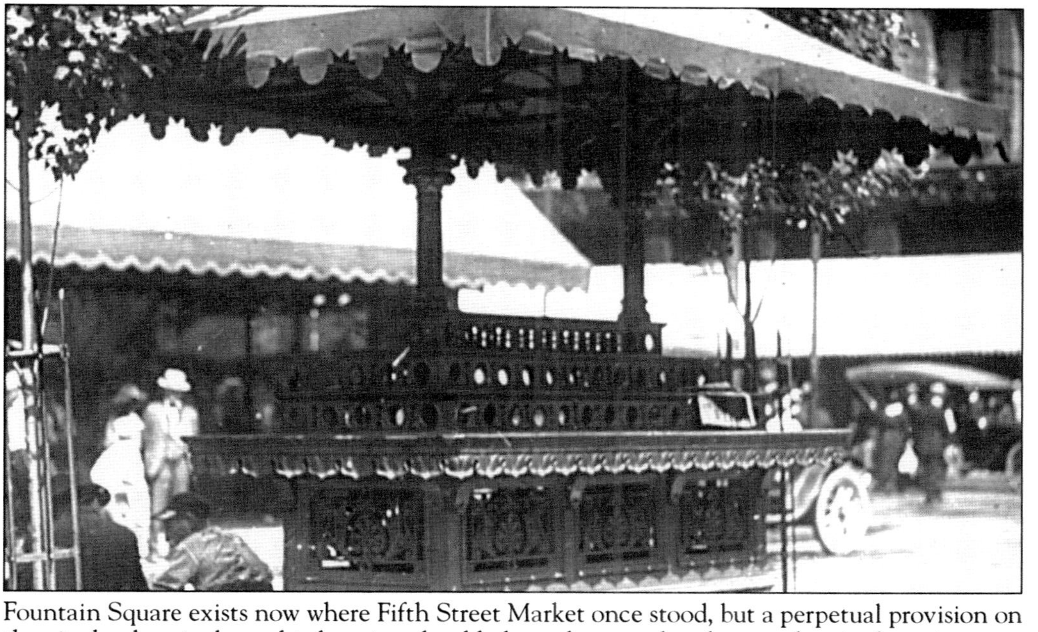

Fountain Square exists now where Fifth Street Market once stood, but a perpetual provision on the city books stipulates this location should always be a marketplace or the city loses its grant for the space. Consequently, flowers are sold for a short time each year from this permanent six-by-nine-foot iron structure designed by architect and Cincinnati native James W. McLaughlin. (Courtesy of the Cincinnati Public Library.)

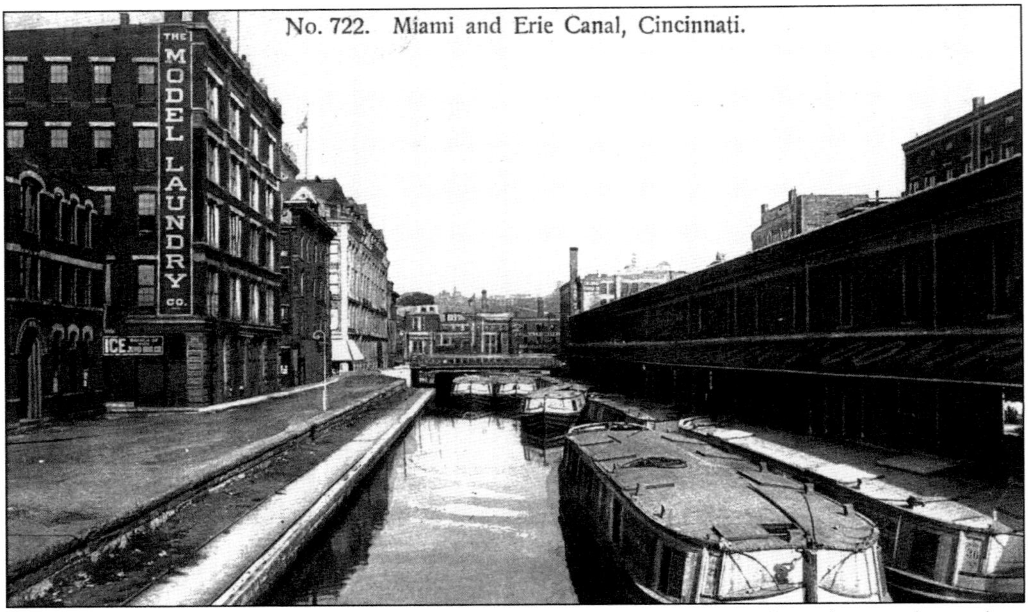

Established in 1829 and replaced by Court Street Market in 1864, Canal Market was located on Court Street between Vine Street and Walnut Street. Canal Market received its name because of its close proximity to the Miami and Erie Canal located only one block north. Produce and livestock traded at the market came hauled in boats down the canal, perhaps on boats such as these stacked up along the Miami and Erie Canal. (Courtesy of the Cincinnati Public Library.)

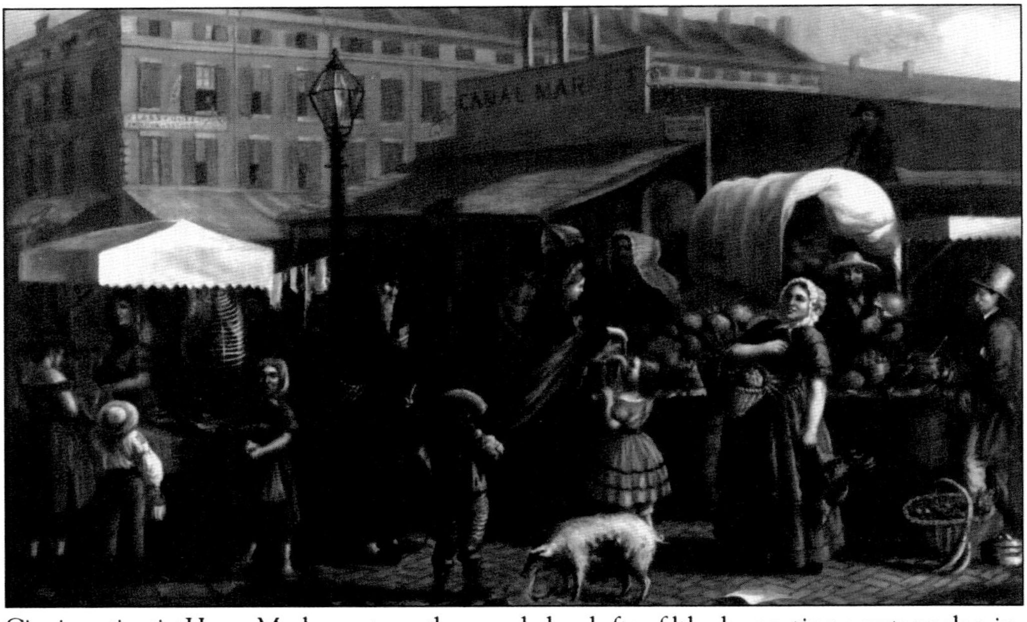

Cincinnati artist Henry Mosler captures the crowded and often filthy, hog-eating-a-watermelon-in-the-streets underside of the 1860 Canal Market. In Mosler's painting, one understands the market as a place where diverse social groups congregate, and this is nowhere more true than in today's Findlay Market. Here vendors, shoppers, animals, male, female, young, old, rich, poor, black, white all rub shoulders in the market. (Courtesy of the Cincinnati Public Library.)

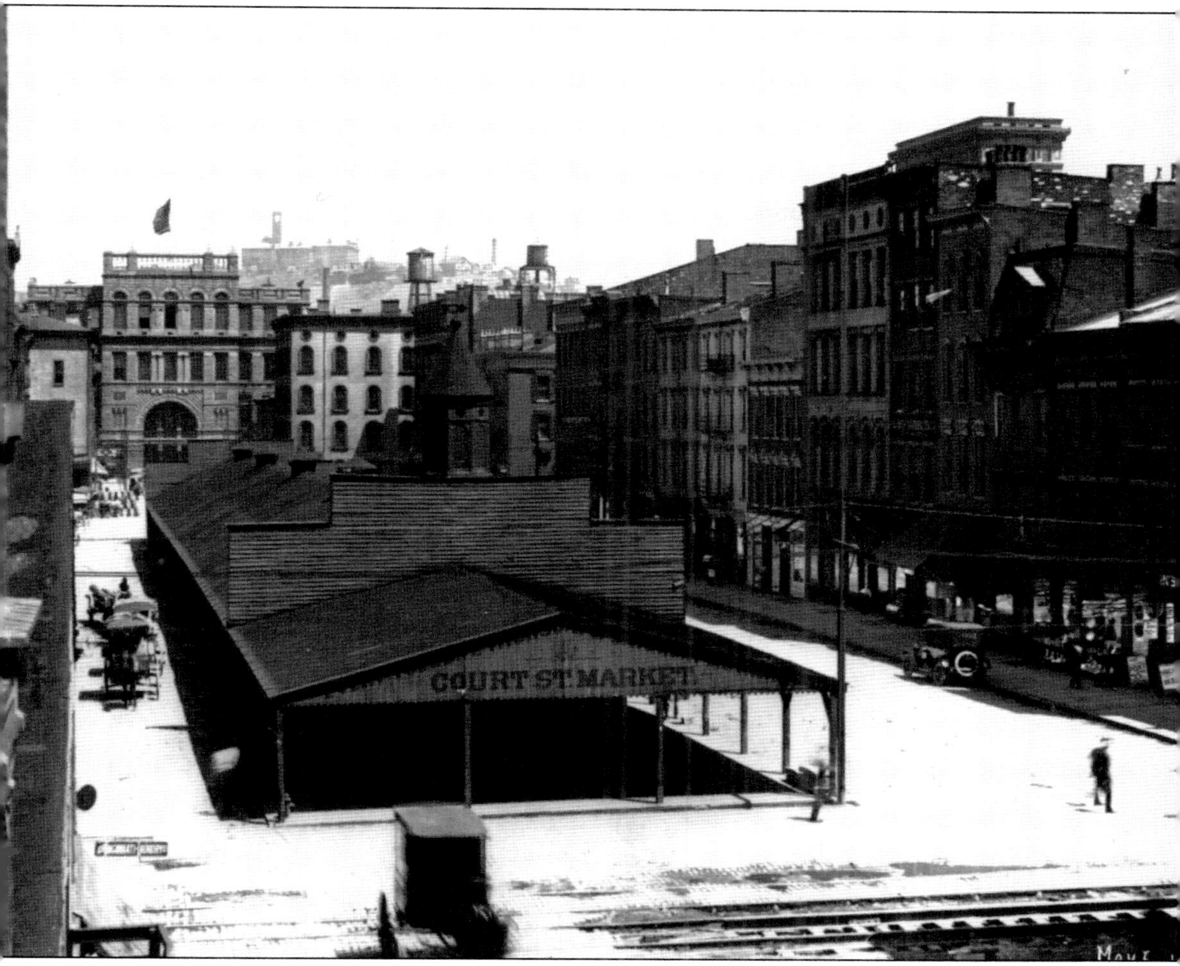

Built in 1864 to replace Canal Market, the wooden Court Street Market was condemned because of its expense to the city. Its roof leaked like a sieve, and it was a sight city officials felt would detract from the newly planned courthouse. Concluding the market was a menace to public health, the mayor ordered the building razed in 1915. The outdoor Court Street produce market, however, continues to operate at this same location two days per week. (Courtesy of the Cincinnati Historical Society.)

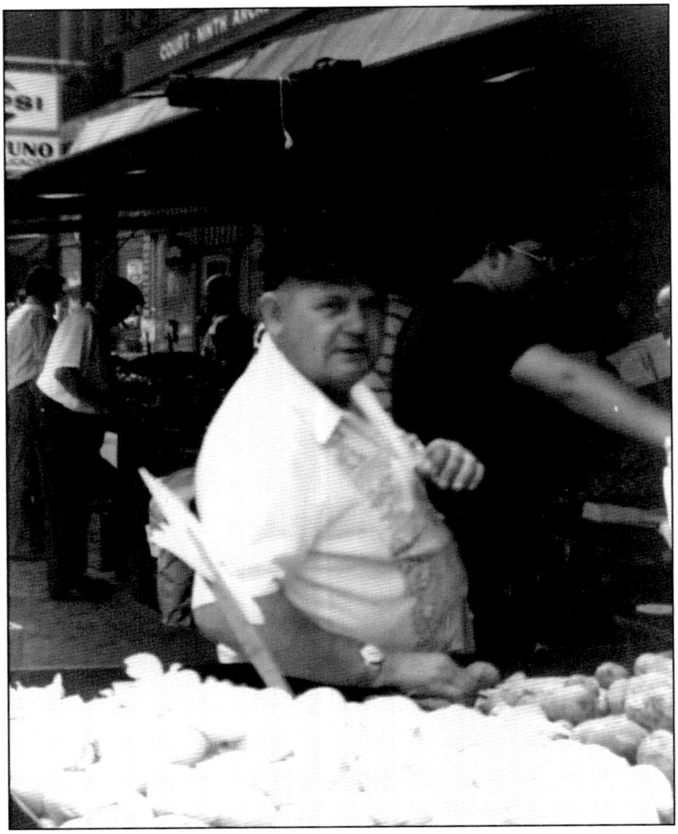

For many years, vendors, including Gene Simpson shown here at his Court Street stand, worked between Findlay Market on Wednesday, Friday, and Saturday and Court Street Market on Tuesday and Thursday. From the market, the sounds of vendor chanting filled Court Street: "Berries, now. How many? Anybody want my berries? Berries here. Quarter-a-piece cantaloupe. Quarter, quarter, how many?" Among competitive vendors along Court Street, it was said, "A silent huckster is a hungry huckster." Below is one corner of the old outdoor market. (Left, courtesy of Elmer Simpson; below, courtesy of the Cincinnati Public Library.)

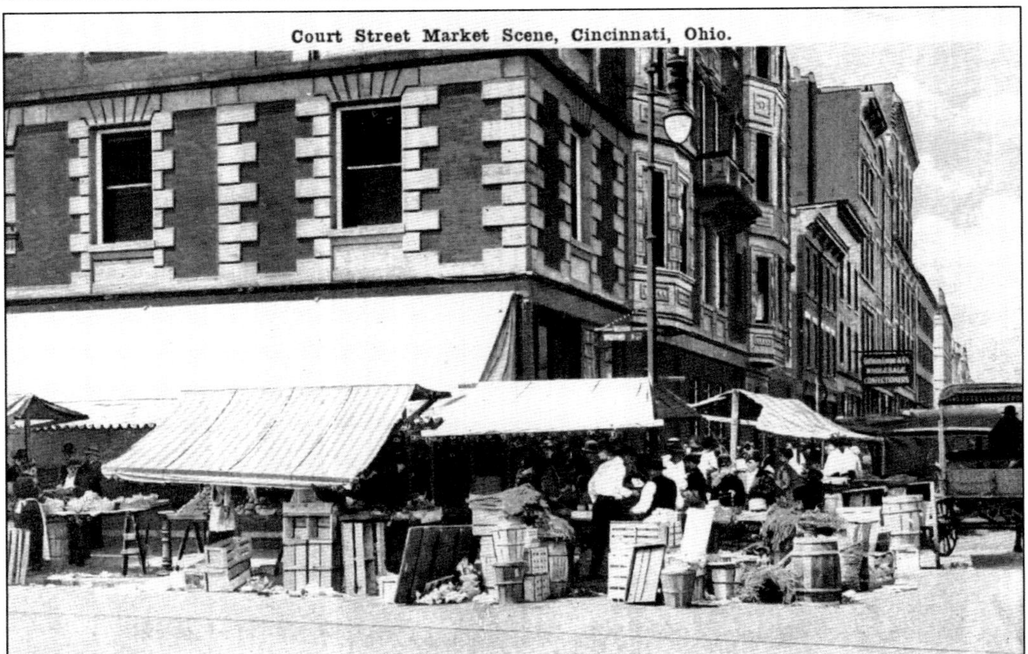

Another vendor who sold at both Court Street and Findlay Markets is Joe Caito, right, pictured at work at his Court Street stand in the 1940s. Frank Gaudio, Caito's grandson, leans onto the display boards beside his grandfather in the photograph below. Frank Gaudio, with his son John Gaudio, continues to operate his business at Findlay Market today. Behind them is the ever-present family truck in which produce was hauled from wholesale market to cold storage to market and back every day. The two are stationed opposite the Philco radio and television store and the Hobart Company, a company that sold the scales and display cases indispensable to market vendors. (Courtesy of the Gaudio family.)

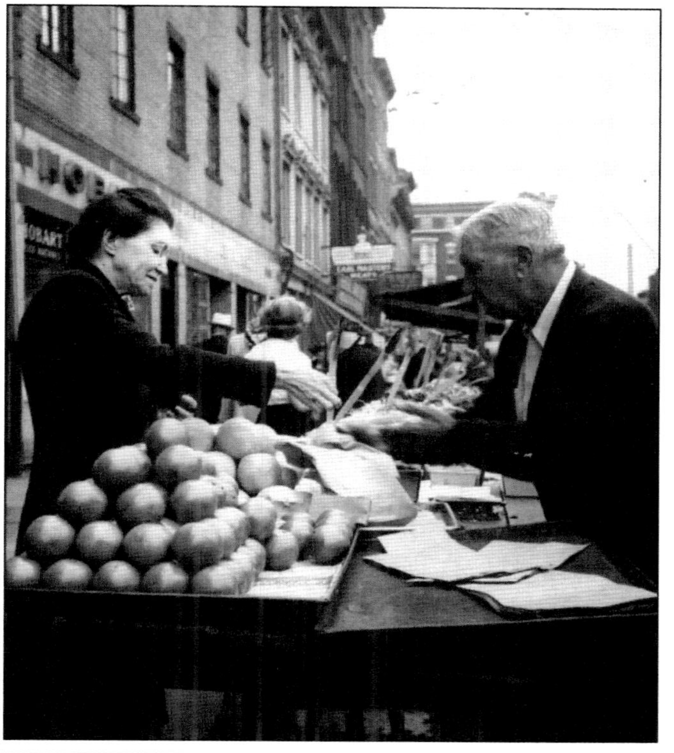

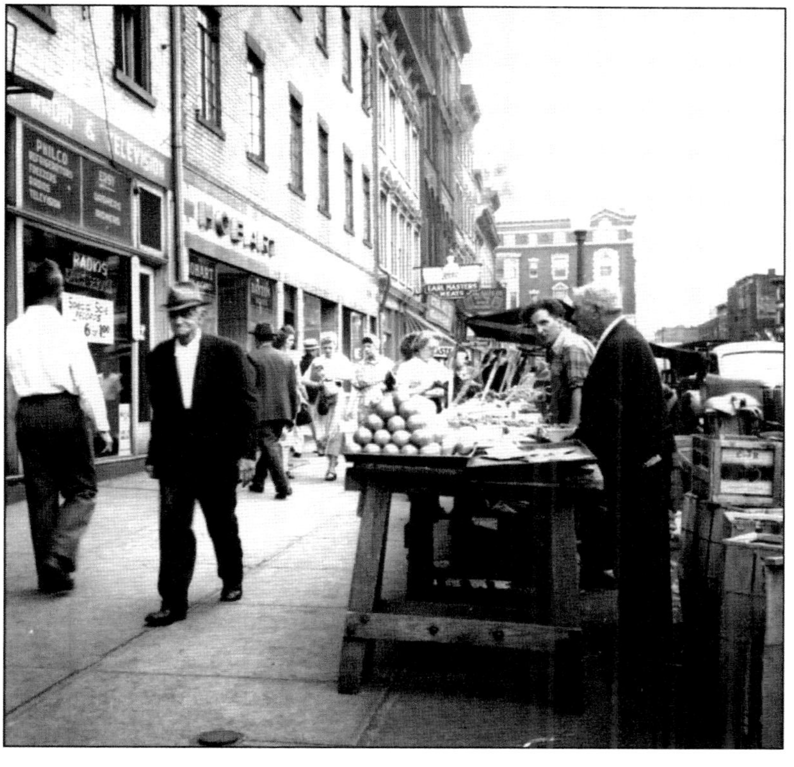

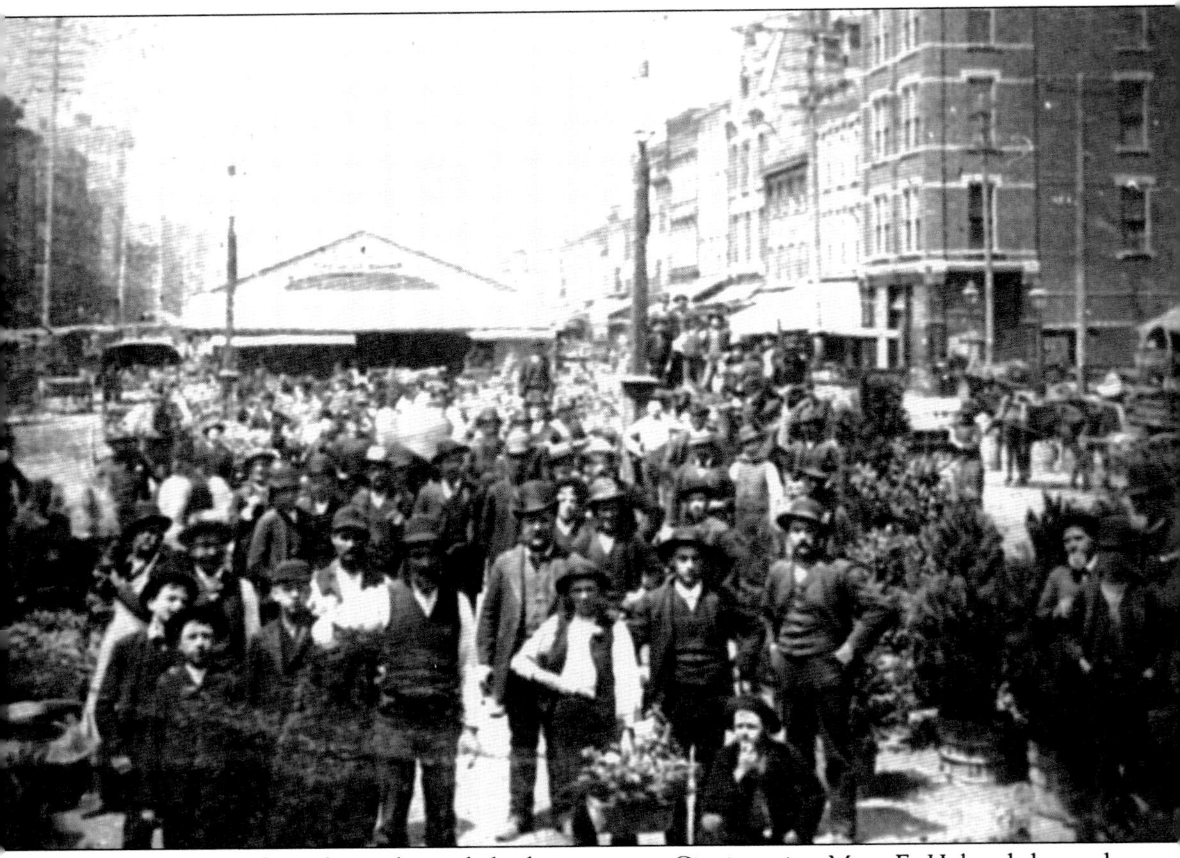

Believing that floriculture elevated the human race, Cincinnatian Mary E. Holroyd donated $10,000 to the city to construct a flower market memorializing her first husband, Jabez Elliot. Prior to enclosing the building in 1890, flowers and the vendors selling them on market were constantly exposed to the extremes of Cincinnati weather, as indicated in the 1880 photograph above of the sunny, outdoor Sixth Street flower market. (Courtesy of the Cincinnati Public Library.)

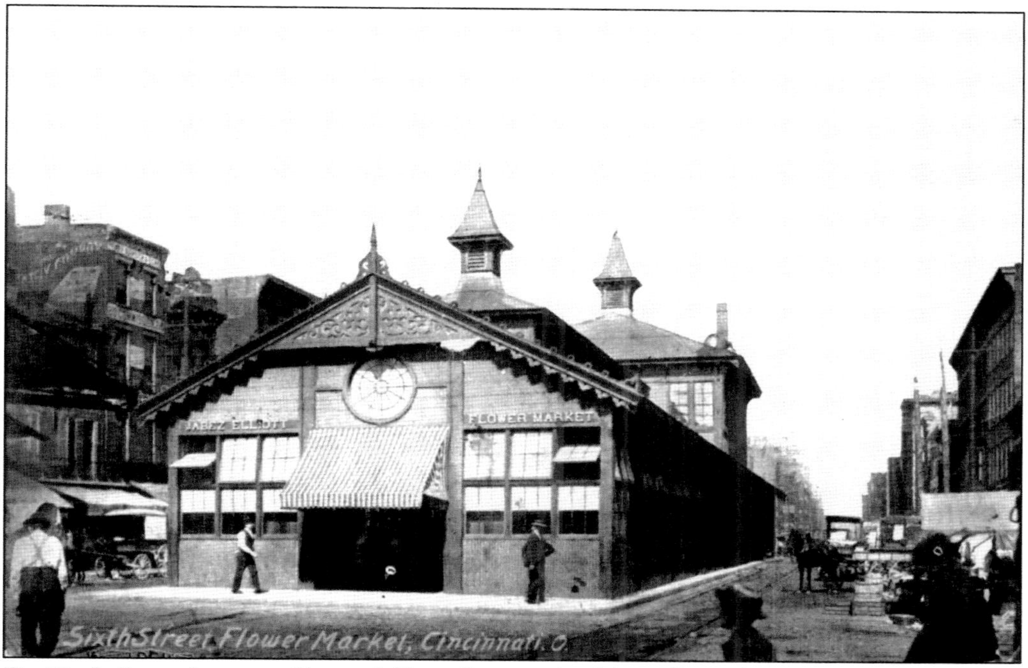

On Sixth Street between Elm and Plum Streets, the Jabez Elliot Flower Market was built in typically German architectural style and was considered the largest enclosed flower market in the United States. This market helped shape Cincinnati into being recognized as "Floral City," one of its most fitting titles. (Courtesy of the Cincinnati Public Library.)

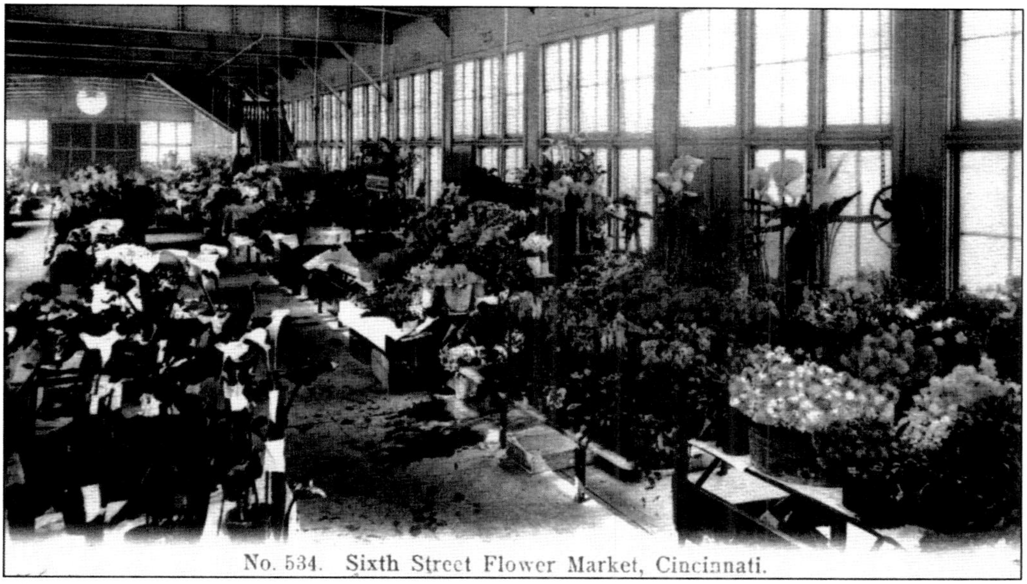

The flourishing use of the automobile spelled the demise of this flower market. Suburban florists drew away "the sweet perfume from the heart of the city," and business at the market declined. As automobile ownership increased, so did the demand for parking, and in 1950, the Jabez Elliot Flower Market was razed to make room for a parking lot, thus removing the intangible asset of flowers to the community. (Author's collection.)

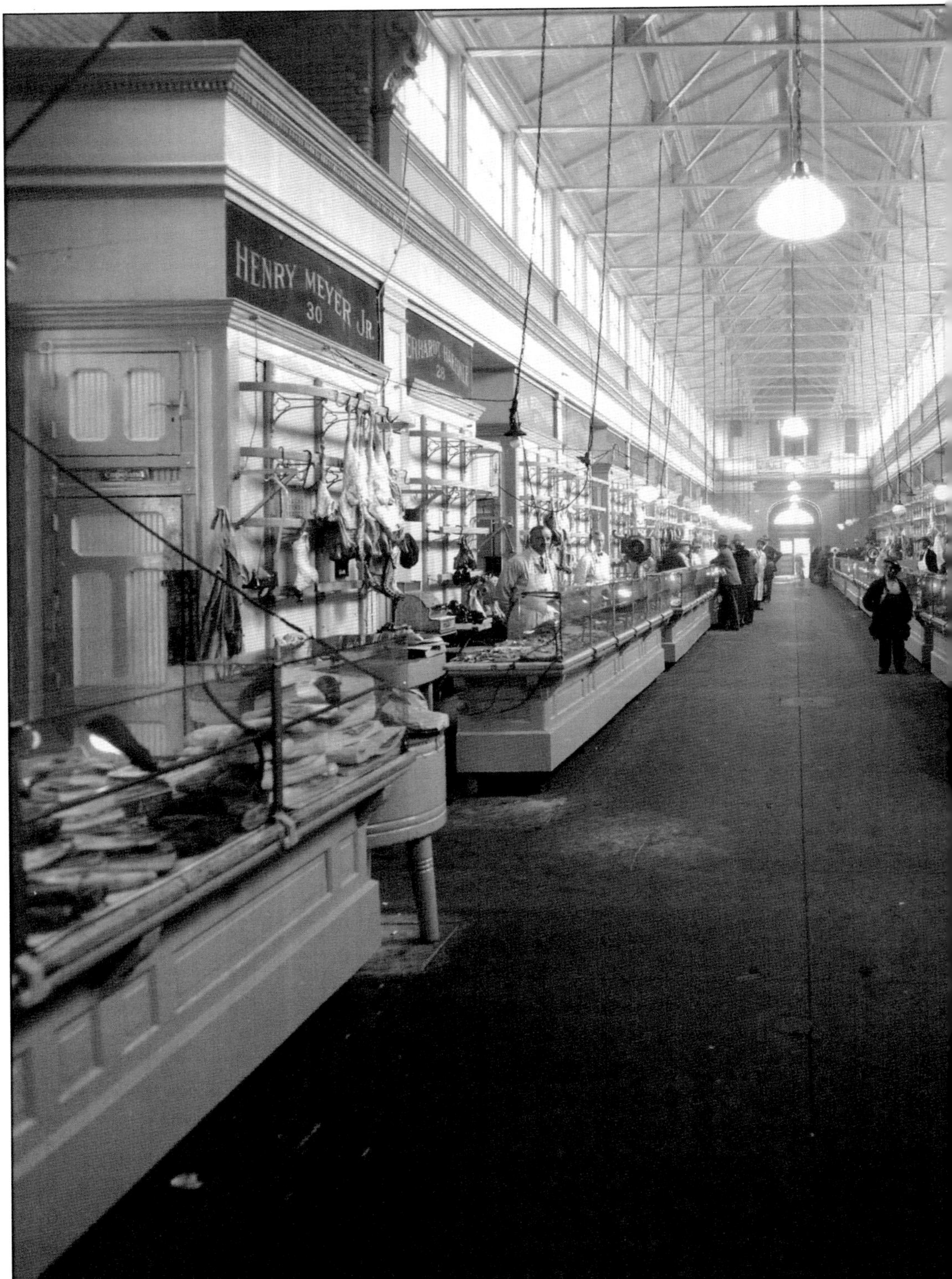
HENRY MEYER JR.
30

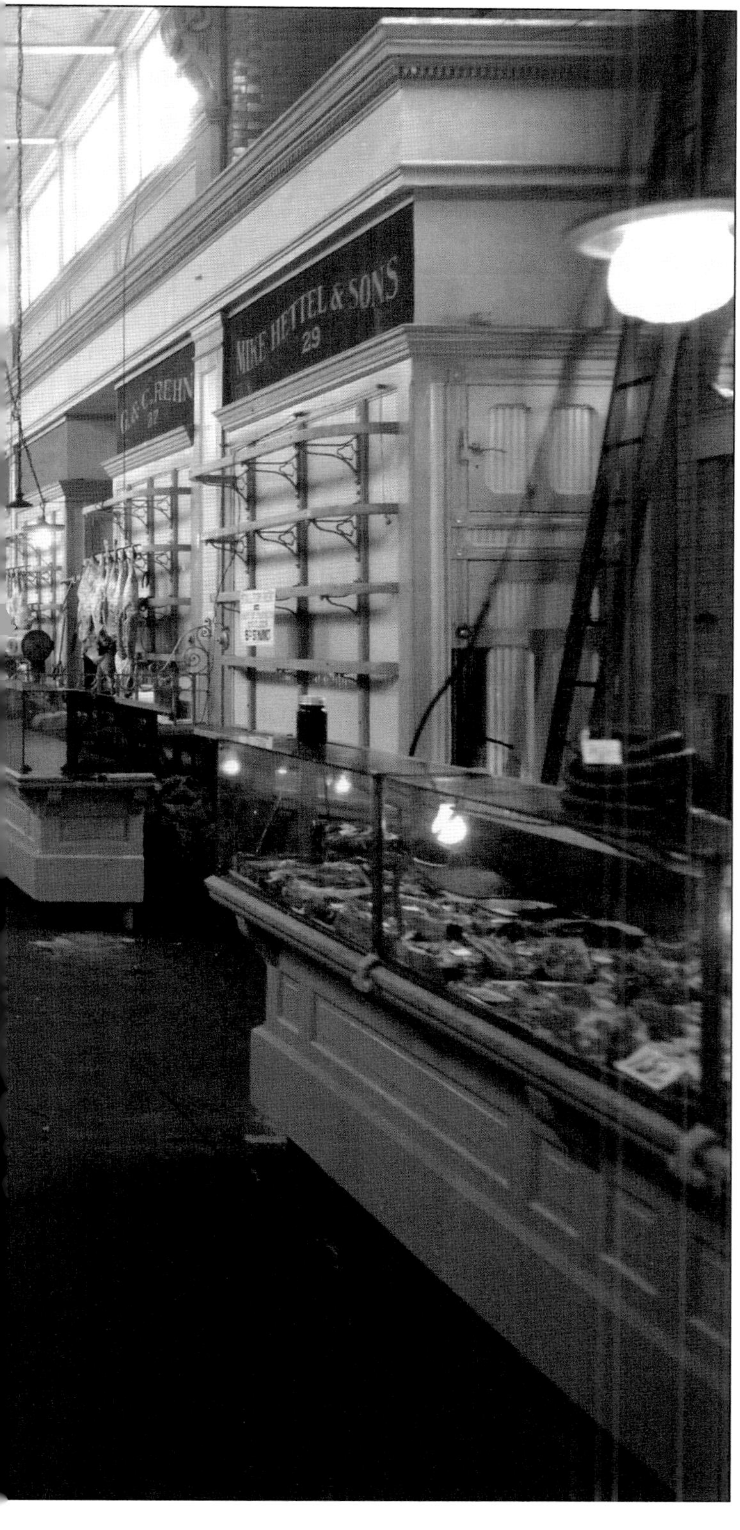

This interior view of Sixth Street Market shows a long stretch of butcher stands, and meat hangs from every hook and heaps every display case and butcher block. Each business is identified by name and stand number on large signs above the meat hooks. The two doors visible on the side of each stand serve as the cold storage system; ice is stored in the small space above; the ice cools the meat kept in the larger space below. A close look reveals this open-for-business market house populated almost exclusively by white males; in this photograph, one sees one woman and one man of color. (Courtesy of the Cincinnati Historical Society.)

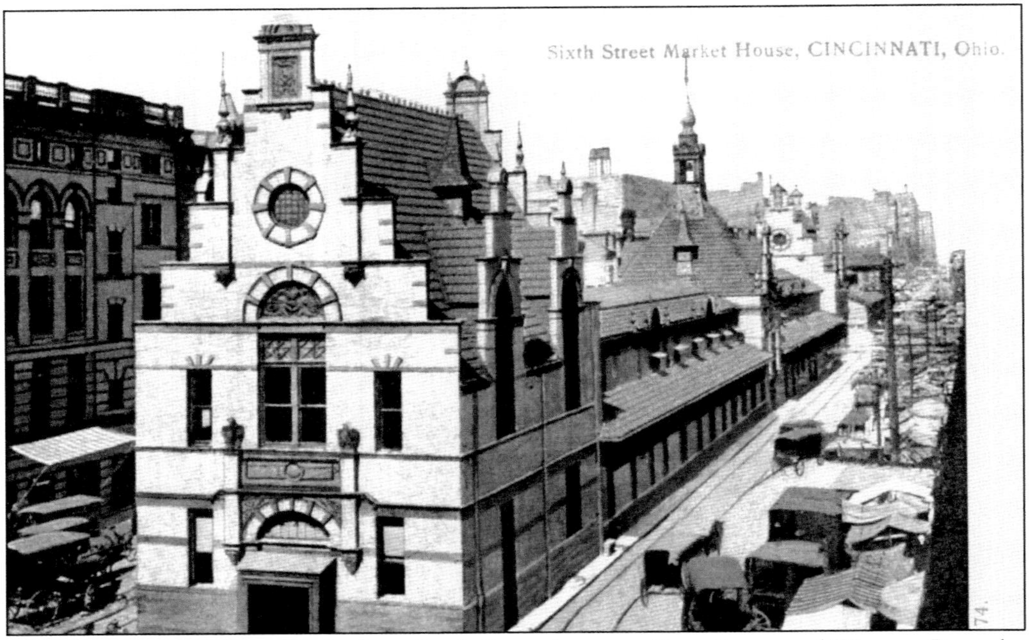

Also known as "Western Market" on Sixth Street between Plum Street and Western Row, the 1895 Sixth Street Market house accommodated 64 indoor stalls and was Cincinnati's largest public market. The unheated masonry structure also housed the office of the superintendent of markets, weights, and measures, the official responsible for managing Cincinnati public markets. The building was replaced by a parking lot in 1959. (Courtesy of the Cincinnati Public Library.)

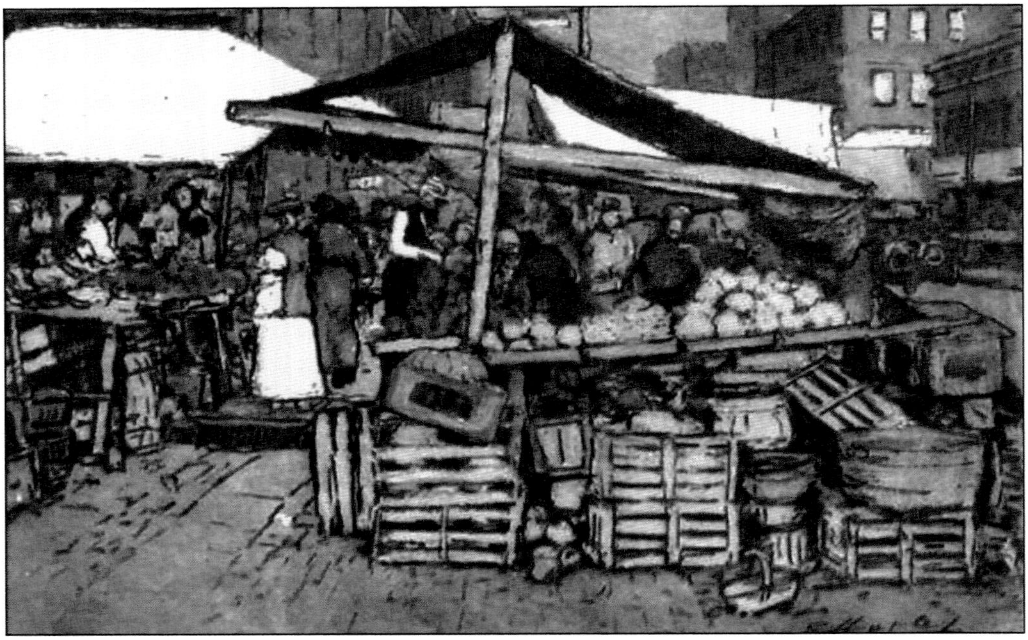

Cincinnati artist Edward Timothy Hurley captures the open-air spirit in his *Sixth Street Market* etching. While merchants sold meat, poultry, and dairy from rented indoor stalls, produce vendors set up their portable stands curbside outside the market house. (Author's collection.)

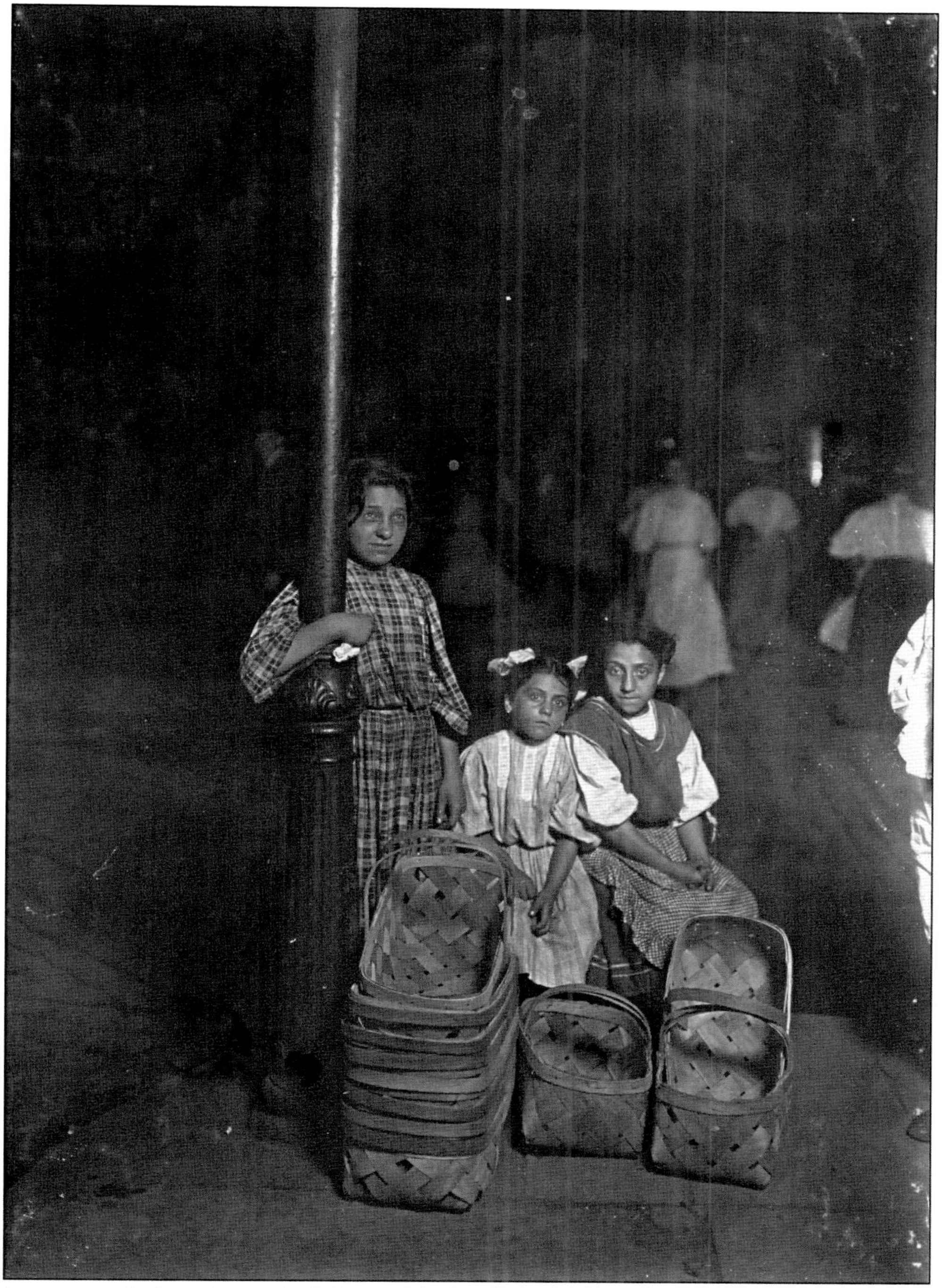

There was a darker side to Sixth Street Market than that so colorfully celebrated by Edward Timothy Hurley, however. In 1908, photographer Lewis Wicke Hines used his camera to document egregious child labor practices in Cincinnati. Here he records Marie Costa, who had sold baskets on this Sixth Street spot for 11 straight hours. Hines's work for the National Child Labor Committee helped to end child labor abuse. (Courtesy of the Library of Congress.)

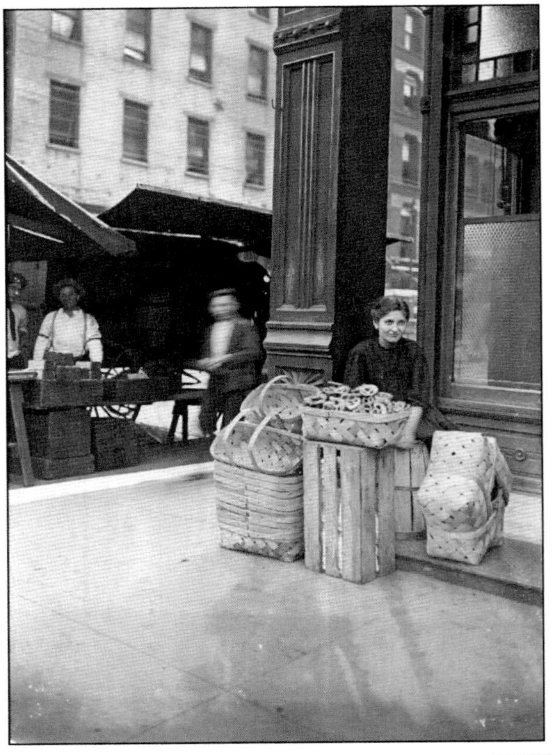

Lewis Wicke Hines records that Lena Lochiavo, this 11-year-old basket and pretzel seller, had been sitting outside a saloon entrance at this Sixth Street Market site since early morning and was not allowed to leave until all her goods sold. Children have always worked with their families on market, and still do, but in these photographs, Hines drew national attention to the plight of those slaving away their childhoods. (Courtesy of the Library of Congress.)

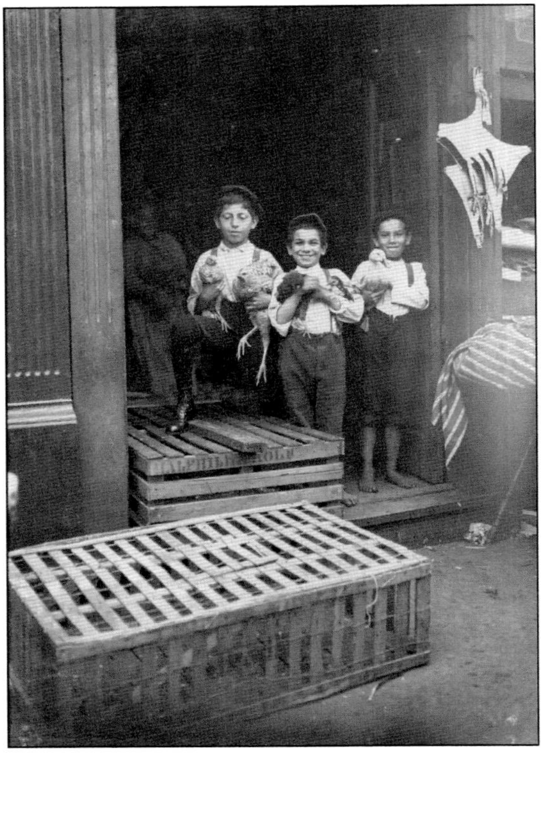

Not all Hines's subjects appear to think of themselves as overworked. The three chicken sellers here seem happy to show off their chickens and their duck. One boy wears shoes while the other two are barefoot, and an older woman watches from the shadows inside the doorway. The chicken-containing crates are a common sight in market images from this period, with boys often propping their feet on them. (Courtesy of the Library of Congress.)

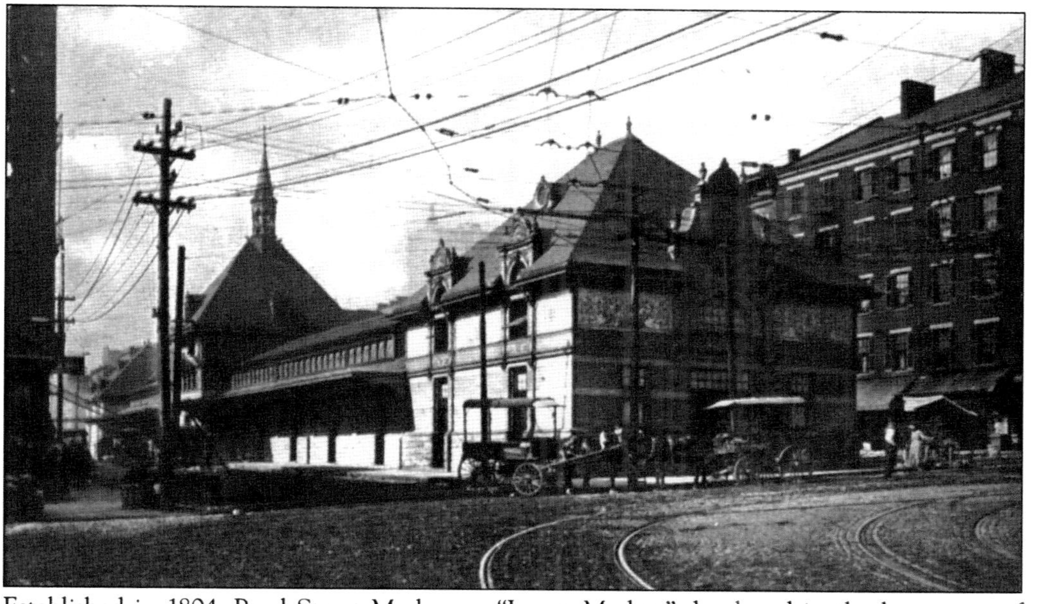

Established in 1804, Pearl Street Market, or "Lower Market," developed in the lower part of town near the Ohio River because Cincinnati hills made hauling uphill difficult for horses with loaded wagons. Citizens walked along boards stretched over muddy streets to reach the old market. The building shown here replaced the old market in 1897; the last remnant of this building disappeared to make room for Riverfront Stadium in 1970. (Courtesy of the Cincinnati Public Library.)

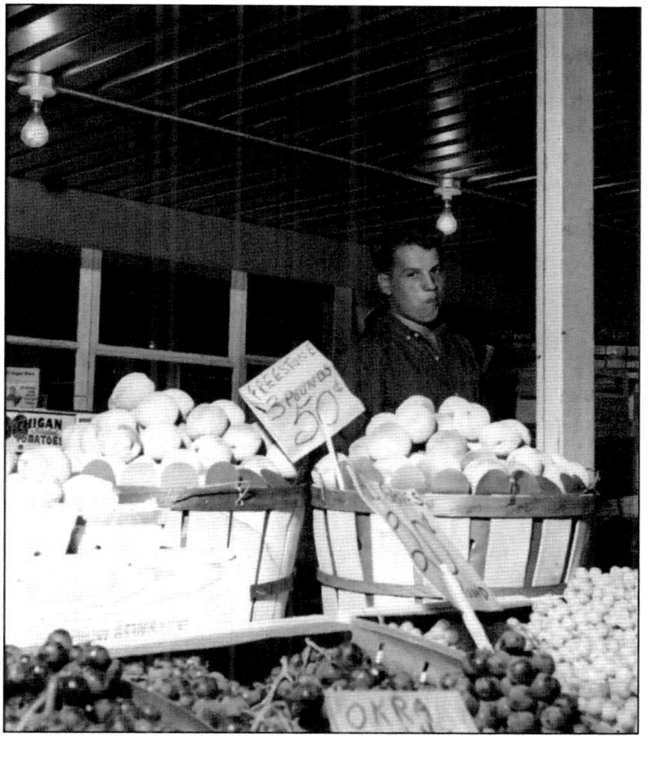

In the mid-1950s, 16- or 17-year-old George Roth sells produce for his uncle William "Little Willie" Roth at the Kellogg Avenue farmers' market. During the 1950s, George handled the business at the Kellogg market while his uncle worked at both Findlay and Court Street Markets. His uncle William has died, but George Roth still sells produce with his sister, Debbie Roth Gates, and Elmer Simpson at Findlay Market. (Courtesy of George Roth.)

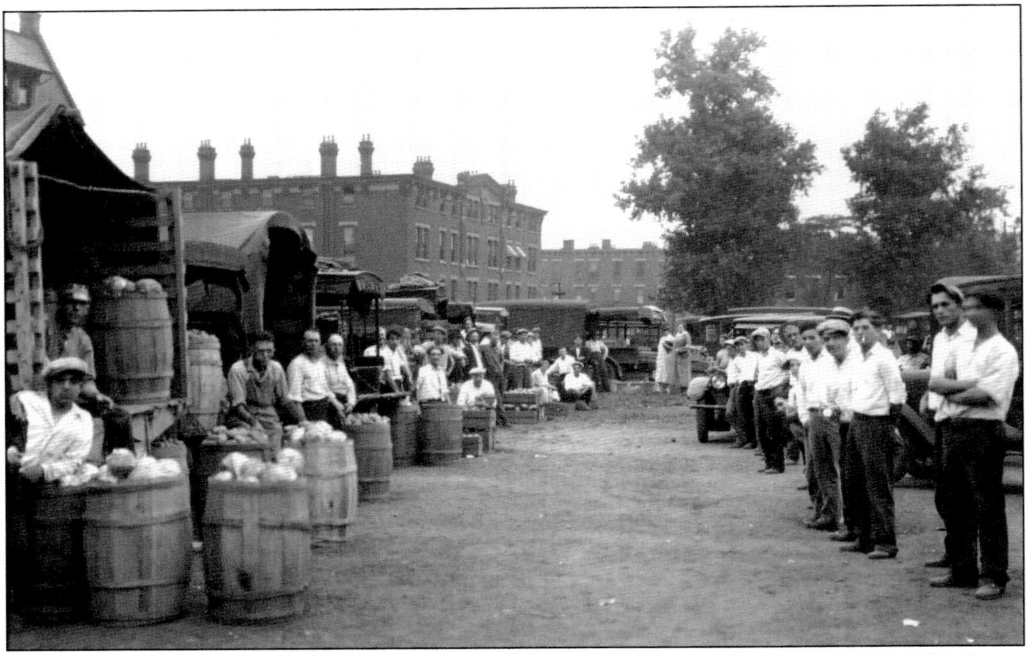

In 1926, the Parkway Farmer's Wholesale Market moved from Court Street to this Twelfth Street and Central Parkway location in the old city hospital lot behind the music hall. The market was open Monday through Saturday from 7:00 a.m. until midnight when hundreds of farmers bargained with both independent shoppers and city grocers. But in 1951, when the city needed the space for more parking, the farmers were relocated to the Ohio River's banks. The wholesale market moved again to clear room for Riverfront Stadium, and in 1967, the farmers struck out to Kellogg Avenue near Lunken Field where a small farmers' market operates today. Above, men sell from tarp-covered trucks; below is the market around 1937. Only a few women and one man of color are present in the photographs. (Courtesy of the Cincinnati Historical Society.)

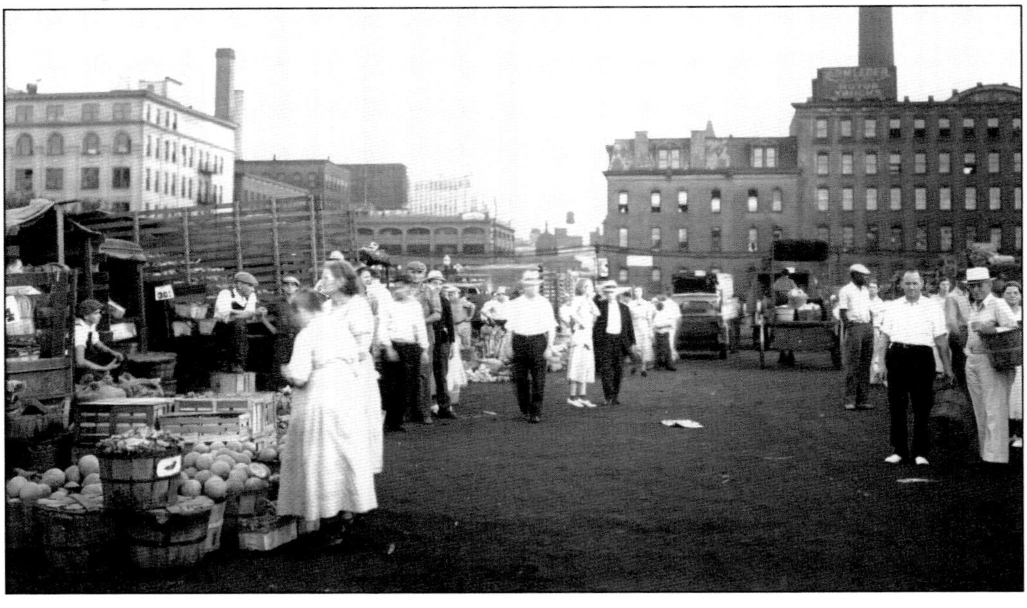

Five

THE CITY AND THE MARKET

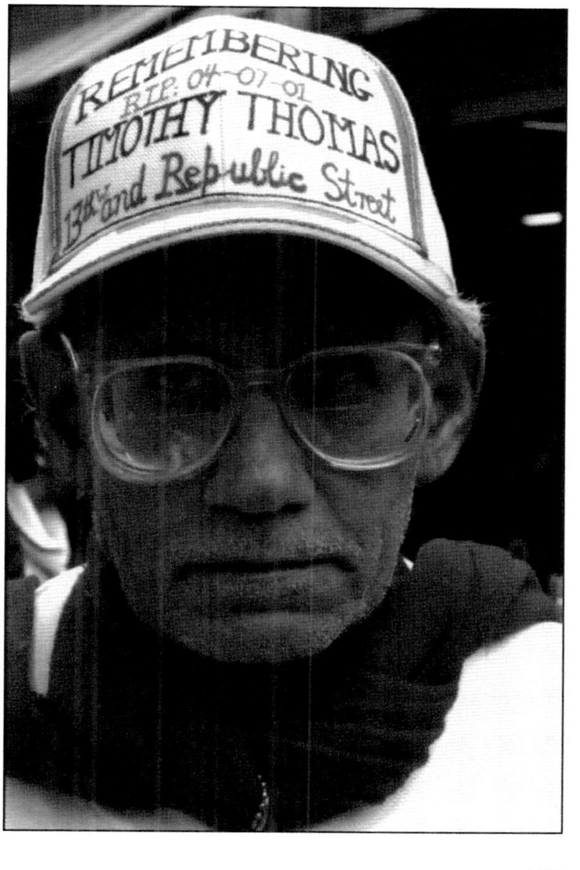

In April 2001, 19-year-old African American Timothy Thomas was killed in Over-the-Rhine by a Cincinnati police officer. The tragedy set off days of civil unrest in Cincinnati, and Over-the-Rhine, the neighborhood to which Findlay Market is so central, became the site of protests, riots, and calls for calm. Findlay Market, seen in the background here, became the focal point for many Cincinnatians' expressions of grief and anger and resolve. (Author's collection.)

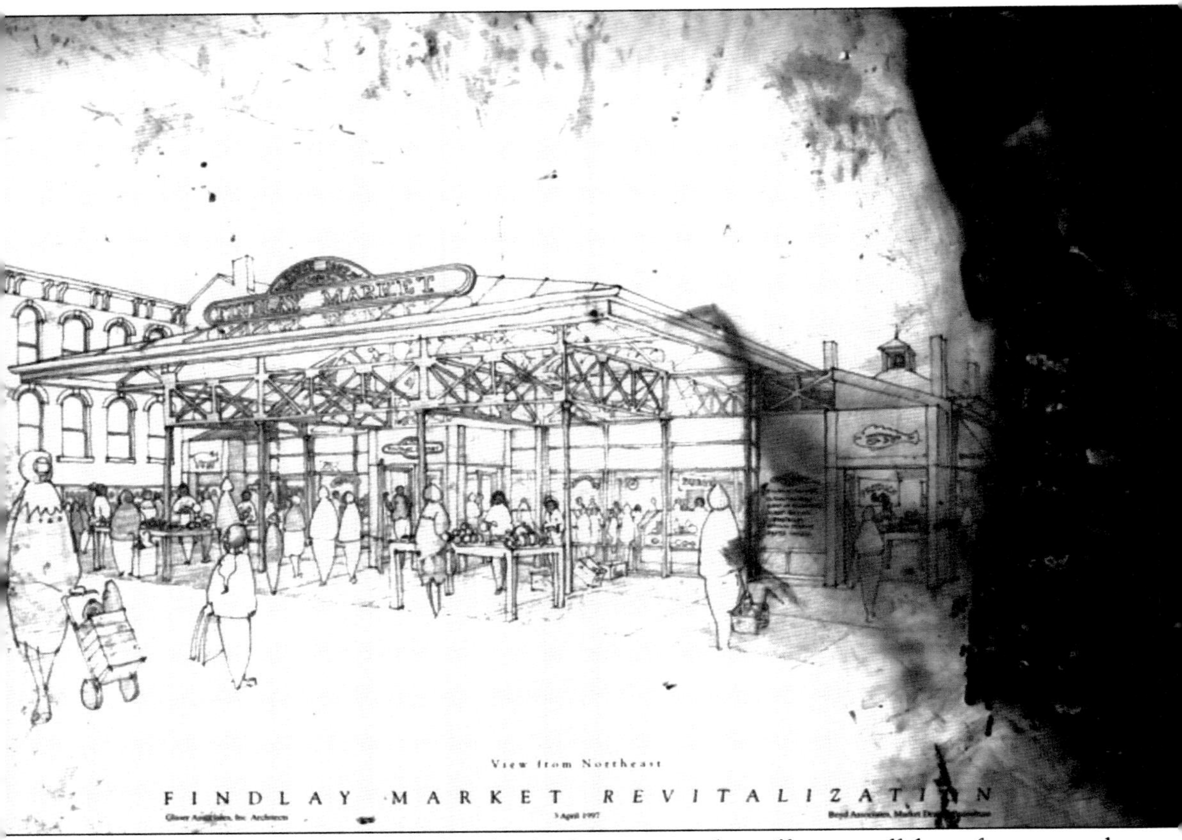

Timothy Thomas's death at the hands of a Cincinnati police officer set off days of protest and riots in Findlay Market's Over-the-Rhine neighborhood, and although the market house itself was spared, a number of Elder Street businesses were significantly damaged. The poster above outlining the proposed Findlay Market revitalization plan hung in an empty storefront and was burned by fire there. (Courtesy of the Kornbluh collection.)

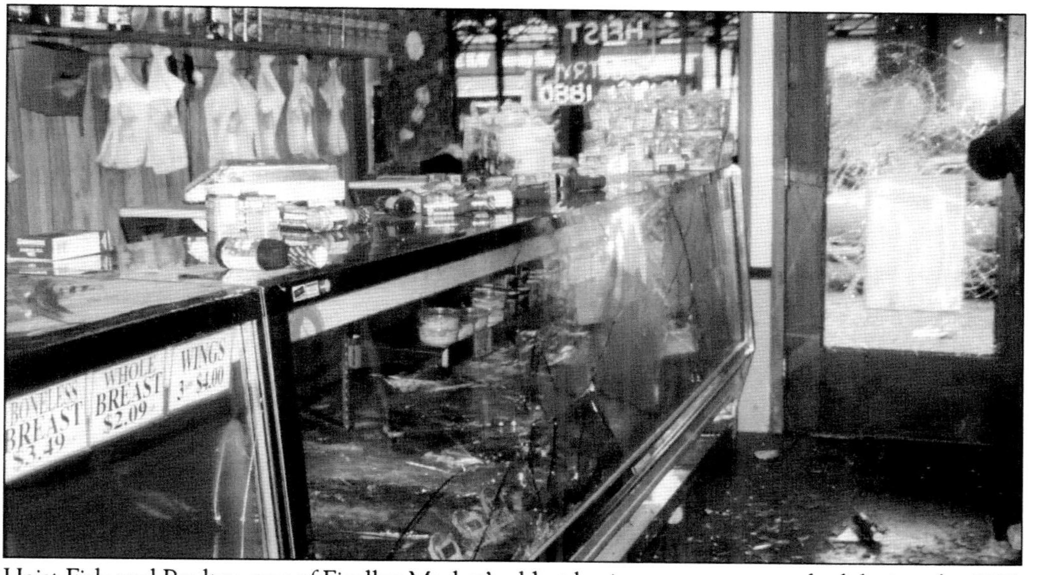

Heist Fish and Poultry, one of Findlay Market's oldest businesses, was ransacked during the 2001 riots. Outside the window in the image below, a television camera operator films the damage. The riots brought national media attention to Cincinnati's racial tensions. (Courtesy of the Heist family.)

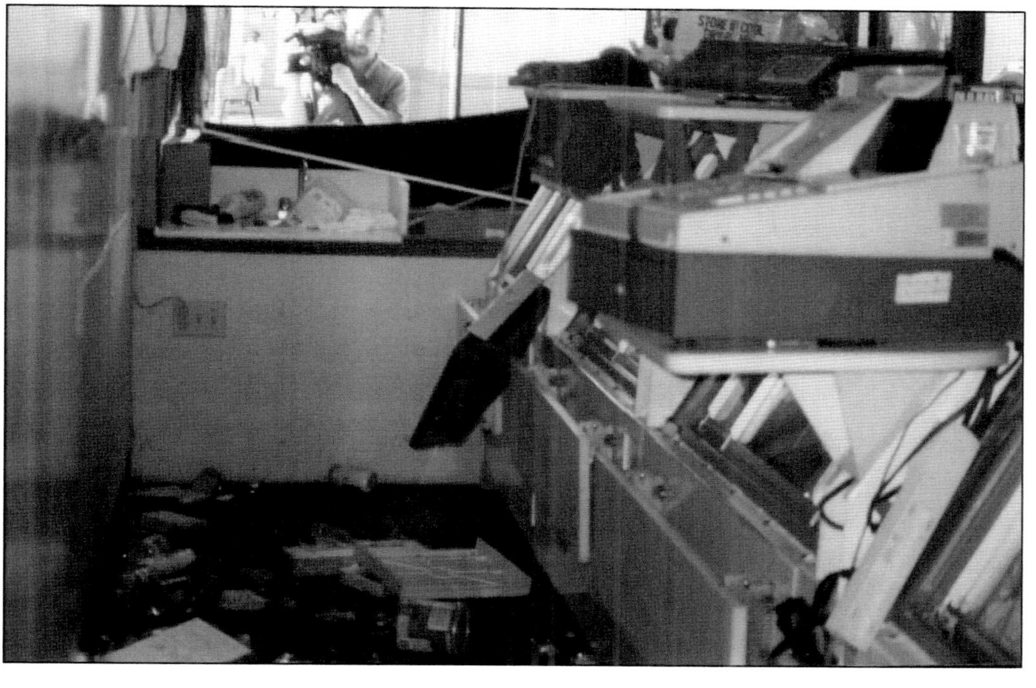

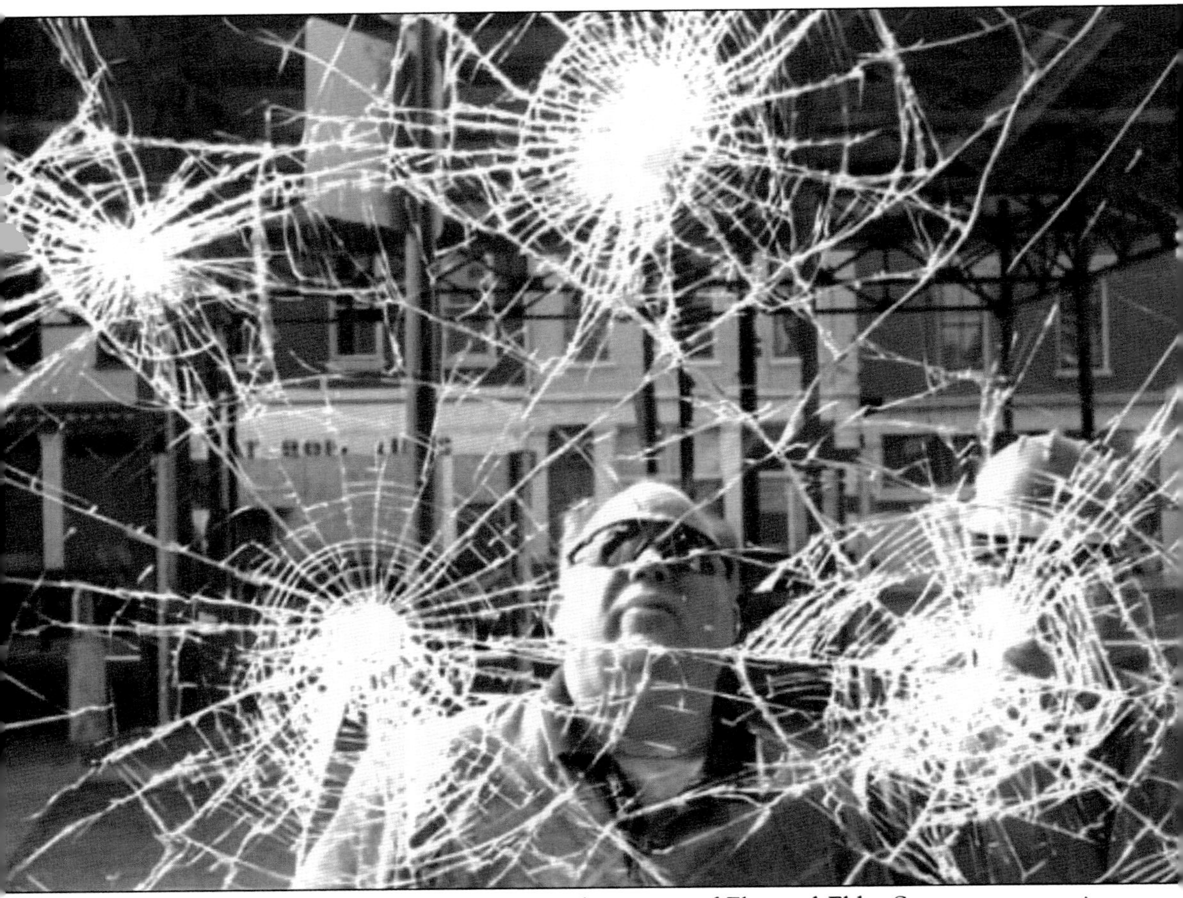

Gary Mallin, owner of Leader Furniture at the corner of Elm and Elder Streets, assesses riot damage to his store. Eventually, and after days of civil unrest near Findlay Market in response to the 2001 killing of Timothy Thomas, Mallin was forced to board up his entire storefront until calm was restored. (Author's collection.)

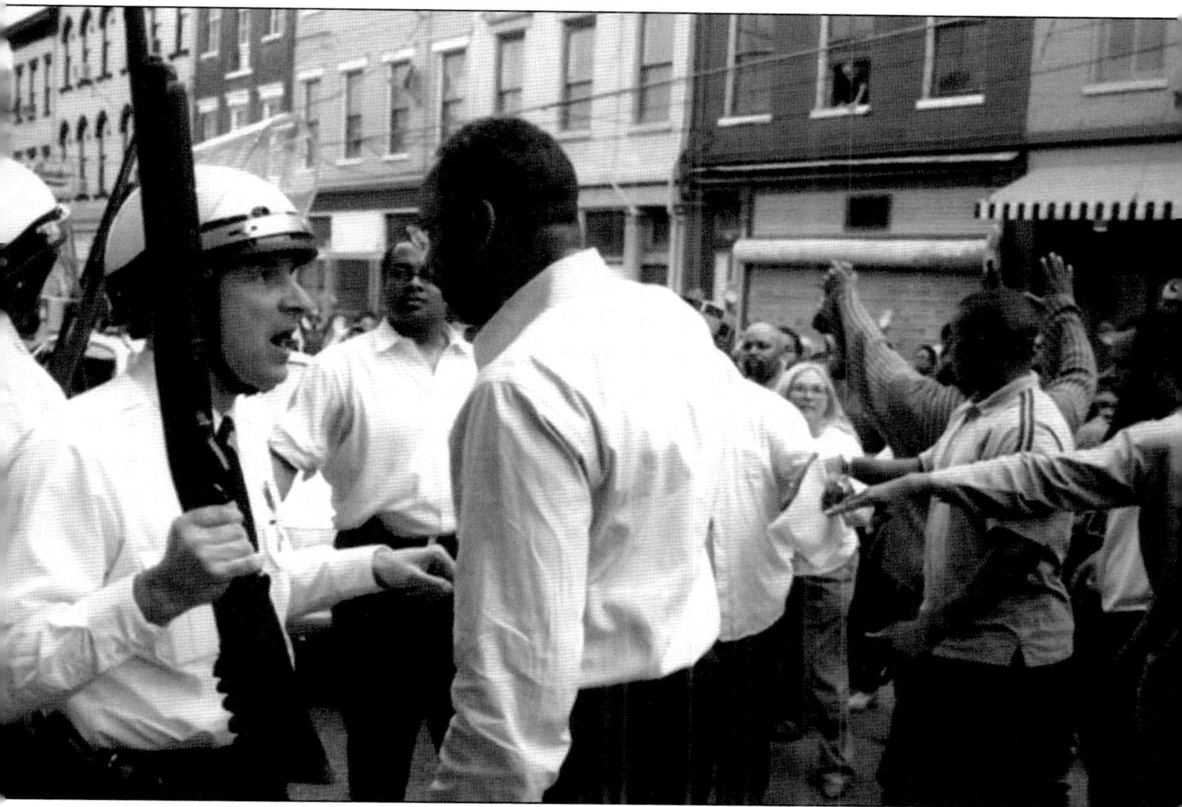

Rev. Damon Lynch III, pastor of New Prospect Baptist Church in Over-the-Rhine, leads a group of concerned citizens and church members in a nonviolent protest following Timothy Thomas's killing. Days of rioting, protest, and curfews brought Cincinnati and Cincinnati's racial tensions to the attention of the national media. Here the group meets a Cincinnati police supervisor at the Findlay Market house. (Author's collection.)

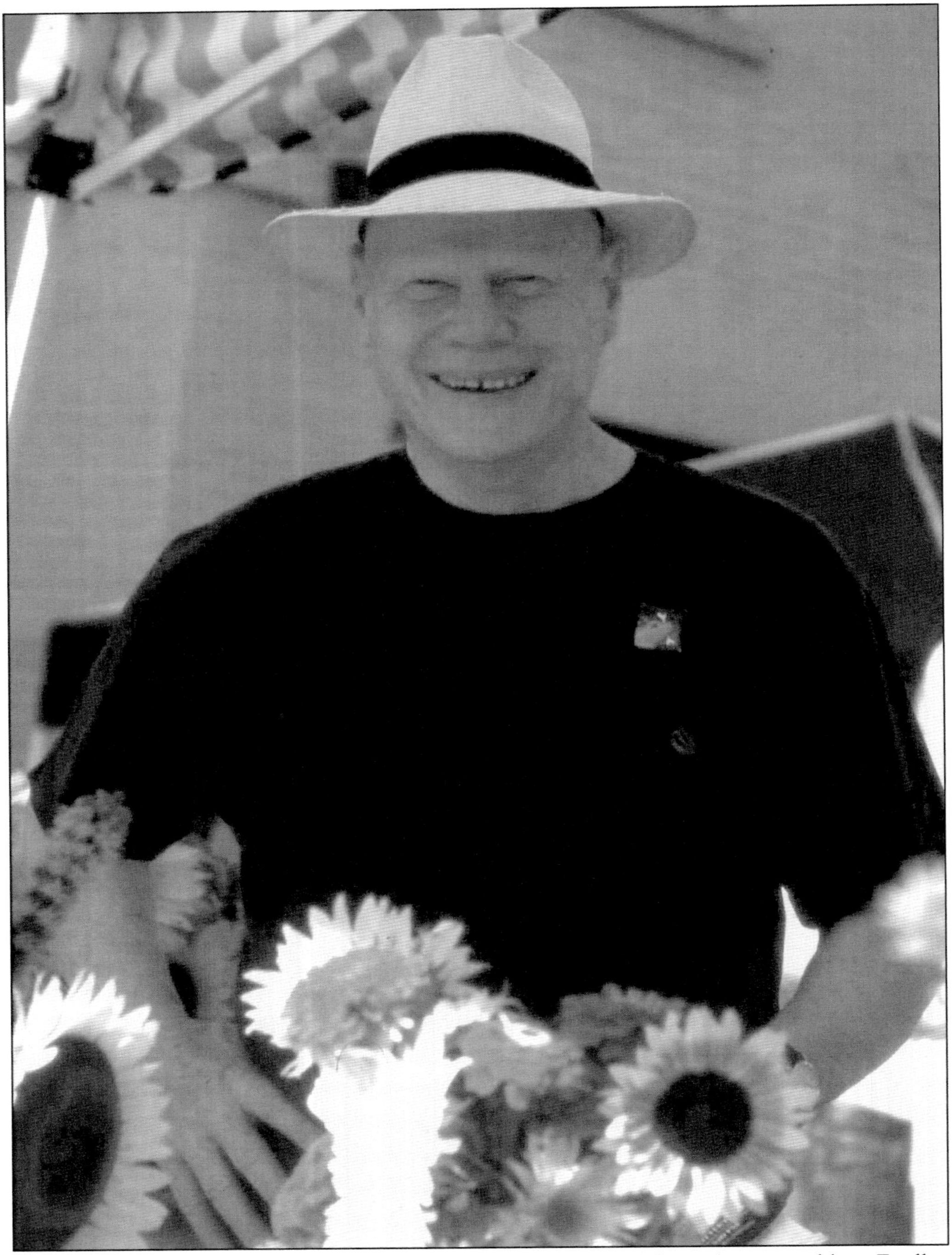

Cincinnati politicians would hardly be worth their salt if they did not shop at and love Findlay Market. Above, former Cincinnati councilman and all-around Cincinnati supporter Jim Tarbell poses amid sunflowers on sale at the market. Tarbell embodies Cincinnati's urban dweller and is a Saturday fixture at and unflagging supporter of Findlay Market. He is often seen riding there on his scooter. (Photograph by Jane Gahl.)

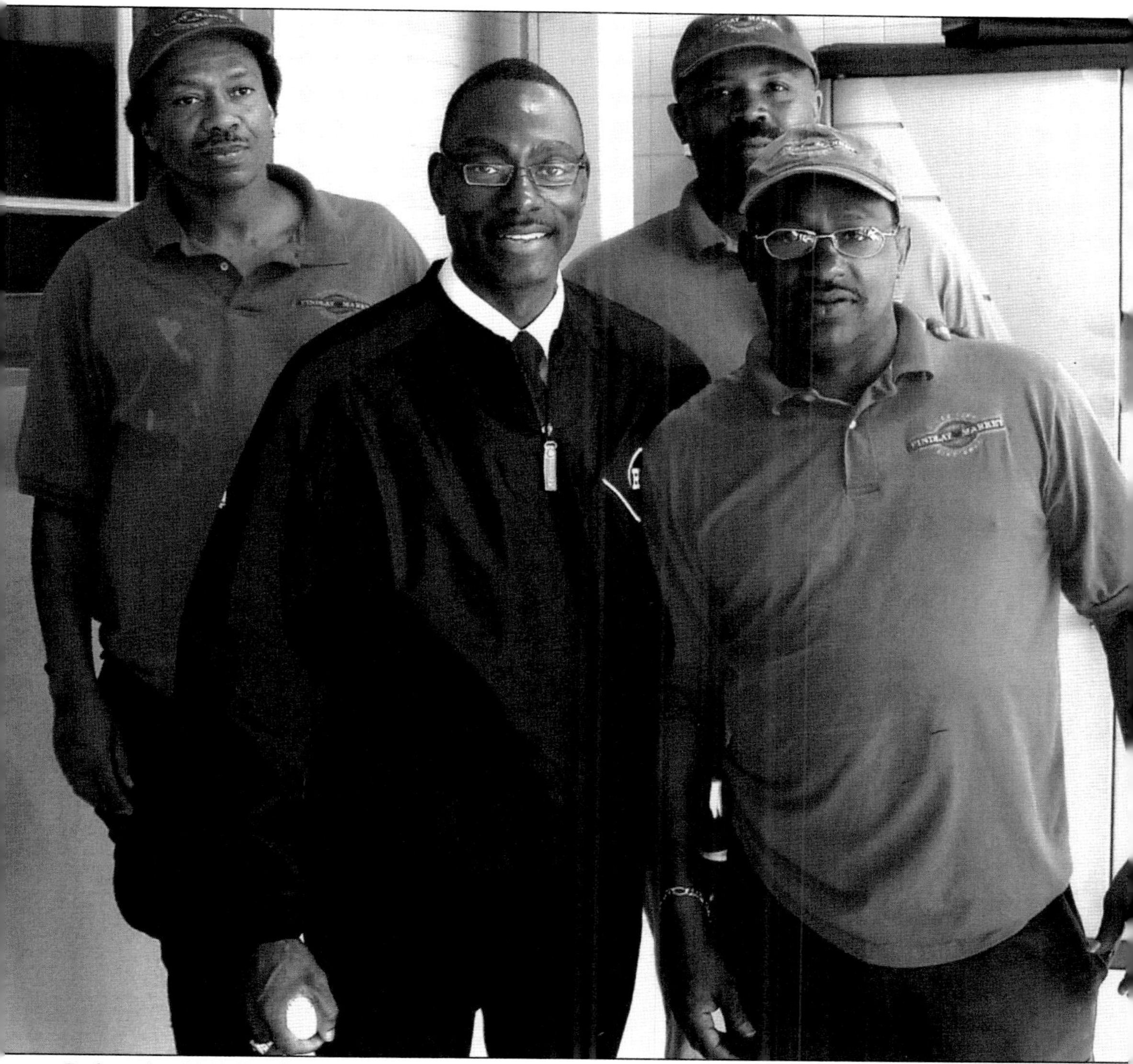

Before the 2007 Findlay Market opening day parade, current Cincinnati mayor Mark Mallory (front left) poses with Rick Rhodes (front right), Clarence Smith (rear left), and Ebb Cooper (rear right), all employees of the Corporation for Findlay Market. Later this day, Mallory made the opening day pitch. He holds the first-pitch ball in his hand here. (Courtesy of the Hudson family.)

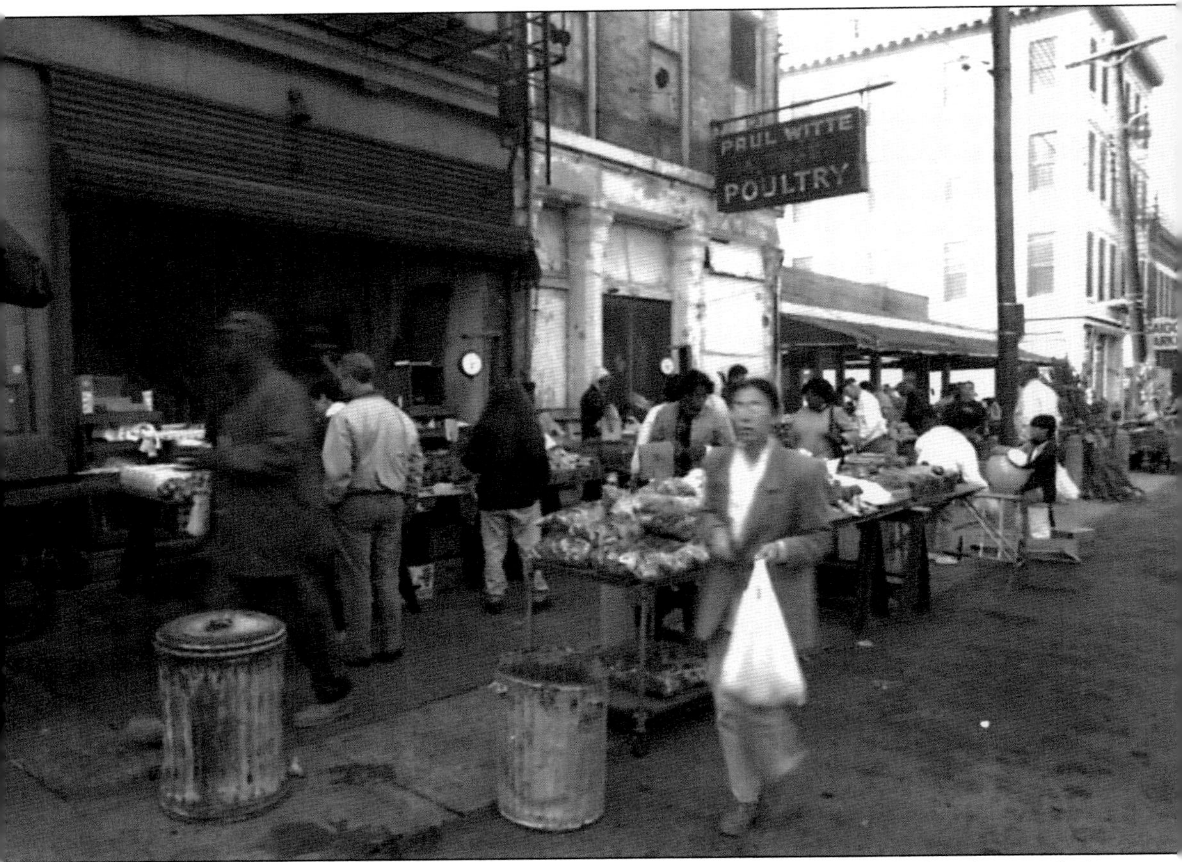

Although the market is bustling in this image, it is also clear the neighborhood around the market house has deteriorated. Vacant buildings have taken on a sunk-in look, and for a number of years, many Cincinnati citizens were reluctant to visit the market. Because so many Cincinnatians had that impression of Over-the-Rhine, groups of artists began to use the Findlay Market area as a canvas. (Photograph by Marty Milligan.)

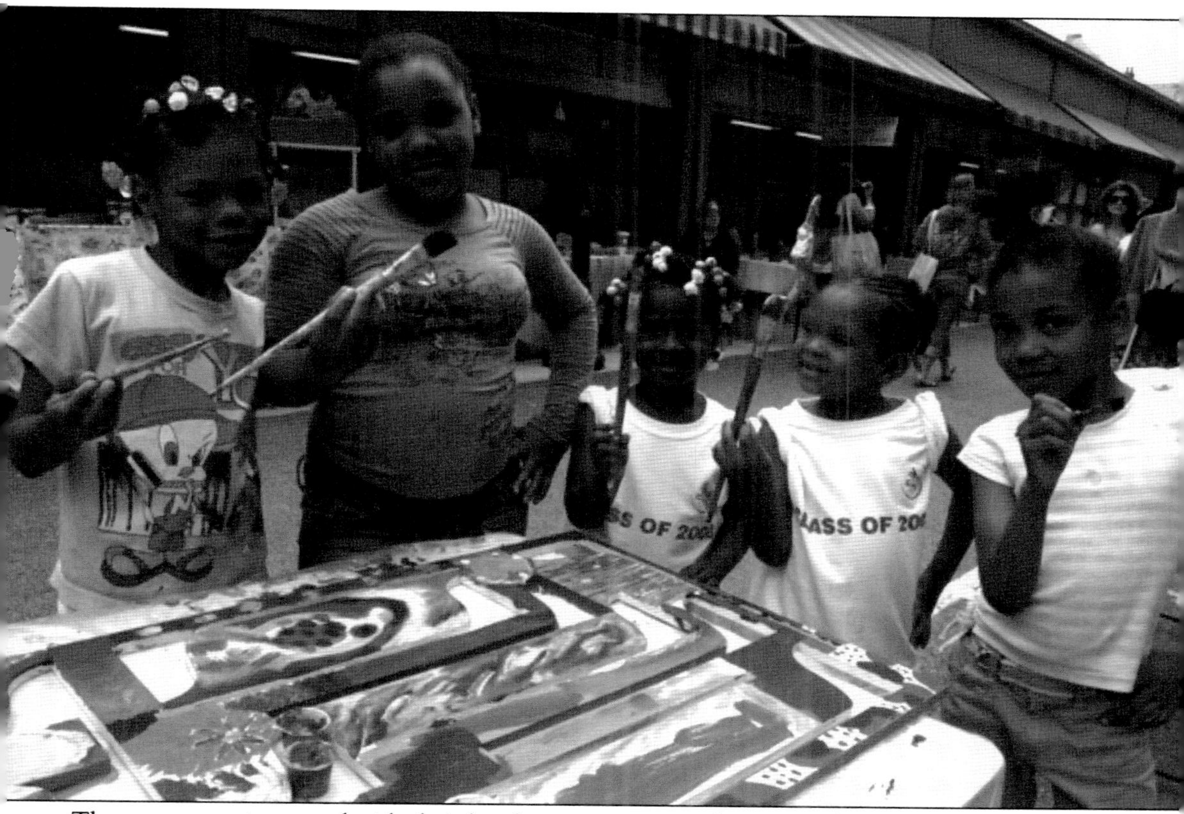

These young artists posed with their brushes participate in the Art in the Market collaboration between art students and educators from the University of Cincinnati's College of Design, Architecture, Art, and Planning, the university's Community Design Center, the Citizen's Committee on Youth, Impact Over-the-Rhine, Cincinnati's at-risk youth, and Findlay Market. Since the mid-1990s, these Art in the Market collaborators have conceptualized, designed, created, and installed a number of large-scale public art projects in and around the Findlay Market area with the goal of uplifting the market's environment and reversing the increep of blight while also instilling in residents a sense of ownership and pride in their neighborhood and market. The project provides art education to urban students while also offering real-life work experience for those students employed each summer to see the projects to fruition. (Courtesy of Flavia Bastos.)

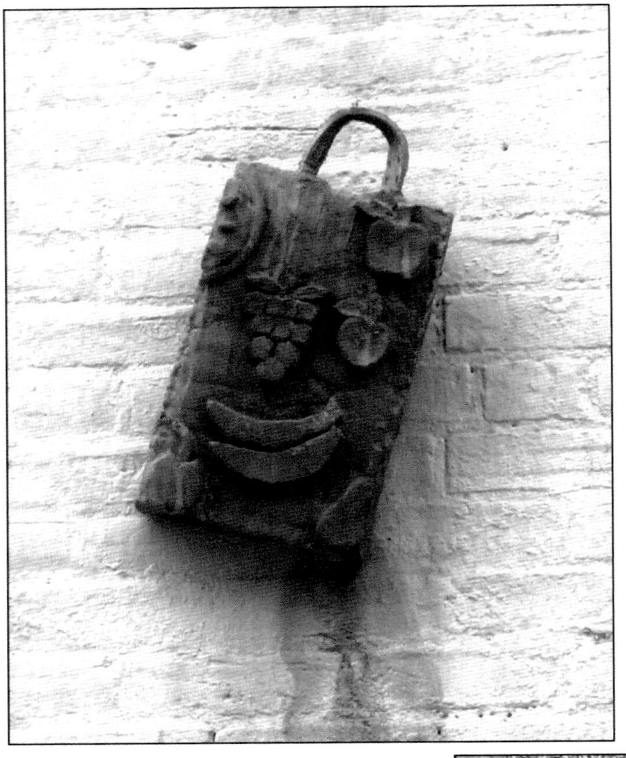

Shown here are two Art in the Market projects installed at Findlay Market. At left is an example of the shopping bag project. This early Art in the Market project celebrates the multicultural character of the market and the exchanges that occur in the marketplace. A collection of aluminum-cast shopping bags is hung in a wavelike line along a wall of Saigon Market. Each bag is individually designed and decorated with Asian imagery and other market-related symbols. Below, and installed subtly among a copse of young trees in the parking lot beside the farm shed, is the totem pole project. The totem poles blend with the trees, but each of the four poles is decorated with metal pieces depicting a narrative based on the lives of the youth who worked on the project. (Photographs by Karen Hutzel.)

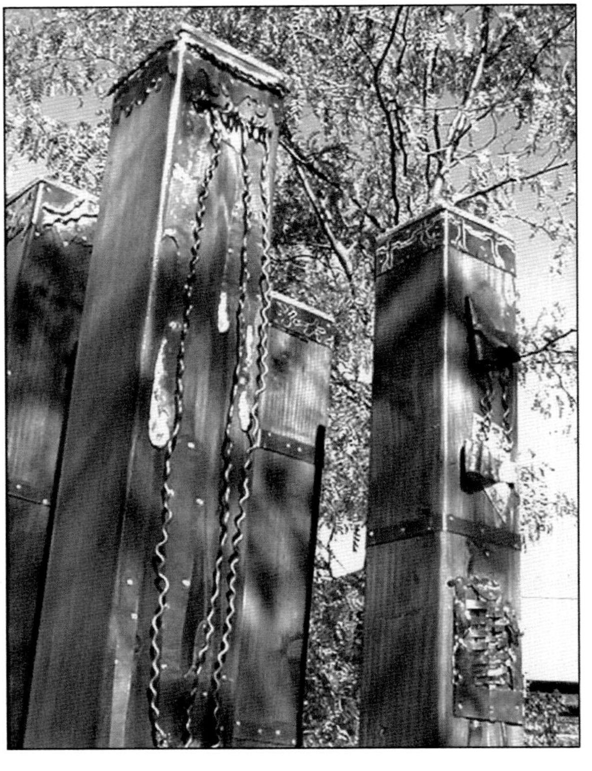

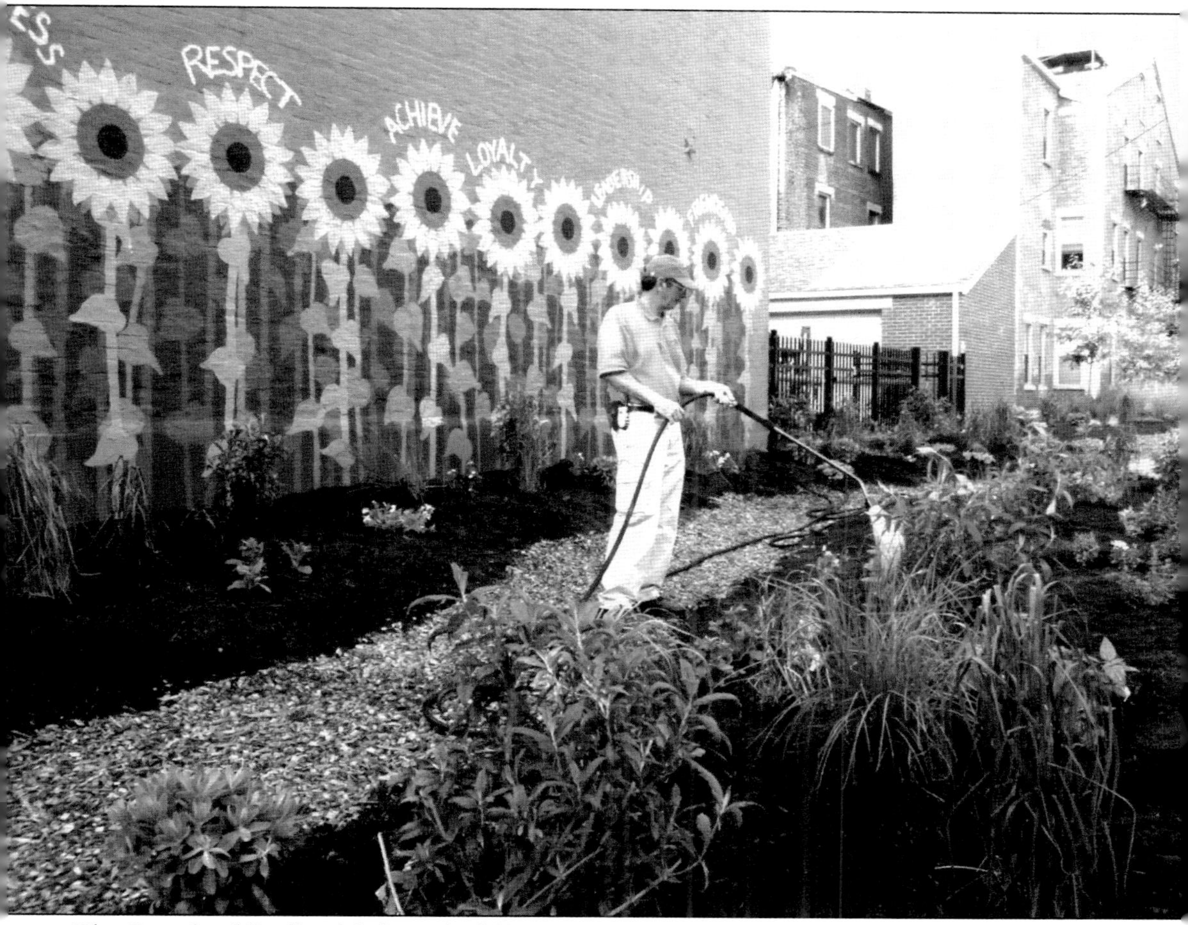

The Friends of Findlay Market asked Keep Cincinnati Beautiful for assistance in improving Findlay Market's south parking lot so customers would feel safe and comfortable parking their cars there while shopping. The collaboration resulted in a painted mural and the installation of the butterfly garden, pictured here being watered by George Wright. Once the garden was installed, Keep Cincinnati Beautiful released butterflies into it. (Courtesy of Keep Cincinnati Beautiful.)

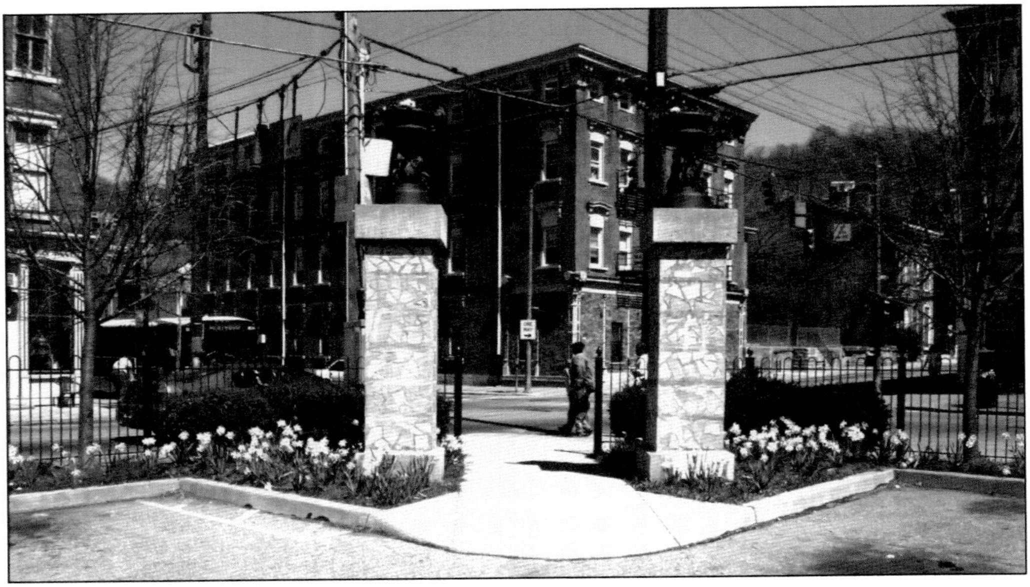

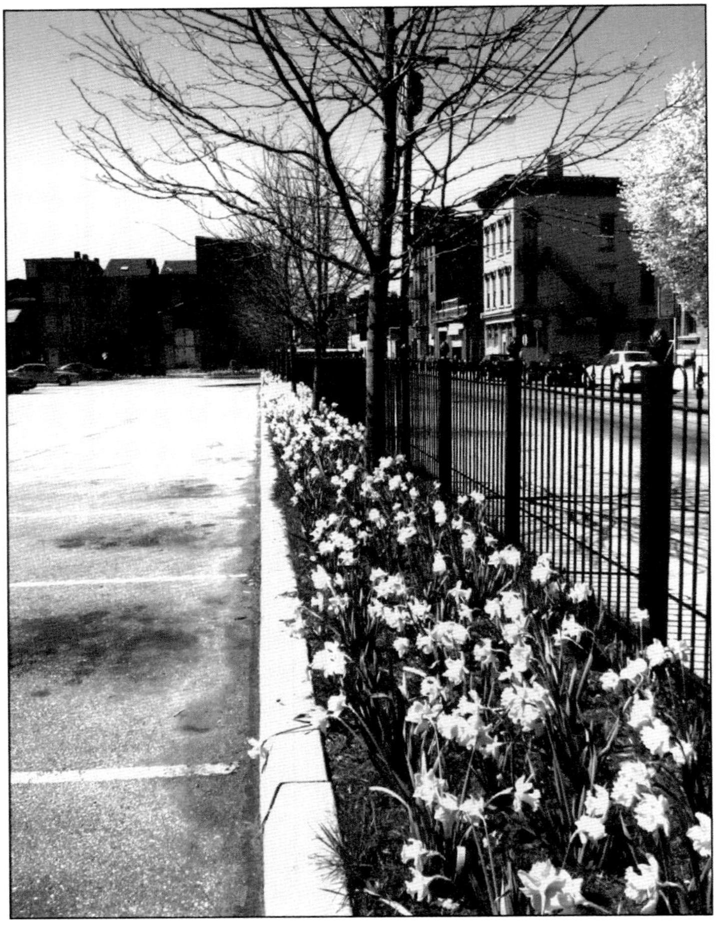

These are the entrances to Findlay Market's north and south parking lots. The daffodils lining the lots were installed by Keep Cincinnati Beautiful to bring a splash of color when the market and the city spirits pick up steam each spring. (Courtesy of Keep Cincinnati Beautiful.)

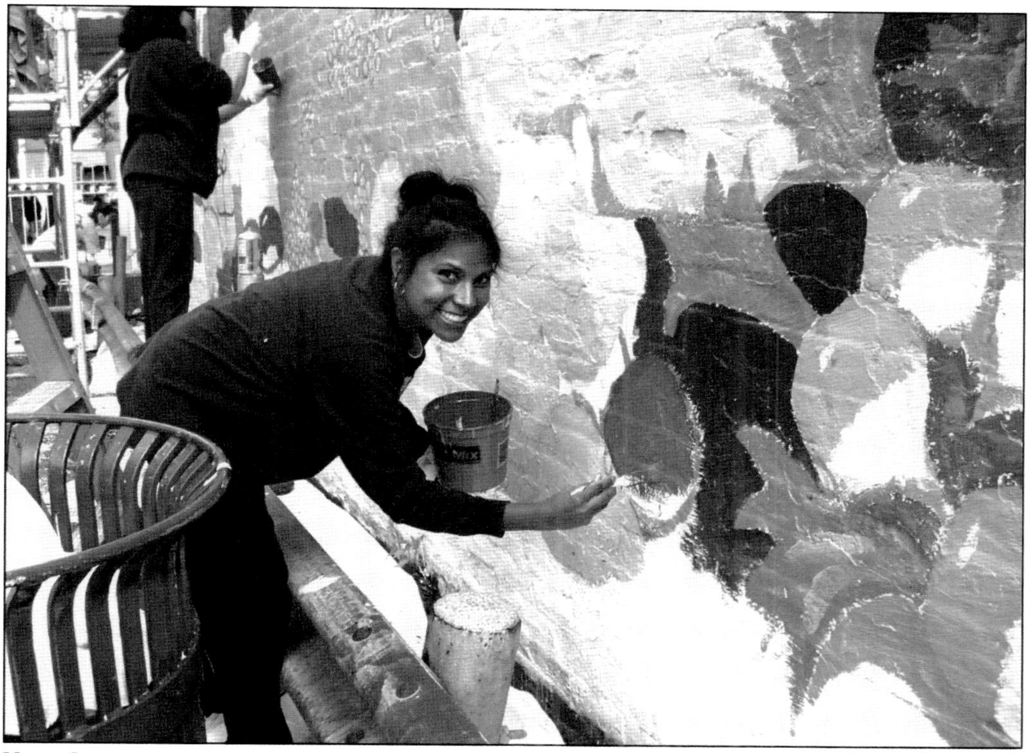

Keep Cincinnati Beautiful volunteers paint one of several colorful wall murals on the buildings around the Findlay Market area. These art projects involve a number of grassroots groups and utilize the talents of many neighbors to improve the image and lift the spirits and rejuvenate Over-the-Rhine. (Courtesy of Keep Cincinnati Beautiful.)

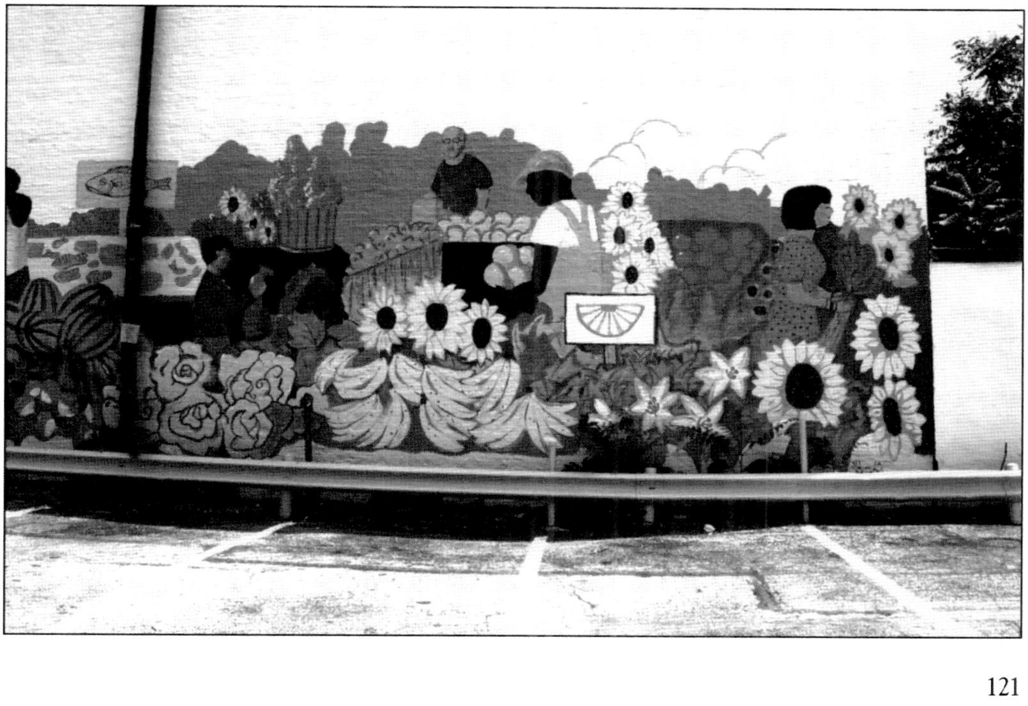

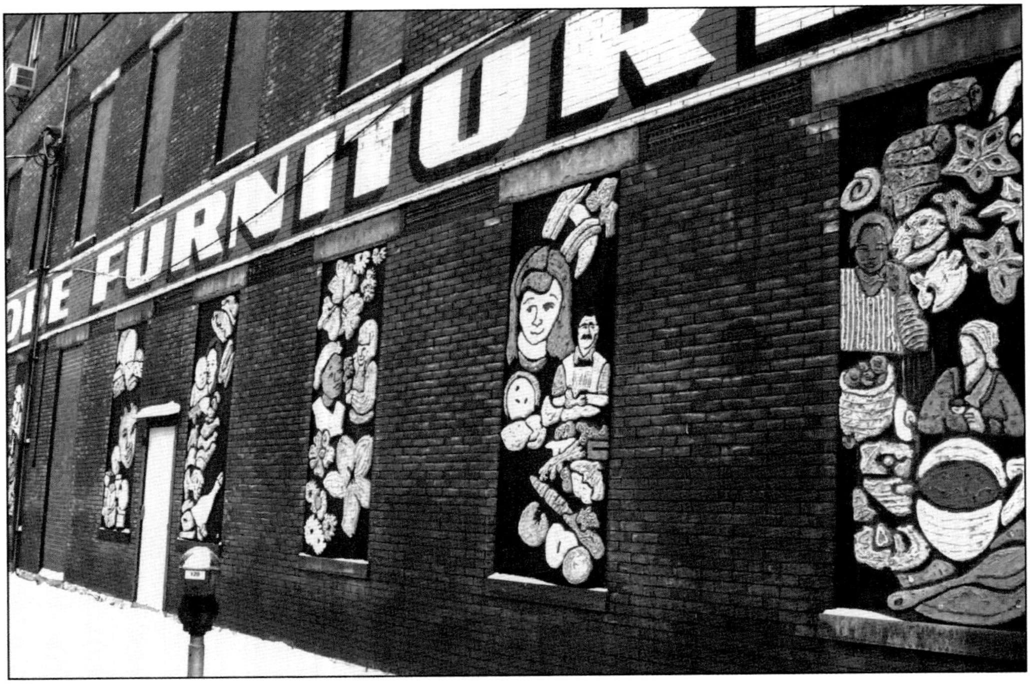

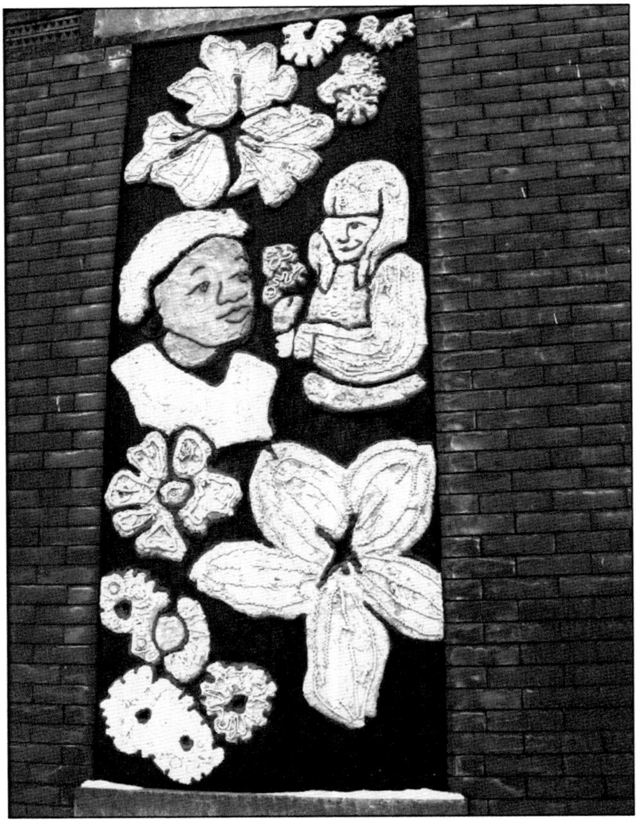

The Globe Furniture building at the corner of Elm and Elder Streets is as much a visual landmark to Findlay Market as any other building in the area. Once the furniture business moved from this location, however, the Art in the Market group isolated the long row of drab, bricked-up windows (above) and turned them into detailed mosaics (left). (Courtesy of Flavia Bastos.)

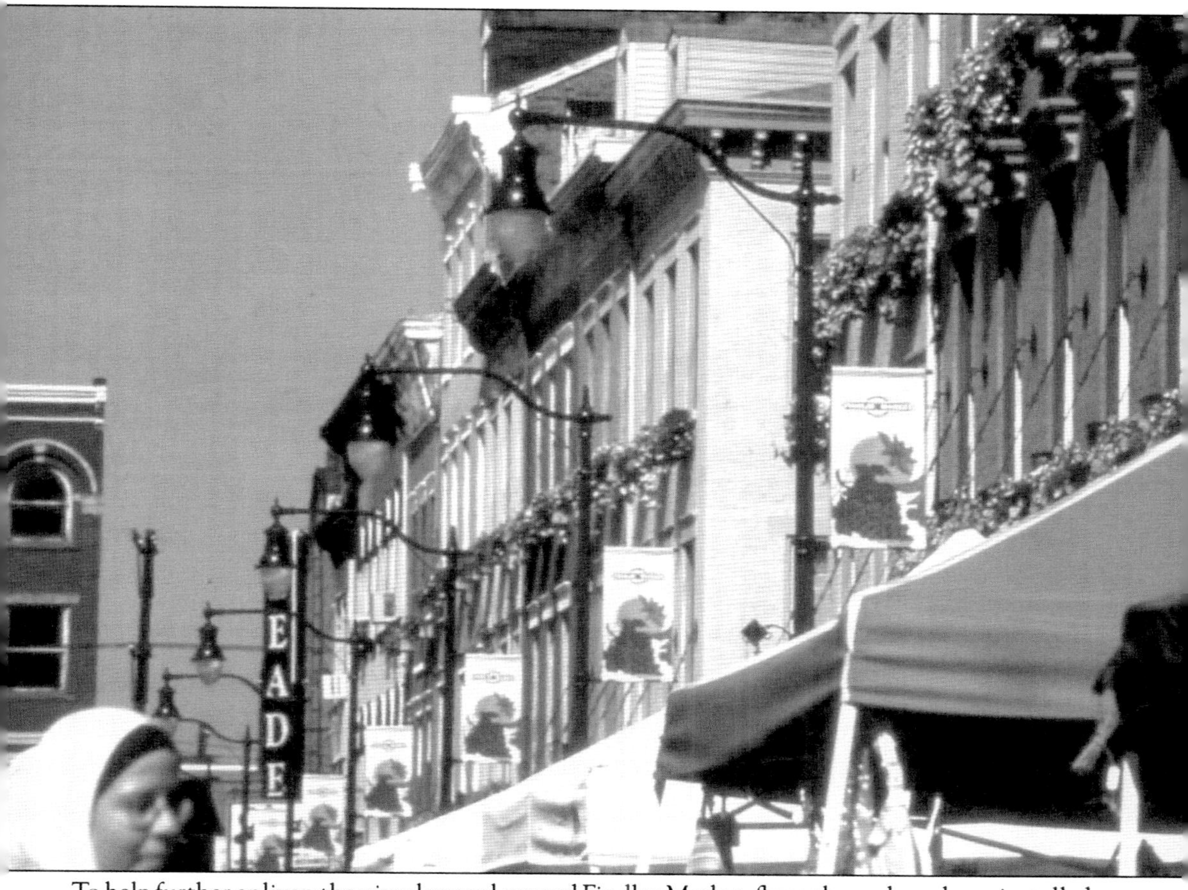

To help further enliven the visual appeal around Findlay Market, flower boxes have been installed on the windows all around the market house and in the windows along the streets connecting the market house and the farm shed. Street banners add color too, and the new streetlamps not only light up the place but recall the early market lamps. (Photograph by Jane Gahl.)

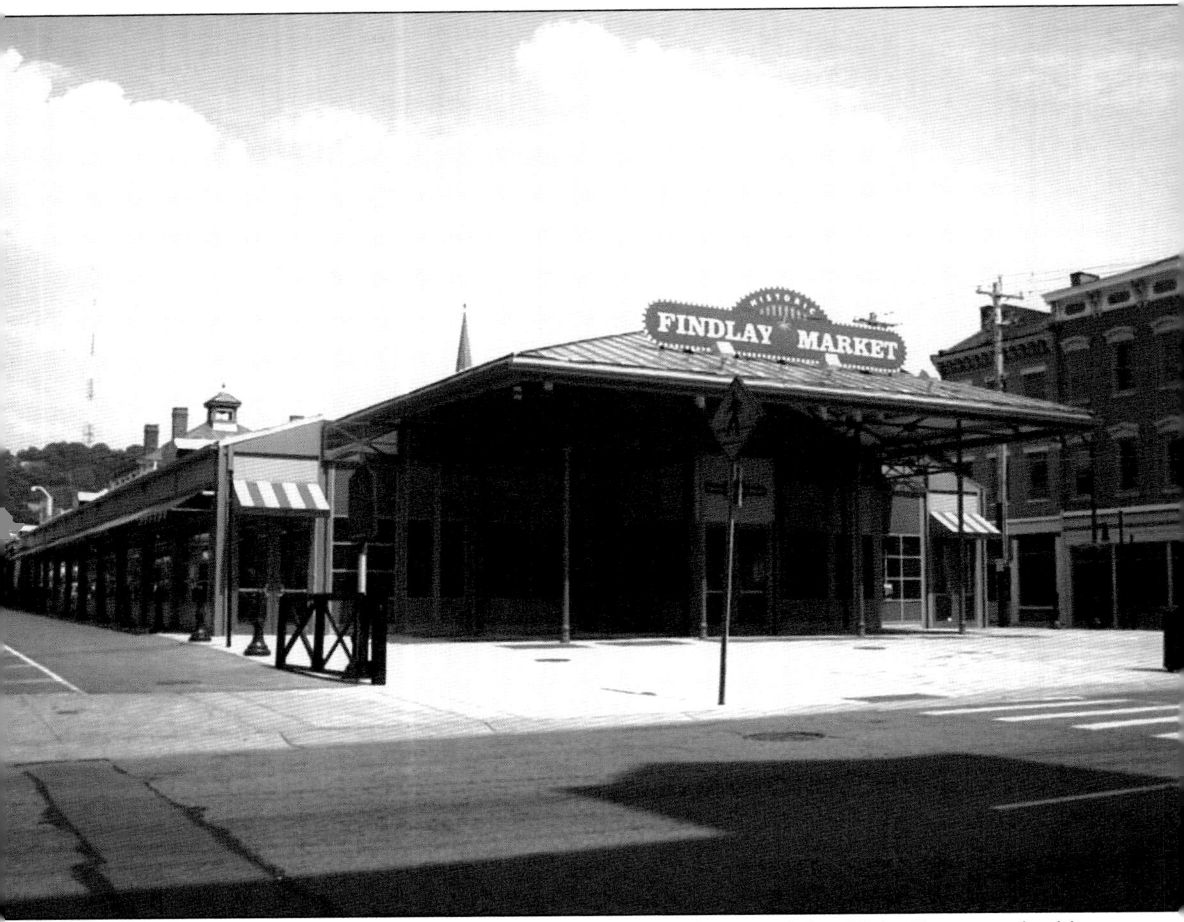

This is the Findlay Market house as it looks today from the site of the Globe Furniture building at the Elm and Elder Streets entrance. Of course, a shot this uncluttered had to be taken on a nonmarket day. (Author's collection.)

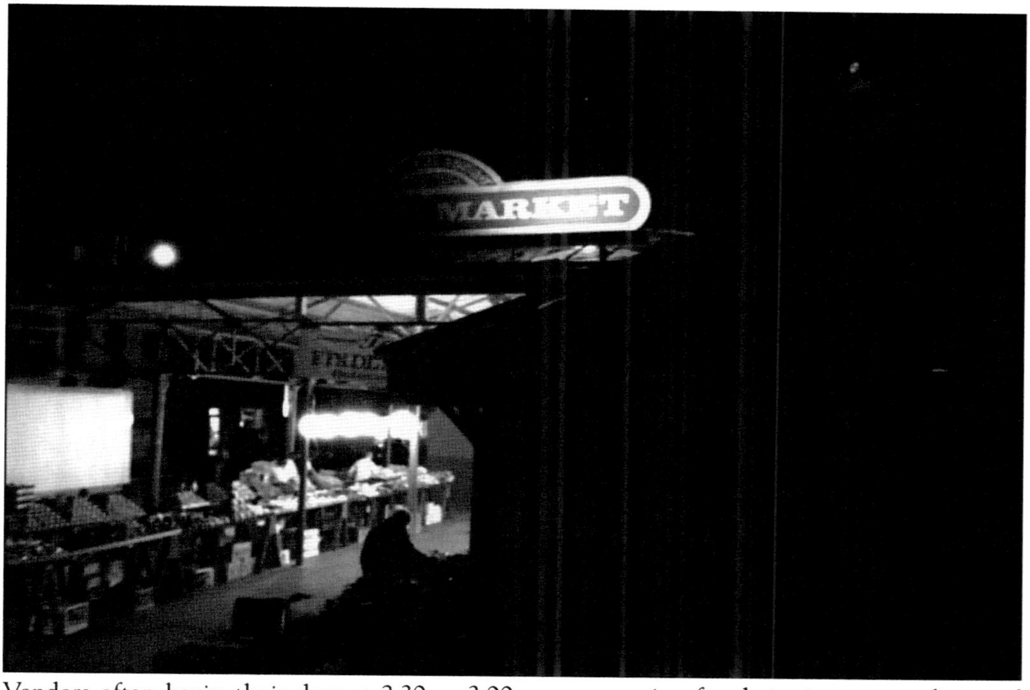

Vendors often begin their days at 2:30 or 3:00 a.m., preparing for their time on market, and pictured here is the daily predawn scene missed by most shoppers. This is the day in, day out work of generations of Findlay Market merchants. While most of the city of Cincinnati sleeps, Findlay Market hums. (Photographs by Marty Milligan.)

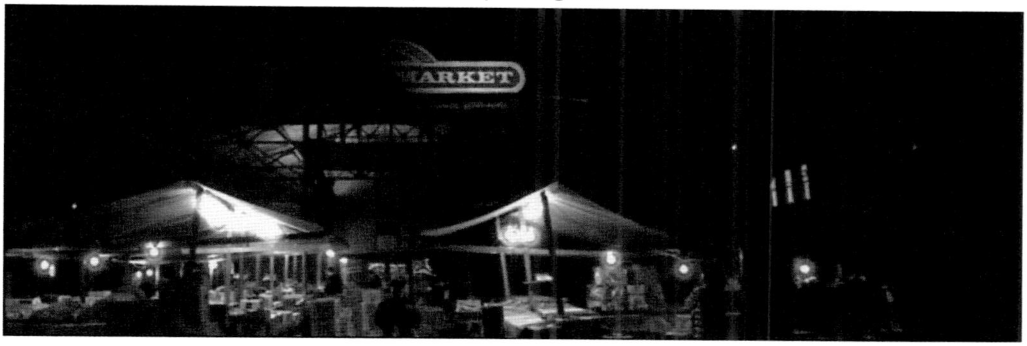

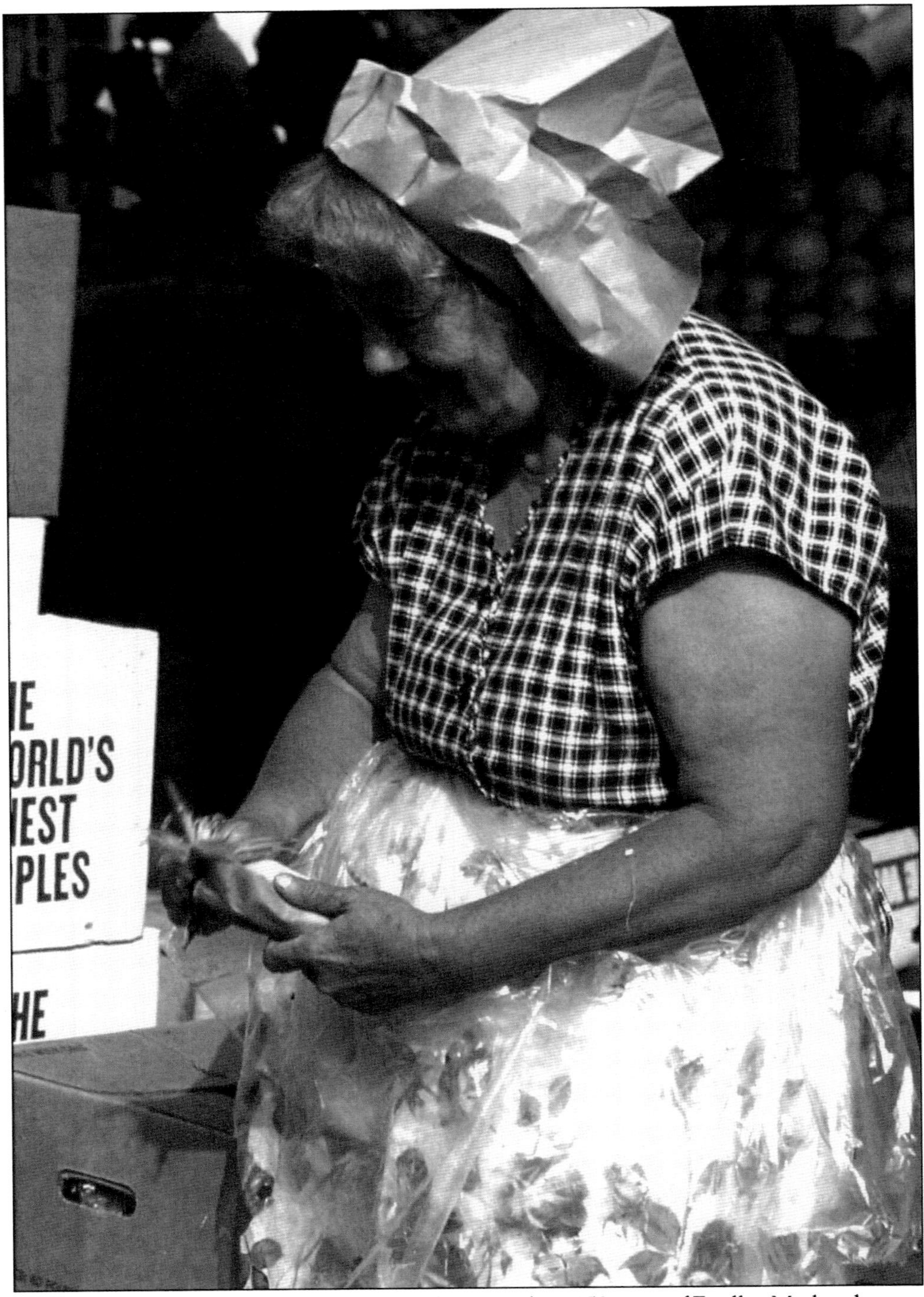

One thing that has changed very little over the more than 150 years of Findlay Market, however, are the characters who work and shop there, and it is still those characters who make Findlay Market such a draw. Here a vendor detassels corn while wearing a paper bag for a sun hat. (Photograph by Jane Gahl.)

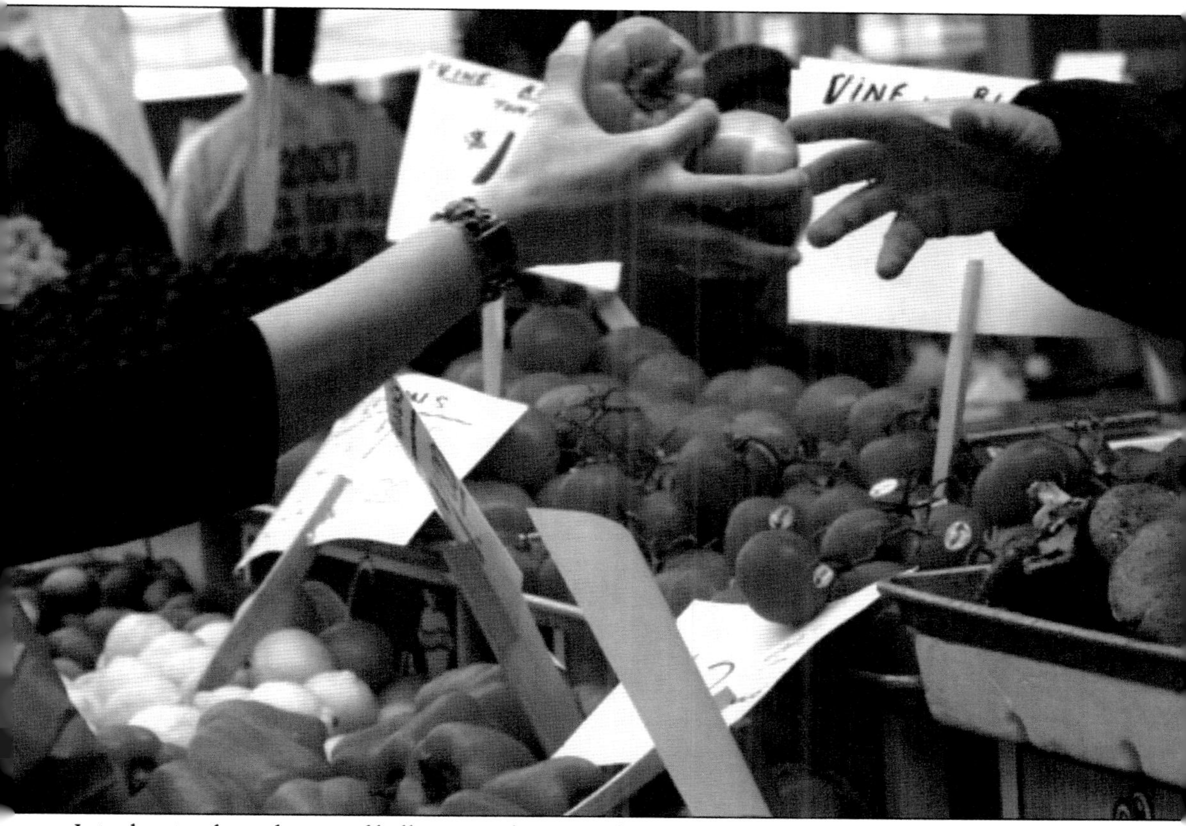

It is the simple exchange of bell peppers between shopper and merchant hands that symbolizes the heart of Findlay Market. The honest, one-on-one exchanges and personal relationships that have developed over generations put the unqualified shine on this market. (Photograph by Kelli Bruns.)

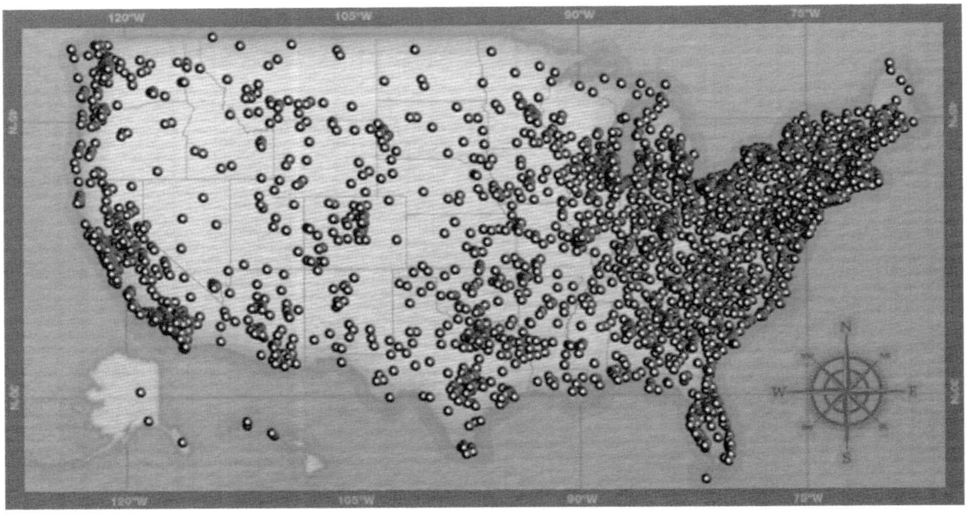